Colonial Presbyterianism

Princeton Theological Monograph Series

K. C. Hanson, Series Editor

Recent volumes in the series

Bonnie L. Pattison
Poverty in the Theology of John Calvin

Anette Ejsing
A Theology of Anticipation:
A Constructive Study of C. S. Peirce

Michael G. Cartwright
Practices, Politics, and Performance:
Toward a Communal Hermeneutic for Christian Ethics

Stephen Finlan and Vladimir Kharlamov, editors
Theōsis: Deification in Christian Theology

David A. Ackerman
Lo, I Tell You a Mystery:
Cross, Resurrection, and Paraenesis in the Rhetoric of 1 Corinthians

John A. Vissers
The Neo-Orthodox Theology of W. W. Bryden

Sam Hamstra, editor
The Reformed Pastor:
Lectures on Pastoral Theology by John Williamson Nevin

Byron C. Bangert
Consenting to God and Nature:
Toward a Theocentric, Naturalistic, Theological Ethics

Richard Valantasis et al., editors
The Subjective Eye:
Essays in Honor of Margaret R. Miles

Caryn D. Riswold
Coram Deo:
Human Life in the Vision of God

Philip L. Mayo
"Those Who Call Themselves Jews":
The Church and Judaism in the Apocalypse of John

Paul S. Chung et al., editors
Asian Contextual Theology for the Third Millennium:
Theology of Minjung in Fourth-Eye Formation

Lloyd Kim
Polemic in the Book of Hebrews:
Anti-Judaism, Anti-Semitism, Supersessionism?

Paul O. Ingram
Constructing a Relational Cosmology

Hamilton et al., editors
Renewing Tradition:
Studies in Texts and Contexts
in Honor of James W. Thompson

Philip Harrold
A Place Somewhat Apart:
The Private Worlds of a Late
Nineteenth-Century Public University

Edward J. Newell
"Education Has Nothing to Do with Theology"
James Michael Lee's Social Science Religious Instruction

Mark A. Ellis
The Arminian Confession of 1621

The Log College
Picture courtesy of the Presbyterian Church of America,
Historical Center, St. Louis, MO

Colonial Presbyterianism

Old Faith in a New Land

❧ *Commemorating the 300th Anniversary of the First Presbytery in America*

EDITED BY
S. DONALD FORTSON III

Pickwick *Publications*
An imprint of *Wipf and Stock Publishers*
199 West 8th Avenue • Eugene OR 97401

COLONIAL PRESBYTERIANISM
Old Faith in a New Land

Princeton Theological Monograph Series 71

ISBN 10: 1-59752-531-6
ISBN 13: 978-1-59752-531-2

Cataloging-in-publication data

Colonial Presbyterianism: old faith in a new land / S. Donald Fortson III

xiv + 236 p.; 23 cm.

Princeton Theological Monograph Series 71

ISBN 10: 1-59752-531-6 (alk. paper)
ISBN 13: 978-1-59752-531-2

1. Presbyterian Church – United States – History – 18th Century. 2. Presbyterians – United States – 18th Century 3. History – United States – 18th Century. I. Fortson, S. Donald III. II. Title. III. Series.

BX 8936 .F67 2007

Manufactured in the U.S.A.

Contents

Preface

THE year 2006 is the three-hundredth anniversary of the first Presbytery in America. In 1706 the Irishman Francis Makemie and a handful of ministers met in Philadelphia to organize themselves into an ecclesiastical body much like the ones they had known in the old country. Makemie and his small band of clergymen initiated what would become a large family of churches that eventually populated the entire United States. Through church planting efforts the new world preachers established the first generation of Presbyterian churches in the American colonies. By 1789 the United States of America had adopted a Constitution and Presbyterians had formed a General Assembly with over 400 churches.

In a number of ways, the story of the colonial church mirrored the development of the new nation. Presbyterianism in America was a grass-roots movement of immigrants who brought with them many old world values but also had new expectations about political participation and religious liberty. Committed to freedom of conscience and representative government, Presbyterians supported the War for Independence and participated in the political process that gave birth to the United States. That same set of ideals directed the formation of a national Presbyterian Church with voluntary participation by Christians of the Reformed persuasion. The American Presbyterian Church's constitution would formally identify the separation of church and state as a safeguard for religious freedom.

Presbyterian colonists recognized that the new world environment would require that some of the ancient patterns would have to be adapted for a new day. Many of the old practices did have essential theological significance but this was a new context and called for innovation to meet current needs. Beginning with the colonial era, Presbyterians consistently maintained the freedom to change their constitutional documents to meet contemporary requirements and to respond to further light from Holy Scripture. Later generations of Presbyterians would differ over where exactly to draw those lines but the principle of *ecclesia reformata semper reformanda* was embraced by the earliest Presbyterians on American soil.

The colonial church was uniquely poised for mission in the new world. The fledgling first Presbytery along with her soon to emerge sister presbyteries would initiate mission work among native Americans and slaves as well as encourage frontier missions to white settlers in the Appalachian regions and the South. Evangelism and church planting were foundational to their identity as God's people called to take the good news to their neighbors. Presbyterians find themselves in a similar context today in a culture that desperately needs the gospel of Jesus Christ and with many young ministers eager to plant new churches across the nation. While some modern-day American presbyteries may appear stagnant, new churches and expanding presbyteries are a reality—many with an evangelistic fervor similar to that of their colonial ancestors.

As the number of churches increased in the eighteenth century, one of the greatest challenges was providing ministers for all the new congregations; by 1789 there were over 400 churches but only 177 ministers. Presbyterians required education for ministers and training was not always readily available. The church would respond to this urgent need in the nineteenth century with regional seminaries. Even with the predicament of vacant pulpits, the colonial churches remained firm in their conviction that an educated ministry was necessary. Contemporary Presbyterians continue that tradition of ordaining ministers who are theologically trained and the examination of ministers' piety and knowledge remains one of the chief roles of a regional presbytery.

A distinctive form of church government also continues as a fundamental element of Presbyterian identity. The ecclesiastical body known as the presbytery is the primary expression of common fellowship where the Reformed theology of the church is experienced. Corporate accountability and mutual participation in mission are the fruit of that doctrine. It was Reformed ecclesiology that first drew the colonial preachers together to form a presbytery in America. That same connectional commitment informs the present-day Presbyterian ethos.

Twentieth-century Presbyterianism experienced repeated divisions over the substance of its corporate theological standards. New confessions and new ordination vows would emerge as the church struggled with what it meant to confess the faith in a new age. Presbyterians of the last century had serious differences over the degree to which clergy should be held to the doctrinal standards of the church. This too was an old question that the colonial Presbyterians dealt with in the earliest decades of the new church in America. Historically, both structure and freedom have been important to Presbyterians and the tension between those two values has not dissipated over the last three hundred years. But one theme has remained constant for Presbyterians—doctrine is serious business.

Much has changed since the colonial era both in society and the church; churchly transformation to meet the demands of these new contexts is imperative. While acknowledging the necessity of ecclesiastical modification, it is also essential that the church maintain her conscious connection to the Christian heritage lest she lose her way in the sea of ever-changing modernity. There are certain Presbyterian core values that have remained unchanged and many of those enduring principles have come down to us from colonial times.

Readers may notice some diversity in the interpretations offered by the contributors as the story is narrated from different perspectives. This kind of variety is nothing new for Presbyterian historians. As early as the nineteenth century, Presbyterians would offer diverse interpretations on the colonial era as they continued to debate the residual issues that had been passed on to their generation.

The contributors to these essays commemorating the first American Presbytery deeply appreciate our ecclesiastical heritage and continue to value the witness of the colonial leaders of the church. While the authors come from different denominations within the Presbyterian family of churches, we all share the common history of this earliest period when Presbyterianism in American was born. Our hope is that these brief glimpses into the colonial period will encourage the contemporary church to faithful service in God's vineyard. It is with a spirit of humility and gratitude for their labors that we offer these essays, believing that these founding fathers have something valuable to say to us.

In May of 1758, Presbyterian minister Francis Alison was asked to preach at the joint meeting of the Synods of Philadelphia and New York on the occasion of their reunion. He exhorted the two groups that day with these words: "We must maintain union in essentials, forbearance in lesser matters, and charity in all things . . . . In a church like ours in America, collected from different churches of Europe, who have followed different modes and ways of obeying the 'great and general command of the gospel,' there is a peculiar call for charity and forbearance."[1] We would do well to heed those words afresh in our time.

[1] Quoted in Leonard Trinterud, *The Forming of an American Tradition* (Philadelphia: Westminster, 1949) 148.

Acknowledgments

The editor wishes to express his sincere appreciation to the contributors who have invested their valuable time to make this book possible. Each of these authors has been a student of Presbyterianism for many years and has added his important research to the accumulated knowledge we have of the Reformed Tradition in America. A special thank you to Dr. Donald K. McKim for his encouragement to pursue this project.

1

Puritans, Presbyterians, and Jonathan Edwards

Samuel T. Logan Jr.

WHY this particular topic? Because the relationship between America's premier theologian and the denomination which grew to prominence in America during his ministry is a crucial one. It is crucial for understanding Edwards; it is no less crucial for understanding the history of Presbyterianism in America.

Edwards spent most of his adult life in the ministry of what was, at the time, called the Congregational Church. It is true that he began his public ministry as the pastor of a Presbyterian Church in New York City. And it is true that, when he was fired from his Congregational pulpit in Northampton, Massachusetts, and invited to Scotland to pastor a Presbyterian congregation, he responded as follows: "As to my subscribing to the substance of the Westminster Confession, there would be no difficulty . . . and the presbyterian way has ever appeared to me most agreeable to the word of God."[1] Further, it is true that the last job Edwards held was as the President of a largely Presbyterian educational institution.

But Edwards was, in fact, for most of his life, a *Congregational* minister. Are the three events cited above, from the very beginning to the very end of Edwards's ministry, the only reasons why his relationship to Presbyterianism bears examination?

Not at all. These three events actually point to more fundamental matters both in Edwards's theology, in the structure of pre-Revolutionary Presbyterianism and Congregationalism, and in the influence of the institution which he served for the last couple of months of his life. It is those

[1] Jonathan Edwards, "Memoirs of Jonathan Edwards," in *The Works of Jonathan Edwards*, Volume I (Edinburgh: Banner of Truth Trust, 1974) cxxi.

more fundamental matters that I will explore briefly here. Perhaps such an exploration will help to elucidate both what American Presbyterianism *has been*, what it *could have been*, and what it *should be*. Perhaps such an exploration will also suggest why it would be appropriate for modern Presbyterians to look to Edwards as "their theologian."

Pre-Revolutionary Presbyterianism and Congregationalism

"The early history of the Presbyterian Church in the United States is involved in great obscurity," argues Charles Hodge. He continues,

> The reason of this fact is obvious. Presbyterians did not at first emigrate in large bodies, or occupy by themselves extensive districts of country. In New England the early settlers were Congregationalists. The history of that portion of our country is, therefore, in a great measure, the history of that denomination. The same remark, to a certain extent, is applicable to the Dutch in New York, the Quakers in Pennsylvania, the Catholics in Maryland. The case was very different with regard to the Presbyterians. They came, as a general rule, as individuals, or in small companies, and settled in the midst of people of other denominations. It was, therefore, in most instances, only gradually that they became as sufficiently numerous in any one place to form congregations, or to associate in a presbyterial capacity.[2]

But if we are going to identify the Presbyterians when they do appear and if we are going to determine how Edwards influenced them and was influenced by them, we must agree upon a definition. Nothing particularly new here, or so it might seem. On the strictly theological side, Presbyterianism is Calvinistic in doctrine. The *Westminster Confession of Faith* defines thoroughly the Presbyterian theological perspective. But, of course, the theological thrust of the *Westminster Confession* is basically shared by numerous other groups, including New England Congregationalists.

Therefore, the focus of our attention must move from theology to ecclesiology. Here distinctions among various early settlers in America seem to become clearer. Here is where, traditionally, historians have drawn the sharpest distinction between Congregational Calvinists and Presbyterian Calvinists. For example, Leonard Trinterud summarizes the important difference between these two groups as follows:

[2] Charles Hodge, *The Constitutional History of the Presbyterian Church in the United States of America,* Part I (Philadelphia: Presbyterian Board of Publication, 1851) 19.

> The issues upon which Puritanism in England had finally divided into Congregationalists and Presbyterians grew out of two seemingly irreconcilable concepts of the Church. To those of the Congregationalist persuasion, the Church of Christ on earth existed only in its individual congregations. The Church Universal was but the totality of these congregations. To the Presbyterian wing of Puritanism, the Church Universal transcended all its local manifestations, being an entity greater even than the sum of its parts. It was the one body of Christ. From these two starting points, each group went on to differ with the other on a number of crucial issues.[3]

But is this interpretation correct? Or, to be more exact, does it correctly represent seventeenth- and eighteenth-century Presbyterianism and Congregationalism (as opposed to twentieth- and twenty-first-century Congregationalism and Presbyterianism)? If Trinterud is correct, it would seem that one would have to be either theologically confused or theologically naive to be able to move back and forth between Presbyterianism and Congregationalism, as Jonathan Edwards did. And I would be hesitant to call Edwards either theologically confused or theologically naive.

But what alternative to Trinterud's view might there be? And would that alternative help to explain Edwards's relationship to Presbyterianism? The answer, of course, is yes!

As Charles Hodge reminds us, Presbyterianism, separatism, and "the middle way" of non-separating Congregationalism all originated in dissatisfaction with the extent of the Reformation under the auspices of the Church of England.[4] The original break with Rome occurred for other than doctrinal reasons, and the subsequent history of the Anglican Church was, to say the very least, checkered. The regents of Edward moved the church in a more thoroughly Reformed direction, Mary sought to return it to the Roman Catholic fold, and Elizabeth, who ruled from 1558 to 1603, took a politically pragmatic attitude toward the church. Those who sought genuine reformation had experienced various forms of persecution under Elizabeth and, even more so, under her successors James I and Charles 1.[5]

What is fairly well known about this situation is that those who opposed the Anglican establishment became known as Puritans because

[3] Leonard Trinterud, *The Forming of an American Tradition: A Re-examination of Colonial Presbyterianism* (New York: Arno, 1970) 16.

[4] Hodge, *Constitutional History,* 212.

[5] See William Haller, *The Rise of Puritanism* (New York: Harper & Row, 1957).

they wanted to purify further the Church of England. What is perhaps not so well known is the degree to which Presbyterianism dominated the early Puritan movement. Once again, Hodge described the situation accurately when he says that the great majority of Puritans in England were Presbyterians. They were Presbyterians because intrinsic to their ecclesiology was the conviction that the fate of the church in England, rather than the fate of the various individual churches in England, was of paramount importance. This *corporate sense* continued to dominate Puritan thinking when individual Puritans moved from England to New England.

The only non-conformists who genuinely rejected the entire Presbyterian way of understanding the church were the separatists. Represented best by such individuals as Robert Browne, John Smyth, and John Robinson, the separatists despaired of achieving adequate purification of the Anglican establishment. They were determined to bring about, in Browne's own words, "reformation without tarying for anie" by forming their own separate congregations in which the appropriate purity was much more achievable.[6] This was the first Anglo-American rending of the previously seamless regional church garment. Its impact has been felt by all Christians, even by those who today regard themselves as Presbyterians.

The Presbyterians and the non-separating Congregationalists among the Puritans rejected the separatists way. They both believed that the biblical teaching about the church required them to see it as an institution in need of reformation, to be sure, but one church nevertheless. The fascinating story is how the difference between Presbyterian Puritans and non-separating Congregational Puritans began and how it developed during this period. And it is this fascinating story which best sets the context for understanding the relationship between Edwards and Presbyterianism.

Basically, the difference between these two latter groups of Puritans arose out of the same pragmatic considerations that led the separatists to renounce completely any notion of the church universal. Both Presbyterians and non-separating Congregationalists recognized that the struggle to reform the Anglican establishment was a difficult one. Ecclesiological differences developed around the question of how difficult the task was perceived to be. To simplify but not, I believe, to oversimplify, those who remained Presbyterian in orientation had more confidence in the possibility of reforming the entire Anglican establishment than did those who became non-separating Congregationalists. Events in Scotland, particularly under John Knox's leadership in 1560 and after, encouraged many of the

[6] Ibid., 182.

Puritans to believe that the ongoing Reformation of the entire national church was possible. The single-minded resistance to such thorough reform by Elizabeth and her two successors convinced others among the Puritans that, while purification of the church as a whole in England was the ultimate goal (because the church was whole), real progress would only be made as individual parts of that whole conformed more completely to the Word of God. Those who took this view became what we now call non-separating Congregationalists.

Before proceeding, let me suggest just one modern application of this 400-year old problem. If one is in a denomination which appears fundamentally flawed and if thorough reform of the entire denomination appears highly unlikely, what does one do? Does one leave for more perfect pastures (separatists)? Or does one step back from the denomination as a whole and form smaller groups within the denomination which better exemplify what the denomination should be (non-separating congregationalism)? Or does one continue to engage fully with all of the power structures of the denomination in an attempt to bring about (unlikely) change (Presbyterianism)? Interesting questions, familiar to many Reformed Christians today. Perhaps the older struggles do have something to teach us after all!

Back to the past—another way to approach the distinctions among these various groups in Britain in the late sixteenth and early seventeenth centuries is to focus on the selection of church officers and the degree to which church and state are co-extensive. Both Presbyterians and non-separating Congregationalists believed that the Anglican way of choosing church officers was unbiblical. Rather than appointing local church officials from the lofty reaches of an ecclesiastical hierarchy, both Puritan groups believed they were most appropriately chosen by church members. But the Presbyterians among the Puritans were actually closer to the Anglicans than they were to the non-separating Congregationalists in their understanding of the co-extensiveness of church and state.

Following the model that was being developed in Scotland, Presbyterians identified church and state quite closely, not in terms of jurisdiction or authority, but in terms of membership. For both Anglicans and Presbyterians, citizenship and church membership were correlative if not synonymous. Presbyterians determined to achieve what they regarded as necessary reformation by changing the method of selecting clergy and by taking the presbytery out from under the direct control of the political Sovereign.

Non-separating Congregationalists, in essence, did not believe that the Presbyterian method would work. They were convinced that as long as those who elected elders were themselves potentially un-Reformed, the officers they chose to lead them might very well continue to be un-Reformed. Therefore, non-separating Congregationalists earned their Puritan appellation by focusing initial attention on the purification of local congregations. They did not, however, in any way abandon the goal of reforming the national church. Since they continued to concentrate so much energy on that ultimate goal, it is quite proper to regard them as having very strong Presbyterian leanings.

Obviously, the process by which non-separating Congregationalism came to focus its purifying attention on local church membership was a very long and complicated one. What has just been suggested is a summary of ecclesiological developments over a half century and across three thousand miles of salt water. The details of this shift have been told thoroughly and quite well before.[7] The objective here has been simply to summarize this development for the purposes of comparing Puritan non-separating Congregationalism to Puritan Presbyterianism. From this comparison, both differences and significant similarities between the two groups can be seen. And it is precisely these similarities and differences which determine our understanding of Edwards and Presbyterianism.

As a matter of fact, however, this comparison suggests in simplified form a point which cannot be stressed too strongly: Presbyterianism in early seventeenth-century Britain was a very different thing from Presbyterianism today (especially in the United States). Likewise, the non-separating Congregationalism of that same period should not be regarded as identical with Congregationalism (either United Church of Christ or Conservative Congregational Christian Conference) in the United States at the present time. As a matter of fact, it may well be that twentieth-century American Presbyterianism has more in common with seventeenth-century non-separating Congregationalism than it does with seventeenth-century Presbyterianism. This is just one of the reasons why Edwards was able to move so easily between the two.

As we move into the second quarter of the seventeenth century, the differences both between earlier and modern Presbyterianism and between earlier and modern Congregationalism become even clearer. A close examination, for example, of the political nature of the *National Covenant*

[7] See, for example, Perry Miller, *Orthodoxy in Massachusetts, 1630–1650* (Gloucester, MA: Peter Smith, 1965); and Edmund Morgan, *Visible Saints: The History of a Puritan Idea* (Ithaca, NY: Cornell University Press, 1963).

signed at Greyfriars Kirk in Edinburgh in 1638 and the affirmation of the *Solemn League and Covenant* in 1643 reveal a concept of the co-extensiveness of church and state that has no place in modern Presbyterianism. Perhaps even more to the point of this essay is the degree to which non-separating Congregationalism represented both a corporate sense and a view of church membership with which modern Presbyterians would be both familiar and comfortable.

A central question, therefore, might very well be, why did English Puritans (of the non-separating Congregationalist variety) come to America in such large numbers at the beginning of the second quarter of the seventeenth century? Answering this question will illumine the degree to which they had Presbyterian leanings and address more directly the kinds of issues and commitments which we see emerging in the life and ministry of Edwards.

John Winthrop was a layman but he was also an extremely influential leader among the Puritans who migrated from England to Massachusetts Bay. A native of East Anglia (within which was located both Cambridge University and the greatest concentration of Puritan sentiment), Winthrop represents very well the classical non-separating Congregationalist mind-set. Deeply distressed over the failure of the English church to complete the Reformation, he felt mandated by Scripture to deal with the results of that failure in corporate terms. Like most other Puritans, he believed that God related not just to individuals but also to corporate units of which various individuals were parts. Specifically, Winthrop shared the Puritan understanding of a national covenant. This meant he believed that a nation that lived in disobedience to God could expect to be judged by God.

While on business in London on May 15, 1629, Winthrop wrote the following letter to his wife.

> My good wife, I prayse the Lorde for the wished newes of thy well-fare and of the rest of our companye, and for the continuance of ours heer: It is a great favour, that we may enioye so much comfort and peace in these so euill and declininge tymes and when the increasinge of our sinnes giues vs so great cause to looke for some heauye Scquorge and Judgment to be comminge vpon us: the Lorde hath admonished, threatened, corrected and astonished vs, yet we growe worse and worse, so as his spirit will not aliwayes striue with vs, he must needs giue waye to his furye at last: he hath smitten all the other Churches before our eyes, and hath made them to drinke of the bitter cuppe of tribulation, euen vnto death; we sawe this, and humbled not ourselues, to turne from our euill

> wayes, but haue prouoked him more than all the nationals rounde about vs: therefore he is turninge the cuppe towars vs also, and because we are the last, our portion must be to drinke the verye dreggs which remain: my deare wife, I am veryly perswaded, God will bringe some heauye Affliction vpon this lande, and that speedylye: but be of good Comfort, the hardest that come shall be a meanes to mortifle this bodye of Corruption which is a thousand tymes more dangerous to vs than any outward tribulation, and to bringe vs into neerer communion with our Lo: Jes: Christ, and more Assurance of his kingdome. If the Lord seeth it wilbe good for vs, he will prouide a shelter and a hidinge place for vs and ours. . . . [8]

To Winthrop the individual was primary, but he was very conscious of the degree to which the group was also real before God. This affected his understanding of the church and the state and led to his decision to travel three thousand miles to try to set up a holy commonwealth in which both church and state would live in obedience to the Word of God. Paramount among the many reasons for the transition by the Puritans from England to New England was this corporate sense. This notion is in basic agreement with the Presbyterian understanding of the church and was at the very heart of what has been called "the great migration."

It must also be remembered that the group of Puritans that came to Massachusetts Bay was different in some crucial ways from the group which settled at Plymouth. The Plymouth group (known to later generations as the Pilgrims) was comprised primarily of separatists. As one reads William Bradford's journal, *History of Plimoth Plantation,* and contrasts it with Winthrop *History of New England,* one is struck continually with the degree to which the former breathes a spirit of individualism (both in personal and church life), while the latter is much more conscious of corporate realities. Therefore, when we speak of the movement of this Presbyterian-like corporate sense from England to New England, we must be very clear that we are referring, not to the settlers at Plymouth, but to the much larger colony established some ten years later around Boston, Massachusetts. It is this latter group that influenced in a major way the development of American Presbyterianism and within which Edwards lived and ministered.

[8] John Winthrop, "Letter to His Wife," May 15, 1629, in *The Puritans: A Sourcebook of Their Writings*, ed. Perry Miller and Thomas H. Johnson (New York: Harper & Row, 1963) 466–67.

But if Winthrop and those who came with him felt that the body of which they were part in England was increasingly corrupt, and that the sickness of that body threatened their own spiritual health, what exactly did they do after arriving in Massachusetts to achieve a healthy body? In a word, they sought to safeguard membership in both church and state in order to protect and provide for biblical holiness in both. The Puritans *never* confused church and state. To their way of thinking, each had its own distinct function and stood in a corporate relationship (in covenant) with God. Both church and state were required to be obedient to God's Word. As reflected in Winthrop's letter to his wife, both church and state should expect the favor of God if they obeyed his Word. His judgment was certain if they disobeyed it.

The actual structure of church and state in New England in the early 1630s is described in great detail in Edmund Morgan's brilliant volume, *The Puritan Dilemma: The* Story *of John Winthrop.*[9] To summarize that structure briefly, the franchise was restricted to male members of Puritan churches. Furthermore, membership (and the ability to participate in the sacrament of the Lord's Supper) in those churches was limited to those individuals who demonstrated doctrinal orthodoxy, lived sanctified lives, and perhaps most important, were able to describe their experience of grace. The third requirement became a "cause celebre" in later Puritanism and in the ministry of Edwards. It would not, in fact, be too much of a stretch to argue that it was his renewed insistence on this third requirement that led to Edwards being fired from his church. But more of this later.

Several things need to be said about this church-state structure. First of all, only those who could vote could hold political office. By structuring their society in this way, the Puritans hoped to make significant progress toward building a society that genuinely held the glory of God as its first priority. From the beginning, however, ministers were prohibited from holding political office. The official lines between church and state were drawn clearly for all to see. Winthrop's journal traces in great detail the relationships between elected political officers and church officers. While frequent disagreements between the two groups arose, there was no confusion between them regarding their respective roles, rights, and responsibilities.

The second point focuses on the question of fairness. Many modern scholars question the restriction of the franchise to church members.

[9] Edmund Morgan, *The Puritan Dilemma: The Story of John Winthrop* (Boston: Little, Brown, and Co., 1958).

They accuse the Puritans of narrow-minded bigotry. In response to such a charge, it must be stated clearly and openly that political liberty was not the highest priority for the Puritans. The highest priority was the glory of God. If achieving the glory of God required the sacrifice of other legitimate values, the Puritans were willing to make that sacrifice. Modern America, however, with its near deification of individual freedom cannot understand a mindset which genuinely sought to worship the Creator rather than the creature. Edwards, on the other hand, understood this as well as any human being who ever lived.

Having said this, nevertheless, it is necessary to understand the degree to which the Puritans in Massachusetts Bay were more or less narrow than their counterparts in England. In other words, we must take an historical "reality check." It is absolutely true that the Puritans sought to set up a society based on a rather narrow franchise, but this was common in the seventeenth-century world. The difference between England and New England was not the percentage of individuals within the society who could vote (in both societies, it hovered around 15 percent) but the way in which those who could vote were chosen.[10]

While in New England a fundamentally spiritual criterion was utilized, in England the criterion was overtly economic. That is, in English society in the seventeenth century, men had to possess a 40-shilling freehold in order to be eligible to vote (and, of course, no women need apply). Narrowness can, therefore, be no more charged against the Puritans than it can against their English counterparts. Indeed, what was true in England was true in most other European countries of the day. By selecting a spiritual criterion for the franchise, the Puritans did make quite clear where their societal priorities rested. Their fundamental values were not economic but spiritual, and this determined the tone of their entire society.

The third point has to do with the specific criterion that the Puritans utilized for membership in their churches. In addition to the normal British Puritan and continental criteria of doctrinal orthodoxy and moral life, the New England Puritans requested applicants for their churches to describe the experience they had of the grace of God. This criterion has been roundly criticized by many historians who have argued that the Puritans were guilty of the old Donatist heresy of perfectionism.

[10] For a comparison of franchise figures in England and New England, see Williston Walker, *The Creeds and Platforms of Congregationalism* (New York: Scribner, 1893) 165; Miller, *Orthodoxy in Massachusetts*, 207; and Edmund Morgan, *American Slavery, American Freedom: The Ordeal of Colonial Virginia* (New York: Norton, 1975) 60.

Nothing could be further from the truth. The Puritans asked candidates for membership in their churches nothing more than "a credible profession of faith," a request made by most conservative Presbyterian bodies today. That this and nothing more than this was sought by the Puritans can be confirmed quickly by even a cursory perusal of the confessions of faith of fifty persons who applied for membership in Thomas Shepard church in Cambridge, Massachusetts, between 1638 and 1645.[11]

Not only were the Puritans not Donatists, but in the matter of church membership, they were actually much closer to conservative twenty-first century American Presbyterians than other seventeenth-century British and continental Presbyterians are to the modern situation. The Puritans of New England believed in the corporate nature of God's people. They sought, both by their church membership and franchise criterion, to do all they could to achieve a holiness of the political and ecclesiastical units.

In this *corporate sense,* the New England Puritans were far more Presbyterian than Congregational, at least as those two terms are normally understood. Indeed, as one examines the way in which the Massachusetts Bay (both church and state) dealt first with Roger Williams and then with Anne Hutchinson, one is impressed with the Presbyterian character of those dealings. When, for example, the church at Salem wished to hire Williams as its teacher, it was strongly counseled not to do so by the other Massachusetts Bay churches. The church at Salem declined to follow that counsel, and the general court entered the picture to enforce the judgment of the churches.[12] In fact, the actions of both the court and the churches was so clearly presbyterian that Williams himself charged the churches of Massachusetts of having given up the principle of congregational independence.[13]

Dealings with Anne Hutchinson were no less definitive. When one church (the Boston church) seemed to be moving in the direction of accepting Hutchinsonian Antinomianism, meetings and Councils of the ministers were called in order to deal adequately with this threat to the doctrinal well-being of the corporate community.[14] Because they were convinced of the essential unity of the civil and ecclesiastical bodies, the

[11] Bruce Chapman Woolley, "Reverend Thomas Shepard and Cambridge Church Members 1636–1649: A Socio-Economic Analysis" (Ph.D. dissertation, University of Rochester, 1973).

[12] Morgan, *American Slavery,* 125–29.

[13] Ibid., 126.

[14] Ibid., 134.

Puritans could not and did not allow challenges to that unity to go unchecked.

It may be that the New England Puritans acted in this manner because, as Cotton Mather remarks, more than four thousand Presbyterians entered New England prior to 1640.[15] But even more likely is the simple fact that these Puritans from the very beginning thought in corporate terms. This made them Presbyterian even if they did not realize it themselves. Once again, it is Charles Hodge who summarizes the situation most accurately.

> The influence of Presbyterian principle in New England is, however, much more satisfactorily proved by the nature of the ecclesiastical systems which were there adopted, than by any statements of isolated facts. These systems were evidently the result of compromise between two parties, and they show that the Presbyterian was much stronger than the Independent element. The two leading points of difference between Presbyterianism and Congregationalism, particularly as the latter exists at present, relate to the mode of government within the congregation, whether it should be by elders or the brotherhood, and to the authority of Synods. As to both these points the early discipline of the New England churches approached much nearer to Presbyterianism than it does at present.[16]

If all of this is true, why were there so many outspoken statements of opposition to Presbyterianism in New England in the 1630s and 1640s? Why specifically did both John Cotton and Thomas Hooker write formal treatises seeking to vindicate the Congregational system as over against the Presbyterian?

To be sure, it would be inaccurate to suggest that New England Puritans actually were Presbyterians in every way. They did seek to maintain, at least in theory, a degree of congregational independence that moves away from a Presbyterian model. Nevertheless, two facts about the Presbyterianism of these New England churches should be kept clearly in mind.

First of all, their corporate sense made it impossible for them to see their churches as completely separate from one another. Each church was part of the whole, and it was in terms of the whole that each church was expected to act. Therefore, the theoretical independence of the churches

[15] Cotton Mather, *Magnalia Christi Americana,* Volume 1 (Edinburgh: Banner of Truth, 1979) 80.

[16] Hodge, *Constitutional History,* 30.

was largely mitigated by the even greater emphasis upon the unity of the body.

Secondly, the reaction which we frequently see in early New England to Presbyterianism was to the Presbyterianism *of that day.* As already suggested, Hooker and Cotton and most of the other New England Puritans identified Presbyterianism with the state-church situation which, in their opinion, had proven inimical to true reformation and biblical holiness. While the state-church model might seem to be successful in Scotland, Scotland was under the political control of England. In New England minds, this very fact made it impossible for the Scottish church to live as fully by the Word of God as New Englanders thought was necessary. Therefore, it was the seventeenth-century version of Presbyterianism that Cotton and Hooker were rejecting, not Presbyterianism as we know it in the twentieth century.

To gain a better understanding of that seventeenth-century version of Presbyterianism, at least as understood by New England, it is necessary only to reread Chapter 23 of the original version of the *Westminster Confession of Faith.* Section 3 of that original chapter reads as follows:

> The civil magistrate may not assume to himself the administration of the Word and sacraments, or the power of the keys of the kingdom of heaven: yet he hath authority, and it is his duty, to take order that unity and peace be preserved in the Church, that the truth of God be kept pure and entire, that all blasphemies and heresies be suppressed, all corruptions and abuses in worship and discipline prevented or reformed, and all the ordinances of God duly settled, administered, and observed. For the better effecting thereof, he hath power to call synods, to be present at them, and to provide that whatsoever is transacted in them be according to the mind of God.[17]

New Englanders feared this kind of arrangement and rejected such Presbyterianism. However, when the Puritans of Massachusetts Bay came to adopt their own doctrinal statement, the *Cambridge Platform of 1648,* they not only adopted without change all of the doctrinal sections of the *Westminster Confession of Faith,* but they also created what has been astutely called "Congregationalized Presbyterianism" or a "Presbyterianized Congregationalism."[18] As a result of this doctrinal stand, New England

[17] *Westminster Confession of Faith,* Chapter 23, III (The Publications Committee of the Free Church of Scotland, 1967) 101.

[18] Trinterud, *Forming of an American Tradition,* 21.

was criticized both by British Independents for exercising too tight control over individual churches and by Scottish Presbyterians for allowing too much diversity among the churches. In fact, however, the New England Congregationalism of the *Cambridge Platform* had remarkable similarities to the American Presbyterianism we know at the end of the twentieth century. And it was this form of Congregationalism that Edwards knew and with which he ministered.

One of the most fascinating discussions of the Puritan attempt to maintain theological unity within its "Congregational" churches and of the degree to which this represented a form of Presbyterianism is Philip Gura's, *A Glimpse of Sion Glory: Puritan Radicalism in New England, 1620–1660.* And one of the most illuminating aspects of Gura's discussion is his consideration of the *Woburn Memorial* of 1663. In that protest, ten individuals petitioned the general court objecting to a recent order of the court in which it was stated that "no person in this jurisdiction shall undertake any constant course of public preaching without the approbation of the elders of four of the next churches, or of the county court."[19] In their memorial, the petitioners arraigned the Massachusetts General Court for encouraging both presbyterianism and Erastianism.[20] Needless to say, the petition was dismissed by the court, but the very fact of its existence seems to verify yet again the ecclesiological model that was being used.

In the 1640s and 1650s, therefore, New England was increasingly Presbyterian in orientation. These were crucial years because it was precisely at the same time that New England Puritans began moving south into Long Island and New Jersey. Leonard Trinterud is just one of the historians who has documented this particular migration. He describes the movement of Francis Doughty, an English Puritan of decidedly Presbyterian views, from Taunton, Massachusetts, to Mespat on Long Island in 1642.[21] Charles Hodge and Lefferts Loetscher also chronicle these early years of Presbyterian settlements in the middle colonies.[22]

The point is that the earliest settlement in this country which could clearly be regarded as Presbyterian was begun by New Englanders drifting down into the middle colonies and bringing with them the theological perspectives and ecclesiological models of early Massachusetts Bay. This

[19] Philip Gura, A *Glimpse* of *Sion's Glory: Puritan Radicalism in New England, 1620–1660* (Middletown, CT: Wesleyan University Press, 1984) 207.

[20] Ibid., 208.

[21] Trinterud, *Forming of an American Tradition,* 22.

[22] Hodge, *Constitutional History,* 357; Lefferts Loetscher, *A Brief History of the Presbyterians* (Philadelphia: Westminster, 1978) 59–60.

was another important aspect in the shaping of the ecclesiastical world in which Edwards lived and ministered.

But that world was not, of course, identical to the world of John Winthrop, and this must be understood as well. In fact, there may be some ways in which early *18th century* New England Congregationalism could be seen as even closer to modern Presbyterianism (as that is normally understood) than to seventeenth-century New England Congregationalism.

On October 23, 1684, the Massachusetts Bay Puritans were notified that the King of England had annulled their charter. This crisis had been brewing for many years, but the event was nonetheless traumatic.[23] Loss of the charter meant the loss of the Puritans ability to structure their society as they saw fit. Concomitantly, it meant a dramatic challenge to Winthrop's corporate ideal of a holy commonwealth because, without the ability to restrict the franchise to church members, the Puritans now, at least in their estimate, had lost the essential means of bringing the church and state in obedience to God. Without such political means at their disposal, the Puritans, who were disinclined to abandon their corporate sense, recognized very quickly that a more formally Presbyterian arrangement was their last best option.

Consequently, Increase Mather, who was in London in 1691 seeking to negotiate the return of some charter to New England, joined with other ministers in sponsoring the *Heads of Agreement.* This plan was essentially a union of Presbyterian and Congregationalist ministers which was designed to make it possible in New England to retain some degree of spiritual hegemony in the church and state. Increasing secularism, centered particularly at Harvard, made it impossible for Mather to sell his plan in Massachusetts. He was opposed by a wide variety of churchmen and the *Heads of Agreement* largely came to nought in his home state.

The concern that had been inaugurated by the loss of the charter and exacerbated by the developments at Harvard had more specific results in Connecticut. There the *Saybrook Platform* was adopted in 1708. Hodge summarizes its content.

> In giving, therefore, the exercise of discipline to the pastors and elders, and in making the determinations of Councils definitive and binding, on pain of non-communion, the Saybrook Platform, unanimously approved by the Assembly which prepared it in 1708, and adopted by the legislature as the discipline of the churches es-

[23] Perry Miller, The *New England Mind: From Colony to Province* (Boston: Beacon, 1981) 130–36.

> tablished by law, comes very little short of Presbyterianism. It is very evident, as this Platform was a compromise between two parties, being less than the one, and more than the other wished to see adopted, that one party must have been thorough Presbyterians. That they were, moreover, the stronger of the two, is evident from the Platform approaching so much nearer to their system, than to that of the Independents.[24]

Hodge's perception is further validated by representatives of the Connecticut churches themselves. On February 5, 1799, after the American Revolution had had its democratizing effect on all of Colonial society, the Hartford North Association of the Congregational Churches of Connecticut, issued a statement identifying the Saybrook Platform as "not Congregational, but contains the essentials of the Church of Scotland, or Presbyterian Church in America, particularly as it gives decisive powers to Ecclesiastical Councils; and a Consociation consisting of Ministers and messengers or a lay representation from the churches (and) is possessed of substantially the same authority as a Presbytery."[25] Because of its crucial nature in relation to the subject of this chapter, the entire text of the Saybrook Platform is included as Appendix A.

Therefore, it would be fully accurate to say that the loss of the charter and the response to that loss in Connecticut resulted in an even greater similarity between the Congregationalism of New England and modern Presbyterianism than has been indicated earlier. Furthermore, the date of the Saybrook Platform is crucial.

Edwards and "Presbyterianized Congregationalism"

Edwards was born in East Windsor, Connecticut, in 1703. He would have been aware of the discussions about the Saybrook Platform and of the fact that his father, Congregational minister Timothy Edwards, was a tireless and vigorous advocate for this system. He would have known that his grandfather, Congregational minister Solomon Stoddard, whose pastoral assistant Edwards became in 1729, was one of the primary sponsors of the Platform. And, given his relationship with both his father and his grandfather, Edwards would have been much affected by their perspective on this issue. As George Marsden summarizes, "Jonathan Edwards never entirely escaped the hold this demanding yet affectionate father had over him. He

[24] Hodge, *Constitutional History*, 34.

[25] The Society of Colonial Wars in the State of Connecticut, "1708—The Saybrook Platform"; http://colonialwarsct.org/1708_saybrook_platform.htm.

followed closely in his father's footsteps and, except for greater reserve, closely resembled his father in standards and attitudes."[26]

All of this means that the *church structure* within which Edwards lived and ministered and which he, in fact, presupposed in his ministry activities was essentially Presbyterian. It was essentially Presbyterian in that it took for granted the inter-relationship of individual congregations. It was essentially Presbyterian in that Edwards himself believed that he performed his ministerial duties within a structure of broader ecclesiastical accountability. During several crucial crises in his ministry, Edwards demonstrated exactly what such accountability entails.

The first of those crises occurred in the church at Northampton. Many explanations have been offered for how America's premier theologian came to be fired by his congregation and this is not the place to rehearse those explanations.[27] For our purposes, the important fact is how the challenges to his ministry were handled, both by those challenging him and by Edwards himself.

George Marsden points to the significant impact of the Saybrook Platform on Edwards's situation when he introduces his discussion of the mechanics of "the separation" with these words: "In order for a church [in Connecticut] to sever its relationship with a pastor it needed the approval of an ad hoc committee of neighboring churches."[28] While this suggests less pre-determined formal structure than would be the case with an official presbytery, the principle of accountability remains clearly established. The Northampton church could not take unilateral action. Its action had to be approved by neighboring churches. The Northampton church was constrained by the authority of those other churches and it was accountable to those other churches. In that sense, the Northampton church functioned in at least a semi-presbyterian environment. And, as Edwards responded, both to the crisis in his church in Northampton and to the later offer from New Jersey, he acted in accord with the provisions of the Saybrook Platform.

The impact of this entire ecclesiastical environment on the unfolding of the crisis at Northampton is described in detail by Marsden. In the end, a Council was called, it met in Northampton June 19–22, 1750, it deliberated much as a presbytery would do, and it decided (by a majority

26 George Marsden, *Jonathan Edwards: A Life* (New Haven: Yale University Press, 2003) 22.

27 Ibid., 341–74.

28 Ibid., 359.

of one vote) that a separation between congregation and pastor was the best way forward.[29] Edwards preached his "farewell sermon" just nine days after the Council's decision.

Not surprisingly, many members of the Northampton congregation were aghast at what their neighbors had done and began a vigorous campaign to keep him in Northampton. First, they sought to pacify Edwards's enemies in order to bring about a reconciliation. When that proved impossible, they began a major campaign to start a new church in Northampton with the clear intention of having Edwards called as its first pastor. All of this was exacerbated by the fact that the majority in the Northampton church, those who had demanded Edwards ouster, had regularly invited him, even after July of 1750, to supply the pulpit of the church on a week-to-week basis. The more one reads of the maneuverings that went on both openly and behind the scenes, the more one could be forgiven for thinking that he was reading about the twenty-first century instead of about the eighteenth. Perhaps the greatest difference between that earlier situation and our modern situation is the way in which the principal—Edwards himself—handled the various options with which he was presented.

In a word, Edwards acted like a *real* Presbyterian. Still following the Saybrook Platform, he again called a Council of ministers, presented all the possibilities to the Council, and, when the Council concluded that he should not remain in Northampton, he accepted that judgment and prepared for a move to the frontier town of Stockbridge. It was a move that neither he nor his family particularly relished. But he did as he felt the wider church was advising him to do. He thus embodied what the "Congregational" church in New England (and especially in Connecticut since 1708) had been all along—a regional church in all but name.

The second of the crises which demonstrated how Edwards regarded his relationship to the broader church occurred in 1757. On September 24 of that year, Aaron Burr, the second President of the College of New Jersey, died. Five days later, Richard Stockton, Clerk of the Board of Trustees of the College and later a signer of the Declaration of Independence, wrote to Edwards offering him the presidency.[30]

Throughout that Fall, Edwards resisted the call to Princeton. His ministry in Stockbridge had begun to bear remarkable fruit and he was getting an extraordinary amount of writing done. He certainly did not want to be saddled with all of the responsibilities which Burr, his son-

29 Ibid., 360.

30 Ibid., 429.

in-law, had been assigned. Discussions with the trustees and his family continued through November and even into December, at which point, Edwards did what, by now, we should expect him to have done—he followed the Saybrook Platform by calling a Council of ministers to ask for their direction. Hearing all of the arguments, both for Stockbridge and for Princeton, the Council of ministers decided that it should be Princeton. According to Samuel Hopkins, Edwards wept . . . and then obeyed.[31]

In hindsight, we know that Edwards went to Princeton to his death. A smallpox inoculation which went wrong killed him in Princeton on March 22, 1758. It probably would be an exaggeration to say that Edwards's presbyterian principles led to his death . . . but it would not be a totally misleading statement. In a cultural environment which was characterized by what Bernard Bailyn has appropriately called "the contagion of liberty,"[32] Edwards never acted as "an independent." In fact, in terms of the way in which he lived his ministerial life, Edwards certainly seems to have acted more "presbyterianly" than some who use the name Presbyterian seem to act today. Perhaps there is a lesson or two here!

Edwards and Princeton

The relationship between the founding of Princeton and the development of Colonial Presbyterianism deserves more attention than it has been given. Only a few salient features of that relationship can be mentioned here, and those only as they related to Edwards's involvement in that institution. His direct involvement, as we have seen above, was brief—just about two months from when he arrived at Princeton until his death. But the very fact that he was invited to serve as the third president of that institution tells us a lot about Princeton and a lot about Presbyterianism in the 1730s and 1740s. (The school of which we are speaking was officially known as the College of New Jersey[33] until 1896 when it became Princeton University. For the sake of simplicity and clarity here, I will simply be referring to this school as Princeton.)

[31] Ibid., 431.

[32] Bernard Bailyn, *The Ideological Origins of the American Revolution,* enlarged ed. (Cambridge: Belknap, 1992).

[33] There is now a different school with the name "College of New Jersey." It is the institution which has had six official names since its founding in 1855 as the New Jersey State Normal School. From 1958 to 1996, it was known as Trenton State College and in that latter year, it became "The College of New Jersey."

The Log College is often presented as the predecessor of Princeton. In some ways, that is true but in other ways, it is not. And Edwards is key to both.

It may be a mistake even to talk about the "founding" of the Log College. It seems likely that the school emerged slowly out of regular but informal meetings held by the Rev. William Tennent, of Neshaminy, Pennsylvania, with young men who expressed a special interest in spiritual matters. That special interest would have grown out of Tennent's own revivalistic preaching and out of similar preaching done in the Raritan area of New Jersey by Theodorus Freylinghuisen. What we do know is that, by the end of the 1720s, Tennent's educational activities had been regularlized to such a degree that those who found his preaching too "enthusiastic" had developed a derisive nickname for those activities—"the Log College," so called because the activities took place in a log house on Tennent's Bucks County farm, which Tennent had received from his cousin, James Logan.[34]

"The Log College"—ah, what a name! It captures so much of the tension which continues even into twenty-first-century Presbyterianism (and Anglicanism and Methodism, etc.). It is the tension between revival and learning, between fire in the heart and light in the head. It is the tension between experimental religion and theological orthodoxy. It is the tension that we all decry but constantly, if unintentionally and indirectly, seem to perpetuate. What shall define us? Theological precision or evangelistic fervor? Of course, we don't want to choose between the two. But somehow we seem so often to do so. Do not the names of two prominent twenty-first-century American Presbyterian denominations suggest as much? Should I join the *Evangelical* Presbyterian Church or the *Orthodox* Presbyterian Church? Perhaps I will select instead a denomination with a more neutral name—the Presbyterian Church in America—and hope to ignore the tension.

But back to the relative safety of the eighteenth century. The Log College was operated by a theologically trained revival preacher. In his own person as well as in his teaching and preaching, William Tennent sought to *be* both evangelical and orthodox and this is the primary way in which the Log College anticipated Princeton. On the other hand, a school

[34] For a fascinating discussion of the relationship between William Tennent and James Logan (William Penn's personal secretary and, effectively, the Chief Operations Officer of the Colony of Pennsylvania until almost the mid-point of the eighteenth century), see E. Gordon Alderfer, "James Logan: Patron and Natural Philosopher," *Pennsylvania History* 24 (April, 1957) 113–14.

which has only one "professor" is bound to inculcate weaknesses as well as strengths in its students. No matter how brilliant and balanced the professor, there is only so much that any one person can be and do. And this suggests one of the crucial ways in which the Log College was less than a full predecessor of Princeton.

Nevertheless, the Log College did its limited work well and, during the 1730s, the Mid-Atlantic region (and beyond) was supplied with increasing numbers of ministers who knew their theology and loved to evangelize. Without question, this was one of the main human reasons why New Jersey and New York and Delaware and Maryland and even Virginia were so receptive to the Great Awakening when it burst upon the country in 1740. Indeed, perhaps the best known of all the Middle Colony Awakening preachers was William's son Gilbert who was himself trained at the Log College. If Alan Heimert is correct in his assessment of the role of the Awakening in the political development of the nation that became the United States and if the Log College really did "prepare the way" for the Awakening in the Middle Colonies, then the overall impact of the Log College was far beyond anything its modest size might have suggested.[35]

William Tennent died in 1745 and, in the very next year, on October 22, a charter was granted for the school which became Princeton. The details of the founding of Princeton suggest that the tension mentioned above was still (perhaps more?) dominant in the life of the church in the mid-1740s. The four "originators" of Princeton were ministers who were known to be of the moderate wing of the New Light/New Side pro-revival party.[36] While each of the four had welcomed George Whitefield into their pulpits and while they all supported the ordination of Log College graduates, they were opposed to the more extreme anti-intellectualism which came to expression during the latter days of the Awakening.

The leader of the four and the man who, in the end, became the first President of Princeton was Jonathan Dickinson, pastor of the Presbyterian Church in Elizabethtown, New Jersey. Dickinson's own career mirrors much of what has been said above about the relationship between Edwards and Presbyterianism. Educated at Yale, Dickinson became the pastor of the Elizabethtown church in 1709, when he was only twenty-one. When he came to Elizabethtown, both Dickinson and his church were

[35] Alan Heimert, *Religion and the American Mind: From the Great Awakening to the Revolution* (Cambridge: Harvard University Press, 1966) 29–30, 43–44, 93–94.

[36] See the narrative of Alexander Leitch, http://alumni.princeton.edu/~ptoniana/founding.asp.

Congregational. By 1717, both he and the church were Presbyterian. Why the change? At least partly because Presbyterianism was the dominant ecclesiastical structure in New Jersey at the time and differed very little from the form of Congregationalism Dickinson had known in Connecticut under the Saybrook Platform.

But Jonathan Dickinson lasted only five months as the school's first president. After Dickinson, Princeton's trustees turned to Aaron Burr, Sr. Burr was born in Fairfield, Connecticut, in 1715/16, and graduated from Yale in 1735. He then became minister of the Presbyterian Church in Newark, New Jersey, one of the churches which, when the split came between the Old Side and the New Side, joined the Synod of New York (which was more sympathetic to the New Side). Burr had, with Jonathan Dickinson, been among the "orginators" of this new school which, they hoped, would bring the best of "Log College theology" to bear on a wide variety of secular and religious subjects. He had supported Dickinson's presidency and, when his friend died, he accepted the responsibility of leading the infant school forward.

Burr lasted in the Princeton presidency somewhat longer than did Dickinson (1748–1757) and, during his time, the college moved to Princeton and became much more stable. For our purposes, Burr's private life reveals almost as much as his public life, for, on June 29, 1752, he married Esther Edwards, the third daughter of Jonathan Edwards. Raised in Connecticut as a Congregationalist, under the Saybrook Platform, having become a Presbyterian in New Jersey and having aligned himself with the New Side Presbyterians in the Middle Colonies, Burr's life and ministry had extraordinary similarities to both his predecessor and his successor in the president's office at Princeton.

And, therefore, when Burr died, the Princeton trustees acted in a way as they thought would best carry forward all that Dickinson and Burr had represented - they elected Edwards as president. Of course, as mentioned above, Edwards lasted in that office a little less than two months. So, if Edwards was president for only two months, what possible impact could this have had on colonial Presbyterianism? Precisely the point!

At the very beginning of this essay, I indicated that I wanted to suggest, among other things, what colonial Presbyterianism *could have been.* Not to put too fine a point on it, if Edwards had remained as President for the same length of time that John Witherspoon (Princeton's sixth President) did, the shape of colonial *and modern* Presbyterianism would, in my judgment, have been far different . . . and far better! Witherspoon was President of Princeton from 1768 to 1794—a total of twenty-six years.

And what twenty-six years they were, encompassing both the Declaration of Independence (of which Witherspoon was the only clergy signer) and the ratification of the U.S. Constitution! No other minister in the American Colonies had as great an influence on what colonial Presbyterianism (and America) became as did President Witherspoon of Princeton!

But would Edwards's influence have been so different from Witherspoon's? Oh, yes! Mark Noll, in his extraordinary volume, *Princeton and the Republic: 1768–1862*, has uncovered and displayed the profound difference between the influence that *was* and the influence that *could have been.*[37] Witherspoon was the first non-American Princeton President and he was the first non-New Side Princeton President . . . and these facts made huge differences in what he brought to Princeton, to colonial Presbyterianism, and to America.

As Noll comments,

> The crowning accomplishment of John Witherspoon's meteoric descent upon America was his new-modeling of instruction at the college. . . . To be sure, Witherspoon set about his work within the framework of the college's traditional purposes. Yet by integrating a new means of integrating learning and faith, by committing the college so thoroughly to the ideology of the American Revolution and dedicating it so completely to the health of the new United States, and even by his own personal success in binding together the interests of learning, patriotism, and Christianity, Witherspoon altered the course of the college for at least the next century. It was a momentous development not just for the college *but also for Presbyterianism* and, to a lesser extent, the new country as a whole.[38] (emphasis added)

In other words, Witherspoon, while working within the general stated purposes of Princeton, made some seemingly slight theological and pedagogical shifts which, in the end, produced massive changes in the character of both Princeton and Colonial Presbyterianism.

Those shifts came largely from Witherspoon's commitment to Scottish Common Sense Realism. Witherspoon did not alter in any way the fundamental doctrinal tenets of Princeton, but he did alter the way in which those tenets could be *known*. And this was where he differed most dramatically from Edwards. Again, Noll makes the point clearly:

[37] Mark Noll, *Princeton and the Republic: 1768–1822* (Princeton: Princeton University Press, 1989).

[38] Ibid., 34.

> The deeper significance of Witherspoon's tenure lay in his reorientation of intellectual activity around the principles of the Scottish Enlightenment, a shift that necessitated the displacement of intellectual patterns associated with Jonathan Edwards and New Side Presbyterian revivalism.[39]

As has often happened in the history of the church,[40] the theological discipline in which this shift first became obvious was the area of ethics and moral philosophy. Here is Noll's excellent extended analysis:

> Witherspoon's intellectual commitments place him at a fairly advanced stage in the development of what Norman Fiering has called 'the new moral philosophy.' With Hutcheson, Alison, and most other eighteenth-century moral philosophers, Witherspoon set aside the Augustinian distrust of human nature; in practice, he denied that original sin harmed the ability to understand and cultivate natural virtue; he regarded the achievements of science as triumphs of empirical inquiry more than as insights into the effulgence of God's glory; and he pictured God more as the originator of material and moral order than as the constantly active creator of the world.
>
> Witherspoon's philosophical allegiance, regarded in this light, was no minor matter. It not only united him with Scottish Moderates and Old Side Presbyterians. It also divided him from the philosophical orientation of the New Side/New Light American Calvinists and complicated the implementation of Princeton's long-term goals. In other words, when Witherspoon set in place a pattern of instruction grounded in Scottish moral philosophy, he materially altered Princeton's traditional approach to ethics, epistemology, and the interconnections of knowledge. In particular, his commitment to Scottish common sense meant that there was no longer any room at Princeton for the influence of Jonathan Edwards. Nothing in the college's early history so significantly shaped its destiny.[41]

So Witherspoon replaced what has been called Edwards's "fiercely revelational" theology with a more "reasonable" faith which contributed significantly both to the general liberalization of Princeton and Presbyterianism and to the founding documents of the United States,

39 Ibid., 36.

40 See Samuel T. Logan Jr., "Theological Decline in Christian Institutions and the Value of Van Til's Epistemology," *Westminster Theological Journal* (1995).

41 Noll, 43.

phenomena which are surely interrelated. After all, if the essential truths are "self-evident," is revelation really necessary at all?

But beyond that, Witherspoon, again through his "common sense realism," led Colonial Presbyterianism very strongly in the direction of a technical orthodoxy which was practically divorced from the revivalism of his New Side predecessors in the President's Office at Princeton. Of course, he did not openly repudiate the work of his predecessors. He largely just ignored it and led Princeton and Presbyterianism away from the very things which were the lifeblood of Edwards's ministry.

Edwards's *Treatise on Religious Affections* remains one of the most important theological works ever written. It shows, more profoundly than any other human work, what is the fundamental character of Christian faith and life. If only twenty-six years of Princeton students had had the opportunity to learn, from Edwards, that God-honoring ministry starts with correct doctrine but does not stop there . . . If only they had had the opportunity to learn, from Edwards, why it is so critical to build on correct doctrine to an unreserved passion for the beauty and glory of Christ . . . If only this had happened, perhaps the Presbyterian Church of the next century (or two or three) would have been BOTH evangelical AND orthodox.

We cannot, of course, re-write history. And the "if only's" have value simply in this—they may make us return to something that *could have been* and lead us to expend our energies to implement what *should be.*

Edwards was all-but-officially-Presbyterian in all the ways that count. May future Presbyterianism be all-but-officially Edwardsean in all the ways that count.

2

Francis Makemie—Presbyterian Pioneer

D. Clair Davis

"IN his twenty-five years in the New World Francis Makemie had become colonial Presbyterianism's chief exponent, its leading literary apologist, main defender of its liberties, foremost overseer of its congregations, and the moving force in the formation of its first presbytery."[1] Schlenther's summary is helpful and accurate. Without Makemie it would be hard to imagine what American Presbyterianism would have become. In so many ways it was his imprint and vision which made it what it is today. But what that means in detail is not easy to say. We know his undoubted commitment to the Westminster Standards, but what were his theological priorities? We know of his untiring support of fledgling congregations, but what did he dream of their future? We know of his vision for a regional church, a presbytery, but did he desire a presbytery focused on evangelism or orthodoxy, Old Side or New Side? We know he was a public-spirited man, as committed to the new society as to the new church, but had he thought through the hazardous implications? Such rhetorical questions could be multiplied, but the answers will always be elusive, for the obvious reason that the written materials left behind are so fragmentary.[2]

So it is not surprising that there has been much speculation, even fiction, around the real Makemie. With such a shortage of material, this writer too will "suggest" how what we know of his agenda turned out

[1] Boyd S. Schlenther, *The Life and Writings of Francis Makemie* (Philadelphia: Presbyterian Historical Society, 1971) 28; all of Makemie's writings are to be found here as well.

[2] All to be found in Schlenther, in a slim volume of 282 pages. Without this book, research would be much more difficult. With it though, the shocking realization comes quickly: this is all there is.

within the setting of later American Presbyterianism. To do that, I will suggest where the theological and culture origins of his thought are to be found, and where he thought the American church should be going.

Life

What we know of Makemie's life is very limited, but we can see the broad outline. He was born about 1658 in Northern Ireland and began his study of theology in Glasgow in 1676. He was ordained in 1682, perhaps as an evangelist, and arrived in Maryland's Eastern Shore (today the Delmarva Peninsula) in 1683, responding to a request for help sent to his Irish presbytery. For many years he carried on an itinerant ministry along the coasts of Maryland, Virginia and North Carolina, and also 1700 miles offshore in Barbados. It isn't clear whether he began many of those churches or not; certainly he gave them much-needed encouragement and his own preaching. From 1692–1698 he lived mostly in Barbados, carrying on commercial as well as ecclesiastical activity, where he became very successful in his export-import business. He also inherited considerable Maryland land from his father-in-law. From his private fortune he generously became the one-man financial sponsor, or "sustentation fund" for the new church plants. In 1706 he organized in Philadelphia the first American presbytery "to meet yearly, and oftener if necessary, to consult the most proper measures for advancing religion and propagating Christianity in our various stations, and to maintain such a correspondence as may conduce to the improvement of our ministerial ability by prescribing texts to be preached on by two of our number at every meeting, which performance is subjected to the censure of our brethren."[3]

The latter part of that presbytery agenda may need some explanation. Our Presbyterian fathers believed that preaching was the most important part of ministry and that it always needed improvement. Preachers who know the difficulties and problems of preaching and also are deeply committed to become better at it were priceless resource people to each other. Reformed people had long been active in organizing small groups within the congregations for the purpose of applying the minister's sermon, and for reporting back to the elders on the value of his preaching to them. Further development of this practice became the regular incorporation of sermon evaluation into presbytery meetings, as those first minutes indi-

[3] From the presbytery minutes, as found in Alan Guelzo, *Roots* in *Tenth Presbyterian Church of Philadelphia*, ed. Philip G. Ryken (Phillipsburg, NJ: Presbyterian and Reformed, 2004) 26–27.

cate. (Probably the first to introduce this practice was John Laski [a Lasco] in the Reformed classis in Emden, Germany).

Also in 1706 Makemie preached to a Presbyterian congregation in New York City. He was immediately arrested by Governor Cornbury for preaching without his own New York license. Cornbury denied that legal precedents in England and the other colonies applied in New York, where he believed he had total authority to advance the exclusive rights of the Church of England. Makemie appeared in his own defense and won a resounding victory for the rights of dissenters in America, demonstrating that they had the same liberties as they had in the mother country. In the midst of efforts to secure more ministers from Britain, he died in the spring of 1708, probably at his Virginia home.

A Pre-Awakening Theology

What can we know of Makemie's theological orientation? We have his interaction with Barbados episcopacy, *Truths in a True Light* (1699), his interaction with radical Quakerism, *An Answer to George Keith's Libel* (1694), and just one sermon, "*A Good Conversation*" (1707). He was irenically ecumenical with the Episcopalians, affirming that they and Presbyterians shared the same classical Reformed tradition, and that he regarded their Thirty-Nine articles, particularly its statement on election, as worthy of respect and being very helpful. In *Truths* he criticized some details, but sought vigorously to foster a truly Reformed ecumenism, transcending the concerns of Presbyterians. He emphasized the common background of all Protestants within the heritage of the Christian church throughout the ages. The Quaker discussion however moved in a much more polemical direction, largely because they had been attacking his (now missing) catechism. He spoke primarily against the Quaker emphasis on avoiding all language not found in the Bible, and thereby to promote a truly biblical religion. He endeavored to demonstrate the impossibility and inconsistency of that agenda, and how it was bound to promote serious doctrinal error. Makemie argued throughout for the necessity of maintaining the true Christian faith, which could be done only within the context of orthodox Christianity. He argued against the inconsistencies of the Quakers, criticizing them for accepting salaries while speaking against them, for example. Much of his argumentation simply pointed out that doctrine has ethical implications, that the tie between doctrine and life must be maintained, in good Puritan fashion. While we could wish for the discovery of his missing catechism, it is doubtful there would be any surprises. Makemie's claim to be a follower of the Westminster Standards must be taken as he would want it taken, at face value. There is no apparent theological idiosyncrasy in his thought which merits further consideration. He is ecumenically Reformed and supports all foundational Christian theology, ranging from the Trinity which all (except apparently Quakers) believe to the specifically Reformed understanding of election.

It is just that one sermon which we have which is so puzzling. No minister would like his theology evaluated on the basis of a single sermon, but it is after all the sermon which precipitated the issue of religious liberty for dissenters in New Yolk, and it is a sermon which he chose to be published. It is the first sermon he preached to the Presbyterians of New York City, people he didn't know at all. One would think that under those circumstances the sermon would be broadly representative of the most basic message that he believed Christians needed to hear. Taking all that into account, the sermon is more than puzzling; it is confusing and unnerving in the extreme, it just does not contain a clear statement of the Gospel. As Edmund Clowney my homiletics professor would have observed: it could have been preached by a rabbi.

The sermon, "The Good Conversation," is a call to a "well-ordered life," a life of obedience to God. Makemie addresses primarily the more obvious public sins of drunkenness, fornication and Sabbath-breaking. Only tangentially is there reference to the heart sins of not loving God or being grateful for salvation in Christ. Much is said about the value of church discipline, Christian education for youth and respect for the civil authority, all as necessary means for fostering good living. There is a wealth of Scripture citations. The primary theme is the holiness of God, and why there is no hope for us unless we also live holy lives. But there are all those amazing gaps, the missed opportunities to speak about the Gospel, of the forgiveness of sins because of what Jesus Christ has done, or the power of the Holy Spirit working in the hearts of the believer to overcome sin. To be sure, he does say that obedience to God is not the meritorious cause of salvation, or anything which in any way deserves salvation, for that would be a "Popish denial" of the merits of Christ. But that discussion is very brief and abstract, not nearly as thorough or as carefully explained as other parts of the sermon. Instead, he stresses that obedience, the good conversation, is the path or map of salvation (165–66). At the very end of the sermon he does allude to the consolation of knowing that the "irregularities" in our lives are accepted by God because of the merits and advocacy of our Savior. But that discussion is also a bare allusion, without any development at all. Taking the sermon as a whole, it must be regarded as seriously unbalanced.

Christian duty and many details of obedience are thoroughly treated, but the work of Christ is barely mentioned. So much is said about the dangers of not understanding what our responsibilities are, in virtually every aspect of life, depending upon our position in society, etc. So little is said about grace, and how it is only by the power of the Gospel and the work of the Holy Spirit in our hearts that we can obey at all.

Now what does that mean? Was this a typical Makemie message? Was he really so sure that the knowledge and application of the Gospel of grace can be assumed, taken for granted in the church and that what people most need reminding of is just their moral duty to God? The most charitable judgment would have to be that this is after all a pre-Awakening sermon. Only forty years later would the Great Awakening disclose the shocking discovery of the terrible gaping hole in the everyday theology of the people, their almost total ignorance of the Gospel of grace and what saving faith is really like.

Makemie's theology was surely balanced and orthodox. Whatever his missing catechism said, it must have been a popularization of Westminster. Within a ministry of proclaiming the comprehensive theology of grace of the Westminster Confession, wasn't he entitled to a judgment call of what people really need to hear most right now? But still—would any Reformed pastor today bring this as his first sermon to people he didn't know?

This will always be the great puzzle of the Awakening. How could the heart of the Gospel be so long overlooked? How could the lessons of the Reformation be forgotten? Why had the Gospel balance of Calvin become so lost? How could pastoral experience not indicate that the real hole in the heart of people in church was the lack of knowledge and experience of the grace of God in Jesus Christ? Why is modern Biblical theology so surprising, that it actually is possible to see Christ everywhere in the Bible? Is it enough, that once a generation the message of grace be proclaimed? Is it really understandable that Christian ministers believe that most of the time what church people need to hear is how far short they come? However those questions are answered, the reality of the missing Gospel will always be startling and unsettling.

Reading all this back from the Awakening is inevitable. Then the New Side discovered what a constant and intentional proclamation of the Gospel would do for the salvation of the lost, the growth of the church and also the priorities involved in the training of ministers. But the Awakening also precipitated the alarm of the Old Side at the potential danger of sound doctrine being replaced with fluctuating human experience. When the dust settled at the end of the Awakening, the Sides of the church could re-unite, presumably on the basis of the common commitment to judge each other's motives with love, and to recognize the need for both a sound understanding of the Gospel and also evangelistic zeal. On that basis the church could exist with one General Assembly—but still see the need for two or later three presbyteries of Philadelphia! New Siders could do ecclesiastical business with Old Siders, but couldn't invite them to speak in city-wide revival meetings. Today we would say there was doctrinal agreement but radically different philosophies of ministry. Sound historians differ radically on the value of the Awakening. When the young Charles Hodge wrote his *Constitutional History of the Presbyterian Church*, he sought to discuss even-handedly the pros and cons of both sides. In response Archibald Alexander, the first faculty member at Princeton Theological Seminary, wrote his *Log College* whose last chapter makes the point that Princeton itself is solidly within the New Side Log College tradition.

Down to the present day there are those within the American Presbyterian church who are sure that doctrinal orthodoxy is threatened by experiential "Pietism." Others remain concerned that the church is ingrown, with no heart for unbelievers outside and no passion for the secular city. They believe that the priorities of a church planting philosophy of ministry are radically different and much superior to a maintenance one. Both sides continue to be convinced of the value of their core commitments and the legitimacy of their presuppositions. Within that context what would a fair evaluation of Makemie's position look like today? Probably it would be this: was not his calling so radically and necessarily directed to protecting and fostering the infant American Presbyterian church, that he could not divert his energies to evangelism? That resembles some situations today. When people have been betrayed by the radically changing theology of the major denominations, then it can seem that what they first need to do is to begin again and reclaim their theological and ethical heritage – well before they can go on to reaching unbelievers for Christ? Or can and must both be done at the same time? For most Presbyterians today I think the last would be the preferred answer. Only the Gospel is true; only the Gospel is the message of salvation which must be proclaimed. Makemie would not have questioned this at all, that is certain; but we can still regret that the Awakening did not come sooner.

Distinctive Presbyterianism

For Presbyterians discussions of Christian theology flow quickly into issues of church government, for they see those issues as also being questions of Scripture interpretation. As in all such questions some are of higher priority than others. How essential to the well-being of the church is its Presbyterian structure? Within the New World setting, with its many imported theological traditions, how important is it that Presbyterianism be well represented, when other Reformed traditions are also present?

What will Presbyterianism look like, when it is not the state church, but only one of many dissenting groups, "denominations," in America? Certainly Presbyterianism by nature could never think of itself as sectarian or narrowly individualistic. It would always be concerned with the broader cultural implications of its faith. While Calvinism never had had the geographical scope of Continental Lutheranism, at least in Scotland and the Netherlands those larger objectives could begin to be carried out. But what could it mean to be Presbyterian in the American colonies, with their many and varied churches?

The New England establishment had long decided that Congregationalism was the best expression of New Testament Christianity. In the South, established Anglicanism thought of itself as being as much a state church as it long had been in England. In America then, establishment was a reality but not for Presbyterians. Consistent separationist sectarianism also existed, with the Baptists and the Quakers. But where was the place for Presbyterianism, neither established nor sectarian? In many ways their answer would become the general American answer: on the one end of the spectrum, is the deep commitment to the "separation of church and state;" but on the other end, the serious expectation of the Christian church to make a difference in the society. To be a *spiritual* entity, but also to express the coming of the *Kingdom*—that is the American expectation of the church, which colonial Presbyterianism under Makemie's direction was to begin.

The earliest settlers of Presbyterian background almost never had immediate access to a local Presbyterian church. Usually the best they could do was to affiliate with an approximation of that, either in New England a Congregationalist church or in the South the Anglican Church of England. The Congregationalist form of the Westminster Standards was functionally very close to the Scottish Presbyterian version. Congregationalists always understood that it would be necessary for local churches to act regionally in many situations. The more routine examination and ordination of a minister was one, when a council with that specific and limited agenda would be brought together. Major doctrinal disputes would require such regional cooperation too. While a New England "consociation" was meeting, it would be hard to see any functional difference between it and a presbytery. That is, Congregationalism could appear to be a kind of temporary or *ad hoc* Presbyterianism. Scottish Presbyterianism, on the other hand, had itself moved in a Congregationalist direction when it finally recognized the right or appropriateness of the local congregation to call its pastor. Throughout the many patronage controversies it had become clear that while a presbytery could determine whether the candidate's theological views were orthodox, and even whether he could satisfy the presbytery concerning his general effectiveness in preaching, still only the congregation itself could be the judge of whether his doctrinal focus and preaching was to *its own edification*. In Presbyterian terminology, the people call and presbytery processes their call. When there was no *outward call* of the congregation the prospective minister and presbytery would have to concede that he didn't really have an *inward call* either.

Perhaps in an area settled both economically and ecclesiastically the line between congregational and Presbyterian regional accountability could remain fairly ambiguous. In those circumstances Presbytery could accustom itself to agreeing with the prior judgments of local churches, very similar to the function of a consociation. Certainly the New England ethos was to duplicate as much as possible the social and economic settled climate of England. People were expected to live in villages and commute outward to their land. Naturally the church building was on the square or next to the common. Single men and women were expected to affiliate and live with families. Presbyterians could also understand that kind of model and could recognize their kinship with the New Englanders. Certainly that was reciprocated, as repeated New England endorsement of Makemie's writings and ministry testifies.

But what if the cramped settled quarters of New England are not the only American geography or model? What would a church for Americans on the move look like? How would a regional church on the frontiers of New Jersey or Maryland or Pennsylvania or Virginia express itself? What if the regional church has a calling to be much more than an administrator of the already existing church, but rather to organize and implement the expansion of the church into new areas? In frontier America Presbyterianism would see itself called to express itself in more missional ways, more resembling the new church of the New Testament. (Attend a meeting of church-planters today, and hear the ways they think and talk: not of how to fine-tune an older style of church, but how to begin ones with intentionally new directions and visions).

For Makemie he saw his calling as encouraging the congregations just beginning, and helping them find pastors. But it also meant protecting and nurturing them within a hostile or at least monopolistic religious establishment. The forces arrayed against them were regional or colony-wide, and it was necessary and appropriate that responses to ecclesiastical oppression be just as broad and comprehensive. This is how we must understand the appeals to colonial legislatures, to allies in New and Old England and to the public in general. All this adds to the significance of the gathering of that first presbytery in 1706 in Philadelphia.

In those days pastors were recruited back in Ireland or Scotland, and had already been approved and ordained there. For the colonial church the issues of the best pastoral training and the requirements for ordination didn't arise as acutely, though it must have been a factor in recruiting those men to come to America. Those were the questions which the Awakening church of the 1740s would need to consider, and which led to the brief division between the Old and the New Sides. But already within the first presbytery the pastoral and missional direction was clear and compelling, and the continuity with those later discussions is clear. Meetings come and meetings go—but the church of a region is always there, and its calling is to bring the Gospel and creatively to wherever it has not yet come.

Working with Congregationalists was more a matter of fine-tuning the differences and moving from a passive to a more aggressive style of regional leadership. But in the Anglican territory of Maryland and Virginia where Makemie ministered primarily, the issues were more problematic. In Barbados Makemie had emphasized the great identity of Anglican and Presbyterian theology, both being aspects of international Calvinism. He praised the Thirty-Nine Articles, especially the clear statement on divine election. But that didn't keep him from raising the usual Puritan, Scots and Scots-Irish theological objections against certain Anglican practices. He did avoid some of the more marginal issues: the title of priest or the wearing of garments with priestly associations; the position of the communion table and whether it was wooden or stone more suited as an altar. He did mention briefly some practices with which he disagrees: the use by ministers of prescribed written prayers could be interpreted to mean being forced to accept ministers incompetent to pray and hence unqualified to lead their flocks. What is the point of kneeling while receiving the Eucharist (if Jesus himself sat for the meal, who are we to be more devout than he)?

Much more crucial were the prescribed Anglican liturgies for Baptism (ministers were required to speak of baptism accomplishing salvation) and for funerals (in a similar way the prescribed prayer assumed the salvation of all baptized people). These required more searching criticism. How could people be called to faith in Jesus Christ as the only way, when at the same time the liturgy created the impression that saving faith was not really necessary? Any hint of "baptismal regeneration" was seen as an enormous obstacle to evangelism. Because of that presumption of some type of automatic salvation, *ex opere operato*, any subsequent evangelistic appeal for a "personal faith in Christ" would be met only with suspicion or incredulity. Presbyterians were bound to think that only through a more consistent church, where doctrine and liturgical and sacramental practice worked together, could the Gospel be clearly expressed,

The other side of church membership, when people's "credible profession of faith" was examined and evaluated in church discipline, was important for Presbyterianism. For Anglicans discipline was administered not at the local level, but through the bishop of the diocese, and then not really by him, but through his lay chancellor. This official was hardly qualified to have pastoral interest in the people involved, but ordinarily just levied fines according to a set schedule. At least that was how Presbyterians saw it, and for them this was a terrible misuse of the order Christ had instituted. Church discipline should not be seen as punishment, but rather as encouragement to spiritual growth and restoration. What needed to be dealt with was much more than the sin, but rather the individual's continuing response to counsel about that sin, as the church instructed him from the Bible. (Today Christians think much more about "discipling" than about "discipline"; that seems to express better the meaning and importance of those concerns.)

Here Makemie's allusions to the dangers of imperfect discipline require some further explanation, though he assumed everyone would know what he was talking about. Misleading discipline had led to confusion and distortion of the Gospel itself. When the local church and its minister were unable to confront people with the disparity between the call and commandments of Jesus Christ and the shape of their own lives, then what could they do? Frequently the preacher saw fit to use his sermon to seem to address in a very searching way the entire congregation, but really to get at the sins of the few who needed to hear it. That was dangerous. Not only was that approach unlikely to arrive on target, but it could lead to tender-hearted people coming to question their own salvation. They might excommunicate themselves! While the Puritan goal was always "to afflict the comfortable and comfort the afflicted," such preaching could easily lead to afflicting further the already afflicted. To see yourself as not really being a believer after all could easily be the final result of a focused process of evaluating your life in terms of the claims of Christ. When the preacher focuses immediately on the state of the heart, not just as the deepest layer in life to be evaluated, but in more immediate terms as the definition of what it is to be a Christian, then assurance and joy in Christ could be quickly lost. Seeing the inadequacy of heart transformation could swallow up the full and complete forgiveness of sins—that is, concentration on one's own questionable regeneration can swallow up the finished work of Jesus Christ in justification.

That could lead further into an unhealthy focus on stereotyped conversion experiences, where people's expectation came to be that everyone needed to go through an extended period of recognizing one's sin, attempting to change oneself, failing miserably, despairing, crying out to God for the Holy Spirit to regenerate you, and then experiencing heart change—and then to question the reality of that change and begin the whole process all over again! Such unhealthy man-centered preaching easily led to detailed instruction of what the sinner needed to do in order to experience God's grace, how to prepare one's heart for God's grace. Though hedged about by many theological qualifications, for many it sounded like: this is what I have to do to induce God to give me grace. It wasn't surprising that Jonathan Edwards came to speak of Arminianism within staunchly Calvinist New England. Much of that is a later story, but it is strongly to Makemie's credit that he could foresee the far-reaching implications and likely effects of imperfect discipline, without and within Presbyterianism.

Much of that confusion comes from theological confusion roots as well as ambiguous discipline. Somehow within the broader Reformed context, the way of salvation, the sequence of salvation, the *ordo salutis*, has historically seemed difficult to understand and especially to implement. What are we to make of the heart-warming sequence of salvation in Romans 8? What can it mean that regeneration is *prior* to faith? Should we attempt to detect a heart-change *temporally* before and outside of a saving trust in Jesus Christ? Is that what we say at the funeral of an infant, that while she never was old enough to believe, that she was still regenerate? Those are the well-worn puzzling paths which have led to multiplied confusion, as the mysterious work of the Holy Spirit in the human heart was sought outside of the Gospel of Jesus Christ.

What then is the right use of the *ordo*? In its proof-text site in Romans 8, the *ordo* is the heart of Gospel encouragement, as it sets forth the great ongoing promises of the Lord. No matter how great and deep the trials and suffering described in Romans 6–8 may be, at the end there is the clear and firm certainty that nothing will ever separate the believer from the love of Christ. God's salvation which began in justification will surely go on and culminate in glorification. However else the *ordo* may work in the Christian heart, surely its point has gone radically astray when, instead of the message of deep encouragement and blessing, the exact opposite is what its teaching had produced. It was intended to bring consolation and joy in the ongoing grace of the Lord. Instead its study brought only doubt and terror in wondering whether that love would ever really begin. It is within that context that Makemie's zeal for helpful discipline is at its best.

Freedom for the Gospel

With all appreciation for other almost-Reformed churches, and with great respect for the common Reformed tradition, Makemie was convinced that having true Presbyterian churches in America was a real necessity. But what if there was political and ecclesiastical resistance to the right of Presbyterian churches to exist? Those very real crises led to the other great contribution of Makemie, his successful struggle for religious liberty in the colonies. There are many sides to his thinking, and indeed for the entire American struggle for liberty. Probably the most basic question is: should people in the colonies assume they enjoy "the rights of Englishmen?" Do the agreements and laws regulating "dissenters" in England apply in the colonies, or are Presbyterian rights there a matter for constant reinterpretation by the royal governors? Makemie argued for the former view and prevailed. A little later this discussion would be repeated within the context of American political liberty. Is "no taxation without representation" a principle which applies to Englishmen wherever they may be within the protection of its government—or is it in the colonies something always at the arbitrary discretion of a ruler?

That is, is there a constitution or something like it, something to which even the ruler must submit, and which limits his power? Without getting into the technical distinction between the written constitution of the USA and the unwritten one of Great Britain, the constitutional understanding of government has been the cornerstone of Reformed political thought. Is God himself bound by his promises? Or does he have the right go back on his Word? What is a *covenantal* promise of God, when he swears by himself or by his holy name, really worth? Over against the arbitrary God of late medieval nominalism, this "constitutional" understanding of God's promises became vital to Protestantism. Medieval theology had degenerated into trying to guess where God's will was ultimately be found, or whether even the attempt to learn it was in itself an infringement on his sovereignty. But if God has bound himself by his Word, then there can be assurance of salvation, boldness in Christ and certain conviction that all the pain and struggle in life is really worthwhile and is for the Lord's own glory and my eternal good.[4]

Too many preachers have attempted to explain God's covenant in terms of a human business contract. His covenant isn't something to be negotiated between God and man, but is rather a one-sided suzerainty covenant. God binds himself by his Word, but is not limited by the redemptive-historical circumstances within which the covenant was proclaimed. Be amazed when God fulfills his promises in a bigger way than we had ever imagined. Instead of Canaan, even of all between Nile and Euphrates, God's people inherit the whole world! As Isaiah 49:6 says, for the sake of his Servant it is too light a thing for God to restore just Israel; salvation is much bigger than that—it includes the Gentiles, and the entire world with them. So God's fulfillment may be greater than we could ever imagine—but it will never be smaller! Now if this is the way the Ruler of the whole world exercises his authority, as a constitutional or covenantal Monarch, must not human rulers also be limited in their authority by whatever constitution or equivalent they have acknowledged? In Calvin's discussion of this point, he does allow that there are societies in which there are no 'lesser magistrates" to protect the people from the usurpation of power by the highest ruler. But when the lesser magistrate exists, he has the solemn obligation to protect his people from tyranny. This responsibility is especially spelled out in the Scots Confession, and was prominent in the thinking of the Scots-Irish church. This is the broader foundation for Makemie's appeal to precedent in English law. Though Makemie endured a great deal to make this fundamental point, including being burdened with all court costs, he inevitably prevailed and won the case for Presbyterians and ultimately religious liberty for all. Liberties for dissenters which applied in England, or Barbados, or Virginia, of course also applied in New York, whatever Governor Cornbury said. That Cornbury himself was convicted of gross misuse of power is also not surprising. The English rule of law is of much more than provincial importance, as the king rules the colonies as well as the mother country. That law is not limited by the ocean or distance from the monarch, but is the foundation for the Christian culture which England sought to maintain.

[4] See Peter A. Lillback, *The Binding of God: Calvin's Role in the Development of Covenant Theology*, Texts and Studies, Reformation and Post-Reformation Thought, ed. Richard A. Muller (Grand Rapids: Baker, 2001).

Not much later the Presbyterian minister John Witherspoon would sign the Declaration of Independence, convinced that without political liberty there could be no religious liberty either. The Awakening taught the awakened the Presbyterian principles of the congregation's right to call a minister who taught them in a way which edified them, even against the wishes of the ecclesiastical establishment. From believing in the right to choose your own minister to the right to choose your own government was not a large step. Makemie himself could not conceive of disloyalty to the British crown, but his fight for the liberty of dissenters contributed much to the ideological background of the American Revolution.

It may help at this point to remember a somewhat later Virginia church planter, Samuel Davies. His arguments for freedom for those outside the established church are virtually identical with Makemie's earlier ones. He repeats the argument that either the Toleration Act of 1689 applies in the colonies, or if it doesn't, then the earlier Act of Uniformity doesn't either. He raises the new issue, "whether a dissenting congregation, that is very much dispersed, and cannot meet at one place, may claim a right . . . to have a plurality of places licensed for the convenience of the sundry parts of the congregation?"[5] In this case Presbyterians were granted religious liberty when in the French and Indian War the frontier Presbyterians were seen as the first line of defense and Davies was valued as a tireless recruiter of troops and general morale-builder, particularly because of his "Curse of Cowardice" recruiting sermon.

Urban Culture and the Kingdom of God

Limited government gives space for dissent. That principle has long been the appeal of "small government" for a religious or any other kind of minority. Does that signal an inherent interest in small government for Makemie? Is a Christian viewpoint necessarily "conservative?" Or do Christians have any interest in encouraging the state to be more active? One look at his remarkable document, *A Plain and Friendly Perswasive*, answers the question. Makemie vigorously urges the government of Virginia to move aggressively away from its rural base toward a society of towns. This is truly remarkable. In nineteenth-century Southern Calvinism the agrarian, ante-bellum society was perceived as significantly better and more Christian than the urban manufacturing society of the North, and the

[5] George William Pilcher, *Samuel Davies Apostle of Dissent in Colonial Virginia* (Knoxville: University of Tennessee Press, 1971) 122; see especially "Toward a Free Exercise of Religion," chapter 7.

Civil War was perceived as Northern aggression against the "family values" of the South. At that time city life was seen as a culture where everything revolves around money; the South sought to affirm resoundingly that a man is more than a producer and a consumer, as urban society seemed to believe. Friendship and family are much more important than business interests, something which is bound to be understood more naturally and easily in rural agrarian life. Such was the viewpoint of almost all Christians in the later South.

In his earlier day Makemie saw that all differently. We must allow for the differences between the almost totally dispersed rural society in his day and the more mixed economy of the nineteenth century. But that doesn't make his concerns irrelevant. He is very forceful in arguing that the interests of church and of society will be advanced more readily in a more urban economy and society. He used almost every argument possible, and regards such a society as preferable for a variety of reasons, economic, political, social and religious. The tobacco market would be fairer when more bidders compete against each other for the crop. An economy based solely on tobacco is inherently unstable. That will demand more and more slaves. Only an urban population will be a growing one, and a larger population will be a much greater protection against French expansionism from the Mississippi. There are many lazy people, who don't want the active life of the cities, but they are short-sighted. Some say that cities will lead to more drunkards, but they can be dealt with in the stocks.

The economy and society would develop more consistently and evenly when the city environment could provide more varied options for employment and investment. Morals would be better when people would be under greater public scrutiny in the city than they could be in isolated country plantations. Finally, church attendance and involvement would work much more effectively within an urban context; a larger, more balanced congregation is needed to support and foster a good Christian church.

What does this mean? Is the Scottish free market of Adam Smith finding a home in America? Isn't the secular appeal of the city over the country the greater anonymity, the possibility of living life without the constant scrutiny of country neighbors; why did Makemie believe that the city was less private? Was that the way it worked in Ireland? However we may look at the comparative advantages of the city and the country today, for Makemie it was obvious. Economic and ethical/religious advance work much better together and they both work best within the context of the city.

In many ways Makemie's book is a textbook example for the later perception of the linkage of Calvinism and Capitalism, as set forth by the sociologists Max Weber and R. H. Tawney.[6] While their contention that Calvinists need economic success to buttress their shaky sense of election is radically misguided, there are other elements of that linkage which seem more solid. Certainly all Protestants believed in divine calling for everyone, not just for the monastic life. Luther spoke of the farm laborer's calling of God to shovel manure. But Lutheranism was almost as agricultural and monocultural as in medieval times. Calvinism on the other hand was a religion for the cities, London, Edinburgh, Antwerp and Amsterdam. There the greater variety of new and older professions within the city fed into the Calvinist zeal for diligence in determining your personal calling. Puritans invented vocational counseling. Discovering God's unique calling for the individual and the new urban specialization can merge into being the same thing.

Newer Calvinist evaluations of what constituted usury made the reality of investment capital possible. Stewardship of God's good gifts could include stewardship of money. If calling equals specialization, and specialization means discovering what you are the best at, that may well lead to increased income. But what was the purpose of that new wealth? There the diaconal element came in. The clear answer was: God gives you wealth in order that you may help the poor. But even that answer can be ambiguous. What is the best way to help the poor? Is it by giving them food and clothing, or is it by providing for them jobs? If providing jobs is the answer, then helping the poor and expanding the business are virtually identical. That would be a fair interpretation of the background of Makemie's zeal to encourage the government to foster the urbanization of Virginia.

Does urbanization help public morals? If we get beyond the question of where is there more privacy, city or country, we can see the deeper issues and can understand Makemie's agenda more clearly. People with similar interests and professions can understand each other better, including the burdens and temptations of those callings. Urban specialization and more understanding mutual spiritual care work well together. While Puritans tended to organize their church small groups along geographical lines, they did know about putting together people in the same calling too. A businessman with sophisticated financial skills can provide greater accountability and direction to another businessman than a farmer could.

6 Max Weber, *The Protestant Ethic and the Spirit of Capitalism*, trans. Talcott Parsons (New York: Scribner, 1958); R. H. Tawney, *Religion and the Rise of Capitalism* (London: Murray, 1926).

One suspects that something of this derives from the urban experience of a Presbyterianism at home in Edinburgh or Belfast.

What are the advantages of the urban church? One needs only to think of the struggles of Charles Hodge in the nineteenth-century to provide adequate salaries for rural pastors. Though he had many innovative ideas, such as a regional sustentation fund for poorly-paid rural pastors, nothing seemed to work. There just isn't enough money in a small rural area to pay a pastor, and no one else really cares.[7] A routine item in any presbytery meeting was: voting to close yet another rural church. One solution would be making use of less-educated part-time farmer-preachers, as with the Baptists or Methodists. Is the Presbyterian "educated ministry" a cultural artifact or biblical wisdom? Should the Christian minister have also a cultural calling as the medical/legal/political adviser for the community, not to mention village schoolmaster? (Today's questions concerning a minister's calling are similar to Makemie's, except that today we think about the urban ministry as less able to sustain a pastor than the suburban one, and consider whether the same educational background is necessary for the city, or whether some "alternative credentialing" may be sufficient).

It is fascinating to reflect on Makemie's desire to modernize the economy of Virginia, within the context of planting vibrant Christian churches. Modernization is what's right for the society, he believed, so that is exactly what Christians are called to promote. Those concerns go far beyond the issues of adequate financial support for ministers. Makemie doesn't limit his discussion to Christian or ecclesiastical reasons for urbanization, but speaks more as a public-spirited citizen. Would we call that today "civil religion," an uncritical linking of modern progress with the cause of Christ? We can anticipate again the defining moments which create the distinctiveness of American Christianity. European Christianity, especially in its Deistic elitist form, had long assumed that only a very few could be affluent, and that poverty within the comforts of religion, with its pie-in-the-sky heaven, would always be the lot of most people. But America was not that way; it is about doing better in a new society than you could have ever done back home. America is about good cheap land, and making your own way. America is the land of unlimited possibility, and "there is no king in America." No wonder that many preachers back home warned against emigration: you'll go to America and get rich and forget God.

[7] Cf. William S. Barker, "The Social Views of Charles Hodge," in *Word to the World: The Collected Writings of William S. Barker* (Christian Focus, 2005) 93–97.

How can confidence in economic and political progress fit with a deep belief in the depravity of the human heart and the absolute need for divine grace? Were the preachers back home right, that inevitably wealth leads to pride and deeply threatens the humility which is the foundation of believing faith? Or is it possible to unite a responsible "progressive" Christian sense of calling to the new world with a radical dependence upon God? Could it be, that the greater your responsibility within your calling, the more obvious to you will be your inadequacy for the task? Poverty and helplessness may drive one to dependence upon God and trust in him; but the enormity of great tasks within a totally different world may do that too.

Makemie's Vision and Ours

Makemie's America was a new kind of society with a new kind of church. For both society and church the issues were not about maintenance but about making a new beginning. But a new beginning with continuity with the past and its many values is what is needed. The Virginia frontier can come to have some of the character of Irish town life. Isolated churches can develop regional consciousness; presbyteries can be pro-active. An American Presbyterian Church can be true to its doctrinal heritage while it comes to know people in its community from other theological traditions. Reformed and still being Reformed works well within that global church, coming to America from so many places. That all was within Makemie's vision, though he would be astounded to see its fulfillment today.

Christians in America were called to be truly public spirited without compromising their firm belief in the need for divine grace. It is not inevitable that when people become richer in America than they could ever have been in Europe, that they will sell their spiritual birthright for a mess of pottage. Is God still showing us how that can happen? Are the "checks and balances" of very diverse American society the product of the Deistic watchmaker God? Or do they rather show their origin from the mutual accountability of a Calvinist culture of discipline and discipling? When all the injustice and oppression in America's society is recognized and evaluated, the Christian conscience of its people and society is still a reason for deep gratitude to God. The American way was to prove much more humane and hence more impervious to the politics of the industrial class struggle. When the post-millennial Kingdom in America collapsed with the comparative failures of the temperance movement and post Civil War Reconstruction, the result was not a turning away from Christianity as irrelevant, as was so easily the case in Europe. There was some withdrawal from political action, as the new pre-millenialism sought to defer the Kingdom of God until after the return of Christ. But from that came a new evangelistic and missionary activism, also directed toward the cities. The significance of the pre-Kingdom age was to preach the Gospel throughout the world. With the demise of the American Kingdom came something much larger, the emergence of God's global Kingdom.

In many ways Makemie anticipated the continuing westward expansion of America, where the frontier could be regarded as both problem and solution. It was the problem for the reasons Makemie saw: it was difficult to plant churches there, especially when one had in mind the full-time Presbyterian "educated minister." Could the Gospel really go to the unchurched frontier; could it cross the Alleghenies, or the Mississippi, or the Missouri, or the Rockies? The frontier was a better fit for the itinerant non college-trained Baptist or Methodist circuit-rider. The Presbyterian minister was not as likely to have the vision for adding more and more church plants to his duties. Regrettably, he was more likely to supplement his income by starting an academy where he could teach Latin and Greek to small boys.

With all those failings of Presbyterian cross-cultural ministry, its unarticulated but still conscious strategy was to bring theological leadership to the community, though not necessarily in Presbyterian churches. With the Baptists and Methodists taking the West, there would be still a kind of Presbyterian community there. That is the sense of Makemie's vision for the development and urbanization of Virginia. He was committed to the expansion of both Kingdom and Church. America he knew would be larger than Presbyterianism, but it would come into its own within a Presbyterian context. The new church in a new world would make use of the rich Calvinist heritage, making use of the freedom fostered by its roots within British and European culture. It would come alongside of all the other churches of Christ within the Protestant and Reformed heritage. Makemie would become the example and advocate for regional vision-casting to plant Christ's church everywhere for God's glory.

Think of Makemie as a Moses, seeing clearly the Promised Land ahead but not himself entering in. Today we share his vision, usually without recognizing where it came from. The Gospel of grace is the greatest gift of God to the Presbyterian Church, but it is much bigger than the Presbyterian Church. The Gospel and God's Kingdom go hand in hand; today we call it word and deed ministry. Makemie saw further ahead in his day than anyone else; his legacy to us is a similar eye of faith for the glory of the Lord.

3

The Log College

David B. Calhoun

WITHIN a hundred years of its closing William Tennent's Log College had reached near-iconic status in American Presbyterianism.[1] This was assured when Princeton Seminary's beloved and highly respected first professor, Archibald Alexander,[2] published his admiring *Biographical Sketches of the Founder and Principal Alumni of the Log College*.[3] Alexander

[1] Regular memorial celebrations were held at the Old Tennent Farm during the nineteenth and into the twentieth centuries. On September 5, 1889, a full day of 13 speeches and 7 hymns was sponsored by the Presbytery of Philadelphia North, including addresses by the governors of Pennsylvania and New Jersey, and Benjamin Harrison, president of the United States.

[2] In a 1946 sermon on "The Log College and the Beginning of Princeton," Clarence Edward Macartney states that "because of the part he played in the founding of the oldest and most illustrious of the seminaries of the Presbyterian Church" Archibald Alexander has "many claims to be named the most influential Presbyterian in the history of our church in America." Clarence Edward Macartney, "The Log College and the Beginning of Princeton" (n.p.: n.d.).

[3] Archibald Alexander, *Biographical Sketches of the Founder and Principal Alumni of the Log College. Together with an account of the revivals of religion under their ministry* (Philadelphia: Presbyterian Board of Publication, 1851). The first edition of this work was printed in 1845 at Princeton. In 1851 a new edition was published in Philadelphia. There were minor changes of wording, a chapter on the College of New Jersey was added, some documents were removed to the appendix, and four illustrations were provided. In 1968 the Banner of Truth Trust reprinted the 1851 edition (with slight changes). In his review of the 1968 Banner of Truth reprint of Alexander's *Log College* Paul Wooley, professor at Westminster Theological Seminary, wrote that in this volume "one feels again the great power of eighteenth-century revival preaching" (*Westminster Theological Journal* 32 [1969] 91). See also *Sermons and Essays by the Tennents and Their Contemporaries* (Philadelphia: Presbyterian Board of Publication, 1855). This volume of sermons was compiled by Archibald Alexander as a supplement to *The Log College*. Charles Hodge's *Constitutional History of the Presbyterian Church in the United States of America* (1839–40) has a less positive view of the Log College men than does Alexander. Hodge charges them with great disorderliness

lamented that in his day every vestige of the Log College had disappeared; but he noted that to preserve "some small relic of this venerable building," a Presbyterian minister had made a "walking-staff" from one of the remaining logs. "As a token of respect, and for safe keeping," the minister had presented the staff to Samuel Miller, Alexander's colleague at Princeton Seminary.[4]

The Founding of the Log College

Soon after 1726, when William Tennent[5] became the pastor of the Presbyterian church on Little Neshaminy Creek in Bucks County, Pennsylvania, he began in earnest to educate his three younger sons and some other young men who wanted to study for the ministry.[6] For several years Tennent trained students in his home and then in a nearby log cabin that he built. The students lived with William and Katherine Tennent[7] and found themselves completely incorporated into the Tennent family—studying, working, eating, and worshiping.

Because he established the Log College, William Tennent is often credited with beginning something new. Archibald Alexander called Tennent's school "the first seminary" in which students were trained for the ministry within the Presbyterian church.[8] Gary Schnittjer claims that "Tennent's private ministerial academy was the earliest documented in

in professional conduct, in ecclesiastical polity, and in doctrinal emphasis. Alexander was deeply pained by Hodge's negative assessment. He wrote a long letter to Hodge expressing his strong conviction that "the Old Side were a great deal worse and the New Side a great deal better" than Hodge had presented them. In time Hodge came to a more positive view of the value of the First Great Awakening. He wrote in 1847: "We believe . . . that we are largely indebted for the religious life which we now enjoy to the great revivals which attended the preaching of Edwards, Whitefield, and the Tennents; and at a later period, of Davies, Smith, and others, in Virginia" (*Biblical Repertory and Princeton Review* 19 [1847] 519).

[4] Alexander, *Log College*, 9.

[5] William Tennent was born in Ireland in 1673 and trained at the University of Edinburgh from which he received his master of arts degree in 1693. He took orders in the Church of England in 1704. In 1718 he came to Pennsylvania and that same year applied for admission to the Presbyterian church, stating that his views had changed. Between 1720 and 1726 he served pastorates in New York.

[6] As early as 1718 Tennent taught his oldest son, Gilbert.

[7] Katherine Kennedy was brought up in a Presbyterian manse in Ireland. Thomas Murphy calls her "the real founder of the Log College." Would the Log College ever have been built, he asked, "without her counsel, her cheer and her self-sacrifices?" Thomas Murphy, *The Presbytery of the Log College*, 118–19.

[8] Alexander, *Log College*, 24.

the American colonies."[9] But Tennent was simply acting within a well-established tradition when he began his "college." He was familiar with the local academies in his native Ireland and in Scotland and with the pattern of ministerial preparation in America.[10]

Some prospective ministers in the colonies were trained in universities in Scotland and Ireland or at Harvard and, later, at Yale. Others enrolled in small local academies, or by private reading and study achieved what could be considered the status of college graduate. Specialized theological and pastoral preparation followed the preparatory education. James Fraser writes, "A classical education, followed by some time reading . . . theology with a respected mentor was what the [Presbyterian] denomination required for ordination, and there were many ways to accomplish that."[11]

To prepare for ordination, some students remained in residence at Harvard or Yale to use the library, attend the president's lectures in divinity, and confer with him from time to time. In some cases the professor of divinity, who for the most part was simply "an auxiliary to the president, . . . assisted by supervising resident graduates in their reading of divinity while also instructing undergraduates."[12] Most ministerial candidates, however, lived and studied with an experienced pastor. These pastors directed students in their reading and gave them opportunities for practical experience in the various duties of the ministry. The pastors' wives provided food,

[9] Gary Schnittjer, "The Ingredients of Effective Mentoring: The Log College as a Model for Mentorship," *Christian Education Journal* 15 (Fall 1994) 88.

[10] For Scottish and Irish influence on the American Presbyterian academies, see Douglas Sloan, *The Scottish Enlightenment and the American College Ideal* (New York: Teachers College Press, 1971) 38–47. "This study explores one major pattern of Scottish influences on American higher education: the appeal Scottish higher education in the eighteenth century had for many Americans; the extent and importance of the Presbyterian academy movement in America; and the thoughts and careers of representative individual educators who were related to the academy and early Princeton traditions" (ix).

[11] James W. Fraser, "The Great Awakening and New Patterns of Presbyterian Theological Education," *Journal of Presbyterian History* 60 (Fall 1982) 201. Fraser emphasizes the Presbyterian commitment of both the Old Side and the New Side to adequate classical studies for ministerial candidates, as well as theological study, and describes the various avenues open to Americans in the East and on the frontier during the eighteenth century to meet these requirements. "While the institutional forms might vary greatly," he writes, there was "a consensus about the content of the training" (203).

[12] Ibid., 200. In 1803 President Samuel Stanhope Smith brought Henry Kollock to Princeton College as professor of theology. His primary responsibility was to supervise postgraduate ministerial education. Kollock resigned his professorship in 1806 and became the pastor of the Independent Presbyterian Church in Savannah, Georgia, where he served until his death in 1819.

lodging, and sympathetic, valuable counsel. Some pastors became noted as teachers and directed the study and training of several young men at the same time in what came to be called "schools of the prophets."

William Tennent's school continued for less than twenty years.[13] It never had more than one part-time teacher. Only about twenty young men studied at the Log College.[14] Yet Leonard Trinterud calls the founding of this little school "the most important event in colonial Presbyterianism."[15] In 1889 a New York newspaper stated that "what the landing of the Pilgrims was to Congregationalism in this country, the founding of the Log College has been to Presbyterianism."[16]

Why did Tennent's school achieve such status? Gary Schnittjer asserts that "there is no good way to explain the success of the school of logs outside of the unseen ingredient of divine providence."[17] There were, however, at least three factors that contributed to the school's lasting fame.

The Whitefield Connection

George Whitefield's early contact with the Log College and his unstinting praise for the school and its founder elevated the whole enterprise in the minds of American Christians, especially as Whitefield moved from his earlier controversial reputation (which divided Christians, including Presbyterians, over his emphases and tactics) to a revered status, among most Protestants, as a kind of American church father.

During a visit to Philadelphia on Saturday, November 10, 1739, Whitefield first met "Mr. Tennent, an old grey-headed disciple and soldier

[13] The beginning of the school has been dated as early as 1726 and as late as 1735. Tennent died in 1746.

[14] Alexander writes about ten of these in his *Log College*. See the list of twenty-one known Log College students in Guy S. Klett and Thomas C. Pears, *Documentary History of William Tennent and the Log College* (Philadelphia: Dept. of History, Presbyterian Historical Society of the Office of the General Assembly of the Presbyterian Church in the United States, 1940) 174. Leonard Trinterud has revised this list slightly in *The Forming of an American Tradition: A Re-examination of Colonial Presbyterianism* (Philadelphia: The Westminster Press, 1949) 332, fn. 4. Despite many critics, Trinterud's book has endured as an important interpretation of early American Presbyterianism. Trinterud's argument that the emergence of the New Side Presbyterian Church was "the birth of a new order" is far stronger than his analysis of the later decline of "evangelical" Presbyterianism.

[15] Trinterud, *The Forming of an American Tradition*, 63.

[16] Murphy, *The Presbytery of the Log College*, 506.

[17] Schnittjer, "The Log College as a Model for Mentorship," 95.

of Jesus Christ."[18] He "keeps an academy twenty miles from Philadelphia," Whitefield wrote in his journal. Whitefield continued:

> He is a great friend of Mr. Erskine, of Scotland,[19] and, as far as I can find, both he and his sons are secretly despised by the generality of the Synod, as Mr. Erskine and his brethren are hated by the judicatories of Edinburgh, and, as Methodist preachers are by their brethren in England. Though we are but few, and stand alone, as it were like Elijah, yet I doubt not, but the Lord will appear for us, as He did for that prophet, and make us more than conquerors.[20]

After a two-week preaching tour in New Jersey, Whitefield returned to Pennsylvania to visit Neshaminy on November 22, 1739. Three thousand people had gathered in the churchyard to hear him preach. William Tennent Jr. preached while the people waited for Whitefield to arrive, and his brother Gilbert Tennent followed Whitefield with "a word of exhortation." "After our exercises were over," Whitefield wrote,

> we went to old Mr. Tennent, who entertained us like one of the ancient patriarchs. His wife, to me seemed like Elizabeth, and he like Zacharias; both, as far as I can find, walk in all the ordinances and commandments of the Lord blameless. We had sweet communion with each other, and spent the evening in concerting measures for promoting our Lord's kingdom. It happens very providentially that Mr. Tennent and his brethren are appointed to be a Presbytery by the Synod, so that they intend breeding up gracious youths, and sending them out into our Lord's vineyard. The place wherein the young men study now is, in contempt, called the College. It is a log house, about twenty feet long, and nearly as many broad; and, to me, it seemed to resemble the school of the old prophets. . . . From this despised place, seven or eight worthy ministers of Jesus have lately been sent forth; more are almost ready to be sent; and a foundation is now being laid for the instruction of many others. The devil will certainly rage against them; but the work, I am persuaded, is of God, and will not come to naught.[21]

The next year, on April 23, 1740, Whitefield was once again at Neshaminy, where he preached to "upwards of five thousand people, in

[18] Whitefield was 24 years old, and Tennent, 66 in 1739.

[19] Ebenezer Erskine (1680–1754) was a founder of the Secession Church. He was educated at Edinburgh, receiving his master of arts degree in 1697. Tennent received his master of arts from Edinburgh in 1693.

[20] *George Whitefield's Journals* (London: Banner of Truth Trust, 1965) 344–45.

[21] *George Whitefield's Journals*, 354–55.

old Mr. Tennent's meeting-house yard."[22] By this time he was committed to the Tennents and they to him.

The New Side Presbyterian Church Connection

In his journal Whitefield mentioned the Presbytery of New Brunswick, authorized by the 1738 Synod. The presbytery became a refuge for the Log College graduates, and led to a division of the Presbyterian church when it was excluded by the Synod of Philadelphia in 1741. In 1745 the Presbytery of New Brunswick joined the Presbytery of New York to form the Synod of New York, known as the New Side Presbyterian Church.

There were no real differences on doctrinal points between the "New Side" Synod of New York and the "Old Side" Synod of Philadelphia. Both accepted and revered the Westminster Standards.[23] "The theology of the Log College was never questioned," asserts Charles Reed.[24] Gilbert Tennent, wrote Archibald Alexander, was "rigidly orthodox, according to the Westminster Confession."[25] William Tennent Jr. was a man of "sound orthodox principles" according to the author of a memoir of Tennent quoted by Alexander.[26] Members of his congregation in Freehold, New Jersey, noted the care with which he instructed children in the Westminster catechisms. Another Log College man, Samuel Blair, was "a thorough-going Calvinist," according to Archibald Alexander.[27]

Both the New Side and the Old Side held to Presbyterian polity, although the issue of "incursions"—New Side preachers taking their message of repentance and revival into places where, in their opinion, people were not hearing the true gospel—created much resentment and bitterness.

The major issue dividing the church was revival. The Log College men (and eventually the New Side Presbyterian Church) supported and

22 Ibid., 411.

23 William Tennent Sr. and Gilbert Tennent had signed the Adopting Act in 1729. John Tennent signed an unqualified subscription to Confession, Catechisms and Directory in New Castle Presbytery late in 1729.

24 Charles Robert Reed, "Image Alteration in a Mass Movement: A Rhetorical Analysis of the Role of the Log College in the Great Awakening" (Ph.D. diss., Ohio State University, 1972) 64. Reed combines a sociological analysis with a study of communication techniques. He attempts to show what role rhetoric played in the shaping of the Log College history. The dissertation is weak on theological analysis and accuracy.

25 Alexander, *Log College*, 66–67.

26 Ibid., 145. The author of the memoir of William Tennent Jr. was Elias Boudinot.

27 Ibid., 171.

attempted to extend the revival, whereas the Old Side was cool, and even hostile, to it.

Furthermore, the Old Side held that it was sufficient to examine a prospective minister's learning and knowledge; the New Side put equal, if not more, importance on the candidates' spiritual qualifications. Tennent's purpose was to train faithful men for the ministry. He believed that "fervent piety" was the first and foremost qualification of a minister. Tennent never tired of reminding his students that they must "keep close to the written Word of God," and so keep their hearts "in all diligence." He urged them to cultivate in their lives "a Godlike temper which is pleased with anything that makes for the glory of God." He warned them against "mere formality and hypocrisy."[28] The Log College men and the New Side Presbyterian Church "were not satisfied with doctrinal correctness alone; doctrine had to be attached to personal piety."[29]

"The two groups in the Church had come to the parting of the ways, not over dogmas, Church government, or educational standards," but (according to Ashbel Green, a leading Old School polemicist) because of "a determined resolution to endeavour to awaken the Presbyterian Church from a state of great declension in vital piety."[30]

Archibald Alexander, who also supported the Old School in the later schism of the Presbyterian church, was of the opinion that at the time of the beginning of the Log College "the state of vital piety was very low in the Presbyterian church in America." Ministers and people were orthodox but there was a "formality" and "dead orthodoxy" and "strong opposition to faithful, pointed preaching."[31] Alexander believed that the Presbyterian church of his day was more indebted "to the men of the Log College for our evangelical views, and for our revivals of religion, than we are aware of. By their exertions, and the blessing of God on their preaching, a new spirit was infused into the Presbyterian body."[32] Alexander recognized the faults of the New Side ministers, which included "harshness, censoriousness, and bitterness" toward their opponents, but he made clear his sympathy with them.[33]

28 Schnittjer, "The Log College as a Model for Mentorship," 90–91.

29 Reed, "Role of the Log College," 213.

30 Ashbel Green, "Letters to Presbyterians," *Advocate* 11, 414.

31 Alexander, *Log College*, 16–17.

32 Ibid., 40.

33 Ibid., 39.

The New Side prospered during the seventeen years the church was divided; the Old Side (called "The Withered Branch" by Leonard Trinterud)[34] did not. "When Whitefield legitimized the revival and the synod moderates identified with the Log College party, public opinion shifted to the side of the movement," states Charles Reed.[35] The reunited church contained diverse views on the matters that had divided it but, more and more, American Presbyterianism came to embody the New Side outlook—a combination of confessional Calvinism, pietism, and "a new brand of missionary-minded Presbyterianism."[36] The proposals Gilbert Tennent presented in the positive sections of his polemical sermon "The Dangers of an Unconverted Ministry" became the policy of the Presbyterian church.[37] In his sermon Tennent set forth "a powerful defense of the understanding that a Godly minister combined a lively intellect with a passionate, personal faith."[38] The New Side commitment to orthodox doctrine, practical piety, and zealous outreach shaped American Presbyterianism, both North and South, until the early twentieth century. This inheritance from the Log College served to perpetuate the name and reputation of the little school at Neshaminy.

The Princeton Connection

The connection between the Log College, which closed in the early 1740s because of Tennent's age and increasing frailty, and the College of New Jersey, which began in 1746,[39] has often been noted. Chapter 7 in Archibald Alexander's *Log College* is titled "The Log College the germ from which proceeded the College of New Jersey."[40] After the Log College

[34] Trinterud, *The Forming of an American Tradition*, 135.

[35] Reed, "Role of the Log College," 208.

[36] Ibid., 213.

[37] Ibid., 173.

[38] Wilfred Earnest Tabb III, "The Presbyterian Clergy of the Great Awakening" (Ph.D. diss., Washington University, 1992) 81. "This study contributes to the expanding body of research on the Great Awakening in the Middle Colonies. It examines the careers of Presbyterian ministers who supported the Awakening, the so-called 'New Side.' Its central thesis is that these ministers were innovative conservatives who brought change to the Presbyterian Church and ministry while still attempting to conserve clerical privilege and power" (iii–iv). The description of the New Side preachers as "innovative conservatives" is a useful and accurate one. Less certain is the claim that they attempted to protect clerical status.

[39] The first charter was issued in October 1746 and classes were opened at Jonathan Dickinson's manse in Elizabeth, New Jersey, the following year.

[40] Alexander, *Log College*, 76.

closed there was no school where the New Side Presbyterians could train their pastors, but this need was quickly addressed, and soon New Side leaders were planning to create a school. "The ministers who now exerted themselves in the establishment of the New Jersey College were all friends of the Log College," wrote Archibald Alexander; "and most of them had received their training, both in classical and theological learning, within the walls of this humble institution."[41]

Before the College of New Jersey moved to its permanent location in Princeton in 1756, it existed for a few years on the pattern of the Log College—as an academy headed first by Jonathan Dickinson in Elizabethtown and then by Aaron Burr in Newark.[42] In 1889 James McCosh, former president of Princeton College, wrote: "The Log College was a well among the hills from which a great and beneficent stream has risen. The Log men, the Tennents and Blairs, were heroes. . . . The college in the wilderness insisted on two great principles: . . . a native ministry and an educated ministry. This led indirectly to the establishment of the college at Princeton."[43]

A number of Log College alumni became key figures in the early years of Princeton College. Gilbert Tennent and Charles Beatty served as trustees. William Tennent Jr. was acting president. John Blair became professor of divinity, vice president, and, for a short time until John Witherspoon arrived, acting president. Samuel Finley was president of the college, as was Samuel Davies, who studied at Samuel Blair's academy at Faggs' Manor, a replica of the Log College.

When Princeton Seminary was founded in 1812, it too claimed to be a successor to the Log College. The Log College was both a college and a theological seminary, but its purpose was the training of ministers. When the General Assembly of the Presbyterian Church decided in 1811 to establish a theological seminary, there was considerable discussion concerning the location of the new school. Not a few people were strongly in favor of placing it on the very site of the Log College.

As Princeton College and Princeton Seminary became the key educational institutions for American Presbyterians, the historic significance

41 Ibid., 82.

42 For the relationship between the Log College and the College of New Jersey, see George H. Ingram, "The Story of the Log College," *Journal of the Presbyterian Historical Society* 12 (1924–27) 487–511, and E. R. Craven, "The Log College of Nashaminy (sic) and Princeton University," *Journal of the Presbyterian Historical Society* 1 (1901–1902) 308–14.

43 Murphy, *The Presbytery of the Log College*, 525.

of the little school on the banks of Neshaminy Creek in Bucks County, Pennsylvania, was guaranteed.

Strengths and Weaknesses of the Log College

As George Whitefield noted, there was considerable criticism of the Log College during its time. Some believed that those coming into the ministry from the Log College were without "sufficient qualifications." It was said that the Log College men "decried the usefulness of some parts of learning" that others in the synod thought necessary.[44]

The 1738 Synod decided that all candidates for the ministry who did not possess a degree from either a New England or European university would be required to stand examination before a special commission appointed by the synod. This action was obviously aimed at the Log College supporters, who had just succeeded in creating a presbytery in New Jersey made up mainly of Tennent's graduates and supporters. The Tennents and their friends objected, believing it was a violation of the right of presbyteries to ordain ministers. Within a few months the synod refused to admit John Rowland, a Log College alumnus already licensed by the New Brunswick Presbytery.

"The overture as such was very reasonable and good," comments Trinterud. "It was, however, not wholly fair."[45] Friends of the Log College were extremely reluctant to have their students examined by the synod, Alexander explained,

> either, because they were conscious that they would be found defective in some of the branches usually pursued in the college course; or, because they were of opinion that the major part of the Synod were prejudiced against this humble institution, and against all who were connected with it. Probably both these considerations had their weight in leading them to oppose so strenuously a measure which to us seems reasonable and necessary, to guard the ministry against the intrusion of unqualified candidates.[46]

[44] Schnittjer, "The Log College as a Model for Mentorship," 89, quoting *Minutes of the Presbyterian Church in America, 1706–1788* (Philadelphia: Presbyterian Historical Society, 1976) 211.

[45] Trinterud, *The Forming of an American Tradition*, 74. Fraser comments, "On the surface the resolution seemed fair enough, but its actual consequences were that Yale- and Irish-educated Old Side candidates could enter the ministry without question, while every Tennent candidate had to undergo the harassment of a hostile examination" ("Great Awakening and Theological Education," 193).

[46] Alexander, *Log College*, 47–48.

There was probably some justification in the synod's criticism of the Log College, since William Tennent was specifically educating his students for the ministry and may have passed quickly over areas that he considered less important for this purpose (or subjects in which he had little or no interest or expertise). Evidence from several sources suggests that science, mathematics, modern literature, and philosophy may have been neglected by Tennent. Alexander admits that Tennent and the friends of the Log College probably "lightly esteemed some parts of learning, which other members of the Synod thought requisite."[47]

It should be noted, however, that at this time Presbyterian schools in Scotland and Ireland were weak in the quality of their education. Trinterud states that "Scottish university work in this period was in a deplorable state, and little improvement was to come for some time." "Private schools" founded by Presbyterians in Ireland were "ephemeral and weak."[48] There was no guarantee that graduates from Harvard or Yale were competent in all the required subjects. Trinterud asserts that it was not "wholly unlikely that Tennent would be able to produce 'graduates' fully as competent as his Scottish-educated opponents."[49]

The Log College men and their New Side Presbyterian supporters never suggested a reduction in requirements of general knowledge. They agreed with the Old Side that ministers were to be educated broadly as well as theologically. Ministerial education was viewed as resting upon the classics and liberal arts, the same curriculum considered basic to all learned professions. Douglas Sloan argues that "as far as education was concerned the real difference between the Old Side and the New Side was not over the necessity and importance of education, but, rather, its goals and priorities."[50]

The Log College provided both "college" and "seminary" training. Some of the students spent five years or more studying with Tennent; others three or four years, depending on their academic achievements when they entered the school.[51] What sort of education was actually received at the Log College? Archibald Alexander wrote a hundred years after the

47 Ibid., 45.

48 Trinterud, *The Forming of an American Tradition*, 64.

49 Ibid., 65.

50 Sloan, *The Scottish Enlightenment and the American College Ideal*, 55.

51 Sudents were expected to study for four years at Yale: languages (Latin, Greek, and Hebrew) in year one, logic in year two, natural science in year three, and arithmetic, geometry, and astronomy in year four.

closing of the school that that question could not be fully answered.[52] Nonetheless, Alexander's description of the school's founder and its "principal alumni" give us some information.

The school's one teacher, William Tennent Sr., was trained at the University of Edinburgh.[53] He was an able classical scholar. He spoke Latin fluently and was proficient in Greek and Hebrew. His learning in the arts and science apparently was not so great as his skill in language. Trinterud's claim that "as a scholar and teacher, William Tennent Sr. was unique without an equal in the synod" probably goes too far, but he certainly was among the two or three most able teachers in the Presbyterian church at that time.[54]

The Log College graduates were well known for their broad academic knowledge as well as their theological expertise. Gilbert Tennent passed his exams before the Presbytery of Philadelphia with distinction. Other Log College men who appeared before the Presbytery of Philadelphia did well in their examinations. The Log College graduates all excelled in languages, especially Greek.[55] Samuel Blair was also competent in philosophy and mathematics, especially geometry and astronomy, and had a "large acquaintance" with geography and history.[56] One of Samuel Finley's Princeton students said of him: "His learning was very extensive: every branch of study taught in the college appeared to be familiar to him."[57] Gilbert Tennent's ability was recognized with an honorary master of arts

[52] Alexander, *Log College*, 49.

[53] For the life of William Tennent Sr. see Gary E. Schnittjer, "William Tennent and the Log College: A Common Man and an Uncommon Legacy" (Th.M. thesis, Dallas Theological Seminary, 1992).

[54] Trinterud, *The Forming of an American Tradition*, 53. The Old Side also supported a school for the training of its ministers—an academy founded by Francis Alison in New London, Pennsylvania, in 1742. In 1751 Alison, a successful educator, moved on to the Academy (later called the College) of Philadelphia. The College of Philadelphia, however, never became a Presbyterian school in the way that Princeton College, the successor to the Log College, was. After Alison's death in 1779 virtually all Presbyterian ties would disappear.

[55] Frederick Brink concluded that "Gilbert, William, Jr., John and Charles [Tennent], Samuel Blair, Samuel Finley, and others [Log College students], all display in their sermons a grounding in Greek that is hard to equal." Frederick Brink, "Gilbert Tennent, Dynamic Preacher," *Journal of the Presbyterian Historical Society* 32 (March 1954) 100.

[56] Schnittjer, "The Log College as a Model for Mentorship," 89, 90.

[57] Ibid., 90, quoting William B. Sprague, *Annals of the American Pulpit* (New York: Arno, 1969) 3:100.

degree. It is not known which school granted him this degree, probably Yale or Harvard, or one of the Scottish universities.

The record of the Log College alumni showed them to have been "men of unusual ability, and of passionate zeal in providing educational facilities for others."[58] In sermon after sermon the Log College men insisted that ministers have training in languages, the sciences, and philosophy, as well as thorough grounding in the scriptures and preaching.[59] Students trained at the Log College and later at the College of New Jersey founded other academies and colleges.[60] It is this tradition that earned for the Log College the status of "one of the great educational institutions of colonial America."[61]

Wilfred Tabb asserts that "New Side ministers argued for a very traditional kind of preparation for the ministry: education in the arts and sciences, specialized training in divinity, and an active knowledge of God's grace."[62] The men trained at the Log College were competent especially in theological studies. Gilbert Tennent's impressive knowledge in theology, according to Archibald Alexander, was "entirely derived from the Bible," although Tennent quoted the standard Latin writers of systematic theology "as one who had been accustomed to read them."[63] Samuel Blair's impressive learning in general studies was exceeded only by "his knowledge in divinity."[64]

Tennent's students excelled in preaching and in the practical areas of pastoral work. The "character of Gospel laborers," Tennent stressed, "implies that such have a knowledge of the work, and the skill to manage it right."[65] Young George Whitefield wrote that he had never heard "such a searching sermon" as one given by Gilbert Tennent.[66] Samuel Davies, upon returning from England, reported that he heard no preacher there who was superior to Samuel Blair.[67]

58 Trinterud, *The Forming of an American Tradition*, 74.

59 See Tabb, "The Presbyterian Clergy of the Great Awakening," 94–97.

60 See Macartney, "The Log College and the Beginning of Princeton."

61 Fraser, "New Patterns of Presbyterian Theological Education," 191–92.

62 Tabb, "The Presbyterian Clergy of the Great Awakening," 100.

63 Alexander, *Log College*, 63, 67.

64 Schnittjer, "The Log College as a Model for Mentorship," 90.

65 Ibid., 91

66 Alexander, *Log College*, 32. It was Alexander's opinion that "it is doubtful whether Mr. Whitefield has ever expressed so high an opinion of any other preacher of any denomination."

67 Ibid., 193.

Gary Schnittjer states that Tennent's "distinctive contribution was perhaps what is currently being called 'mentoring'" and, Schnittjer explains, accounts for the effectiveness of the Log College.[68] This method of theological training was not limited to Tennent. As we have seen, other pastors took in a student or two at a time and provided personalized training for them, but Tennent trained a larger number of students for a longer time. He did on a slightly larger and more organized scale what others had done for some time. The important role that mentoring plays in vocational training has become widely recognized today. "The Log College way of education," asserts Schnittjer, "can serve as a pattern for mentoring."[69]

Conclusion

In commemoration of the two-hundredth anniversary of Princeton University, Clarence Edward Macartney preached a sermon at the First Presbyterian Church of Pittsburgh, Pennsylvania, on "The Log College and the Beginning of Princeton." Macartney closed his sermon by saying:

> On a bright spring afternoon I stood in the meadow where the Log College was erected and read the inscription on the monument, which is as follows:
>
> Lux In Tenebris
> Log College
> Organized
> By
> William Tennent, 1727
>
> Here, in the life of a pioneer teacher, sound
> learning, endued with spiritual passion,
> wrought to vitalize knowledge, glorify truth,
> enrich life, and in due time call forth, to the
> welfare of American youth, these worthy
> Christian colleges.[70]

It is remarkable that over 260 years after its closing, a little one-room, one-teacher school that produced only twenty or twenty-one "graduates" should still be remembered. William Tennent Sr. and his school are de-

68 Schnittjer, "The Log College as a Model for Mentorship," 92.

69 Ibid., 93.

70 Macartney, "The Log College and the Beginning of Princeton." The monument at Neshaminy lists the names of 62 colleges that trace their origin to the Log College, beginning with Princeton in 1746.

scribed in a recent dissertation as "a common man and an uncommon legacy."[71] The words "the Log College"—first spoken in contempt—have become an honored expression for the type of ministerial preparation that combines solid learning, deep piety, pastoral skills, and a missionary heart.

[71] Schnittjer, "William Tennent and the Log College."

4

The Adopting Act Compromise

S. Donald Fortson III

Colonial Presbyterians did not adopt a doctrinal statement at the beginning of their organized life together in 1706. All of the early American Presbyterian clergymen had been nurtured in the theology of Westminster Calvinism in Britain or New England and cherished a strong attachment to Reformed doctrine but they had not sensed the necessity of a formal collective creed. Some of the colonial Presbyterians were not so sure about the wisdom of requiring ministerial subscription to man-made statements of faith. The Protestant principle of *sola scriptura* had seemed a sufficient guide for the infant American church; but, there were others who believed that a key ingredient for strengthening the infant ecclesiastical body must be official adoption of a confessional document.

Presbyterians had immigrated to colonial America primarily from England, Scotland and Ireland and they were wary of confessional subscription because of the divisions it had caused in the old country. The Presbyterian bodies in the British Isles had embraced the Westminster Standards as trustworthy expositions of the faith, however, adopting the Westminster Confession and Catechisms had brought with it inherent problems. From the sheer scope of the documents, how could it be expected that a large body of ministers would concur in the vast detail of these confessional statements? And having experienced the oppressive imposition of creeds and formularies by Roman Catholic and Anglican bishops, did American Presbyterians really want to follow that path? Each of the mother Presbyterian bodies had grappled with these vexing problems and the array of old world controversies were fresh in the American consciousness as they considered the question of confessional subscription in the 1720s.

The Old World Context

The Westminster Confession and Catechisms (1643–46), written during the period of the Long Parliament and English Civil War, had become widely-accepted doctrinal standards for English-speaking Presbyterian and Reformed churches by the time Presbyterian immigrants arrived in the new world. These confessional statements had proven themselves over time as faithful summaries of biblical truth, helpful tools for teaching the faith and a means for preserving doctrinal integrity. As useful as these documents had been practically, problems had emerged when ministers were expected to subscribe to the Confession and Catechisms.

In Scotland, the Parliament had ratified the Westminster Confession "as the public and avowed Confession of this Church, containing the sum and substance of the doctrine of the Reformed Churches." In 1693, the Parliament required subscription of all ministers, with this formula: "I do sincerely own and declare the above Confession of Faith, approven by former General Assemblies of this Church, and ratified by law in the year 1690, to be the Confession of my faith, and that I own the doctrine therein contained to be the true doctrine, which I will constantly adhere to."[1] By 1696, the Church of Scotland further declared that no minister may write or publicly speak anything contrary to or inconsistent with the Confession.[2] The Scottish Kirk consistently favored strict subscription to the Confession of Faith with only minor reservations related to government and church/state relations.[3] Many Scottish Presbyterians that immigrated to America brought the tradition of strict confessional subscription with them.

In Ireland, the Synod of Ulster in 1689 had declared: "That young men licensed to preach be obliged to subscribe to our Confession of Faith in all the articles thereof, as the Confession of their faith."[4] Faced with dangerous Arian theology [denial of the Trinity] that had surfaced in Thomas Emlyn of the Dublin Presbytery, the General Synod tightened the subscription formula in 1705; this move created a reaction among some Presbyterians who formed the Belfast Society in opposition to sub-

[1] Charles Augustus Briggs, *American Presbyterian* (New York: Scribner, 1885) 200, 201.

[2] Leonard J. Trinterud, *The Forming of an American Tradition* (Philadelphia: Westminster, 1949) 39.

[3] See J. Ligon Duncan, "Owning the Confession: Subscription in the Scottish Presbyterian Tradition," in *The Practice of Confessional Subscription*, ed. David W. Hall (Lanham, MD: University Press of America, 1995) 81.

[4] Briggs, *American Presbyterianism*, 201.

scription. This in turn produced renewed efforts to push for unconditional subscription in Ireland. In order to secure peace among the brethren, Robert Craighead of Dublin, the moderator of Synod in 1720, proposed a conciliatory plan known as the Pacific Act.

The 1720 Irish Pacific Act was a compromise intended to harmonize disparate parties. The Act begins by denying that there had been any attempt to "lay aside" the Confession and Catechisms, but on the contrary, "we do still adhere to the said Confession and Catechisms." The Irish Synod encouraged the study and use of the Confession "as being a good abridgment of the Christian doctrines contained in the sacred Scriptures."[5] The 1705 Act of the General Synod is reiterated with this understanding of subscription:

> . . . which is thus to be understood as now is practised by the Presbyteries, that if any person called upon to subscribe shall scruple any phrase or phrases in the Confession, he shall have leave to use his own expressions, which the Presbytery shall accept of, providing they judge such a person sound in the faith and that such expressions are consistent with the substance of the doctrine, and that such explications shall be inserted in the Presbytery books; and that this be a rule not only in relation to candidates licensed by ourselves, but all intrants into the ministry among us, tho' they have been licensed or ordained elsewhere.[6]

[5] Briggs suggests that the 1720 Irish Pacific Act (in contrast with the Scotch Act of 1690) emphasizes "Christian doctrines" rather than the distinctive "doctrine of the Reformed Churches"—the language used by the Scots. He adds that the American Adopting Act favors the language of the Irish Articles. *American Presbyterianism*, 200. It appears that Briggs has imagined a distinction that does not exist. While it is true the 1729 Adopting Act speaks of "systems of Christian doctrine," this is obviously inclusive of the Calvinistic system of doctrine in the Confession. Colonial Presbyterian history places it beyond doubt that Americans viewed themselves as a Reformed Church and their creed as more than an affirmation of basic Christian orthodoxy. There is no purpose of adopting the Westminster Standards if one removes the particular Reformed doctrines that constitute the Calvinistic system of the Confession. Scotch and Irish subscription as well as American subscription involved a commitment to historic Calvinism and not mere assent to a generic Christianity.

[6] Ibid., 216–19. Briggs states that the 1720 Irish Pacific Act was foundational for the American Adopting Act of 1729 and demonstrates this by a careful comparison of the two documents. Trinterud likewise argues that the Adopting Act "was modeled in great part after the Irish Pacific Articles of 1720." *Forming of an American Tradition*, 49. The American act is not a mirror image of the Pacific Act, nevertheless, the language of the Adopting Act shows obvious dependence on the Irish document.

The Pacific Act did not satisfy either party in the Irish Church. Ministers declining to subscribe were excluded and organized themselves into the Presbytery of Antrim in 1726. Conservatives in the Synod of Ulster announced that they were no longer able to maintain ministerial communion with the non-subscribers and ejected them from the Synod in 1727. The Irish rupture was prominent in the minds of American Presbyterians as they approached their own struggle over subscription just two years after the Irish schism. In many colonial minds, debate over subscription could mean division in the church.

English Presbyterians also had their own dissension over subscription. Semi-Arianism appeared in England through Thomas Emlyn's friend, James Pierce of Exeter, and stirred a great controversy in 1718–19.[7] In the case of Pierce, three denominations in London (Presbyterian, Congregational, Baptist) were called upon to deliberate on the matter of Pierce and his followers. There were two groups that emerged: those advocating a strong creedal statement on the Trinity and those opposed to requiring subscription to creeds. Unable to secure a joint doctrinal statement on the Trinity, a group of conservative ministers withdrew from the inter-denominational discussions and held their own meeting in which they subscribed to the first of the 39 Articles of the Church of England and questions 5 and 6 of the Westminster Shorter Catechism.[8]

Many Presbyterian and Congregational ministers in England had historically been opposed to creedal subscription, however, the semi-Arian crisis had made it a necessity according to the conservatives. The London ministers now divided into three groups: the subscribers, non-subscribers and the neutrals.[9] The non-subscribing majority made this declaration:

> If after all, a publick hearing be insisted on, we think the Protestant principle, that the Bible is the only and the perfect rule of faith, obliges those who have the case before them, not to condemn any man upon the authority of human decisions, or because he consents not to human forms or phrases: But then only is he to be censured, as not holding the faith necessary to salvation, when it appears that he contradicts, or refuses to own, the plain and express

[7] Mr. Pierce had stated his belief that the Son and Holy Ghost were divine persons, but that they are subordinate to the Father's being which is the fountain of the divinity of the Son and Spirit. Historic Christian belief emphasizes the equality and eternity of each of the three persons of the Trinity. Briggs, *American Presbyterianism*, 195.

[8] Ibid., 196; Trinterud, *Forming of an American Tradition*, 41.

[9] Of the Presbyterians, 50 were non-subscribers, 26 subscribers, and 9 neutrals. Briggs, *American Presbyterianism*, 197.

> declarations of Holy Scripture, in what is there made necessary to be believed, and in matters there solely revealed. . . .[10]

By advocating subscription as the answer to doctrinal deviation, the subscribers alienated non-subscribers and neutrals, therefore, bringing division among the London ministers. All three parties for the most part were orthodox on the Trinity, but could not agree on subscribing to a creed as the proper method of handling the issue. Many of the non-subscribers eventually united with the Church of England; a few ended up embracing Arianism. The situation in London would also influence American thinking on subscription. In the English case, it appeared that unwillingness to subscribe a doctrinal statement might indicate the presence of heresy.[11]

Do We Need a Confession of Faith?

By 1717 the colonial Presbyterian Church had established three Presbyteries that were associated as a Synod but they still had adopted no formal creed or constitution for church government and discipline. Controversy concerning proper order first arose in 1720 over a case of discipline when Robert Cross, a minister in New Castle presbytery, was found guilty of fornication. The case came before Synod which censured Cross by removing him from the pulpit for four Sundays but allowed the restoration of his pastoral ministry if the people would have him. George Gillespie, a fellow minister in New Castle Presbytery, protested the Synod's gentle treatment of Cross. This discipline case and the differences it raised put before the Synod the issue of common standards to regulate their ecclesiastical life.

The origins of creedal subscription among American Presbyterians surfaces in the action of New Castle Presbytery, which in 1724 required candidates to subscribe the Confession in these words: "I do own the Westminster Confession as the Confession of my faith."[12] By 1727 John Thompson, of New Castle Presbytery, introduced an overture to Synod in favor of requiring confessional subscription. Thompson claimed it was not his intention to bring "any heat or contention" to the Synod, but he is concerned for the "vindication and defense of the truths we profess, and for preventing the ingress and spreading of error." The infant Presbyterian

10 Ibid.

11 Trinterud says that the brief controversy in England "became for many the classical illustration of what opposition to constitutionally imposed creeds really meant. Those who rejected subscription were thereafter not infrequently considered secret heretics or hypocrites." *Forming of an American Tradition*, 41.

12 Quoted in Briggs, *American Presbyterianism*, 210.

Church, which has not its own seminary of learning, is defenseless in an era "of so many pernicious and dangerous corruptions in doctrine."[13]

Thompson admits his own consternation that some of the Presbyterian brethren "have the edge of their zeal against the prevailing errors of the times very much blunted." These brothers exhibit "a kind of indifference and mistaken charity, whereby they think they ought to bear with others, though differing from them in opinion about points which are mysterious and sublime, but not practical nor fundamental, such as predestination." Thompson, on the other hand, is convinced that Presbyterians should hold fast to the distinctives of Reformed doctrine. "Now although I would grant that the precise point of election and reprobation be neither fundamental nor immediately practical, yet take predestination completely, as it takes in the other disputed points between Calvinists and Arminians, such as universal grace, the non-perseverance of the saints, foreseen faith, and good works, &c., and I think it such an article in my creed, such a fundamental of my faith, that I know not what any other articles could be retained without it."[14]

For the reasons cited, Thompson recommends that Synod "publicly and authoritatively adopt the Westminster Confession and Catechism, &c., for the public confession of our faith." Further, the overture asked Synod to "make an act to oblige every Presbytery within their bounds, to oblige every candidate for the ministry to subscribe or otherwise acknowledge, *coram presbyterio*, the said Confession of Faith, and to promise not to preach or teach contrary to it." In addition, it was proposed "that if any minister within our bounds shall take upon him to teach or preach any thing contrary to any of the said articles, unless, first, he propose the said point to the Presbytery or Synod, to be by them discussed, he shall be censured so and so."[15] It is noteworthy that Thompson's overture anticipates ministerial objections to articles of the Confession and suggests that these should be discussed by the presbytery or synod. This important point in the proposal would help open the door for the eventual compromise plan that would allow for exceptions to be publicly declared and discussed.

There was initial resistance to the overture that was brought to Synod again by New Castle Presbytery in 1728; it was deferred to the next year when all members of the Synod could be present to debate this all im-

13 Charles Hodge, *The Constitutional History of the Presbyterian Church in the United States of America*, Part I, 1705–1741 (Philadelphia: Presbyterian Board of Publication, 1851) 137–39.

14 Ibid., 140.

15 Ibid., 140, 141.

portant question. The Thompson / New Castle overture was opposed by a number of presbyters, the most influential being Jonathan Dickinson from the Presbytery of Philadelphia. The essence of Dickinson's objection was not disagreement with the Calvinistic theology of Westminster but his resistance to imposing any creed in principle. Dickinson, wrote to Thompson in April 1729, stating that he believed "a joint agreement in the same essential and necessary articles of Christianity, and the same methods of worship and discipline, are a sufficient bond of union . . . we have already all the external bond of union that the Scriptures require of us." He further states that requiring any "unscriptural terms of union or communion is a direct and natural means to procure rents and divisions in the church. . . . we all of us know that the subscription under debate has been scrupled by many godly, learned, and faithful ministers of Christ, that it has made horrible divisions and confusion in other churches...." The sole authority of Scripture will be undermined because "a subscription to any human composure as the test of our orthodoxy is to make it the standard of our faith, and thereby to give it the honour due only to the word of God."[16] Liberty of conscience was a vital principle for Dickinson and he pointed out that there is a "most glorious contradiction" in subscribing "God alone is Lord of the Conscience" (Chapter XX, Article 2 of the Westminster Confession) and then to "impose the rest" of the Confession which would be a denial of that very principle.[17]

Dickinson rejected Thompson's premise that subscription will protect the Presbyterian Church from corruption in doctrine. "Tho subscription may shut the door of the church communion against many serious and excellent servants of Christ who conscientiously scruple it; yet its never like to detect hypocrites, nor keep concealed hereticks out of the church." Dickinson is also concerned about the inordinate elevation of a human document. "Upon the whole then, tho' I have a higher opinion of the Assemblies Confession than of any other book of the kind extant in the world, yet I don't think it perfect. I know it to be the dictates of fallible men, and I know of no law either of religion or reason, that obliges me to subscribe it."[18] The magnitude and breadth of the Westminster Standards make it problematic for any minister. Was it realistic to expect all candidates to strictly embrace the entire Confession and Catechisms? Dickinson demurs, "If all qualified Candidates can well understand the

16 Ibid., 144.

17 Briggs, *American Presbyterianism*, 213.

18 Ibid., 212, 213.

whole of that large Confession, it's a just Matter of shame to me, who have be'n a Minister between twenty and thirty Years; and yet don't understand several Things in it . . . . I'm afraid therefore, that most of our Candidates must subscribe blindfold, or be kept out of the Ministry from invincible necessity."[19]

Instead of imposing subscription, Dickinson suggests that candidates be carefully examined, that strict discipline against immoral ministers be enforced, and "that the ministers of the gospel be most diligent, faithful, and painful in the discharge of their awful trust."[20] A number of Presbyterians sympathized with Dickinson's position, however, the climate of Synod was advantageous for moving ahead with Thompson's overture. Nevertheless, Dickinson's sensitivities set the tone for much of the discussion during the 1729 meeting of Synod which hammered out the subscription compromise. Many of Dickinson's concerns would be incorporated into the final 1729 subscription principles that accommodated the convictions of subscriptionists and non-subscriptionists alike.

In the period immediately leading up to 1729, there was much anxiety over Thompson's overture and the potential for schism. Presbyterian minister Jedediah Andrews, writing to a friend, describes the conflict and his own fears about the future:

> We are now like to fall into a great difference about subscribing the Westminster Confession of Faith. An overture for it, drawn up by Mr. Thompson of Lewistown was offered to our Synod the year before last, but not then read in Synod. Means were then used to stave it off, and I was in hopes we should have heard no more of it. But last Synod it was brought again, recommended by all the Scotch and Irish members present and being read among us, a proposal was made, prosecuted and agreed to that it should be deferred till our next meeting for further consideration. The Proposal is, that all ministers and intrants shall sign it or else be disowned as members. Now what shall we do? They will certainly carry it by number. Our countrymen say, they are willing to joyn in a vote to make it the Confession of our church, but to agree to the making it the test of orthodoxy[21] and term of ministerial communion, they

[19] Trinterud, *Forming of an American Tradition*, 47.

[20] Briggs, *American Presbyterianism*, 213.

[21] Luder Whitlock suggests that the hesitancy to use Westminster as a "test of orthodoxy" may be rooted in the concern for personal holiness as the chief criteria for ministry. See Luder G. Whitlock Jr. "The Context for the Adopting Act," in Hall, *The Practice of Confessional Subscription,* 98. Andrews may also be implying a resistance to requiring ministers to endorse everything in the Confession or face removal from the church.

> say they will not. I think all the Scots are on one side, and all the English and Welsh on the other, to a man . . . I am afraid of the event. However I'll endeavour to do as near as I can what I understand to be duty, and leave the issue to Providence.[22]

Essential and Necessary Articles

It was with great trepidation that the young Synod of Philadelphia convened in 1729. Diverse parties met in Philadelphia, each with strong principles of conscience on the questions at hand. There was dread for the scandal of division that would dishonor the name of Christ and the recent Irish schism over subscription made the potentiality of a split very real. Could the Americans maintain union? With schism as the alternative choice, both sides were willing to accommodate one another for the greater good of the church. Twenty members were present for the Synod meeting, seven were absent.[23] The affair of the Confession was remitted to a committee of eight (Andrews, Dickinson, Pierson, Thomson, Anderson, Craighead,[24] Conn, and John Budd) to craft a recommendation for the Synod.[25] The committee members represented the spectrum of opinion on the question, therefore, a unanimous proposal would have to satisfy all parties if unity was to be preserved.

In the morning session of September 19, the proposed overture on the confession was presented to the Synod. The overture was unanimously adopted "after long debating upon it." The preamble of the Act clearly bore the imprint of Dickinson and exhibited that generous spirit which acknowledged the valid concerns of both parties: freedom of conscience

22 Hodge, *Constitutional History*, Vol. I, 142.

23 *Minutes of the Synod*, 17 September 1729 as printed in Guy S. Klett, ed. *Minutes of the Presbyterian Church in America 1706–1788* (Philadelphia: Presbyterian Historical Society, 1976) 102. All citations of Synod minutes in this essay will come from Klett's edition of the original manuscript minutes. Spelling, capitalization and abbreviations from the manuscripts are preserved.

24 Thomas Craighead was still in Ireland at the time of the 1720 Irish Pacific Act and would have been strongly influenced by both his brother Robert, moderator of the Irish Synod, and his own experience with the Irish controversy and the Pacific Act. See Whitlock, "The Context for the Adopting Act," 98, 99.

25 Briggs says the group was well-balanced with Thompson and Anderson representing the "strong subscriptionists," Dickinson and Pierson the "anti-subscriptionists" and the remaining four, Craighead, Andrews, Budd and Conn, holding a mediating position. *American Presbyterianism*, 216. This appears to be a fair characterization of the committee and helps explain why so many influences are evident in the final outcome.

was essential, at the same time, a formal creed was necessary for the good of the church. The preamble explained:

> Altho' the Synod do not claim or pretend to any Authority of imposing our faith upon other men's Consciences, but do profess our just Dissatisfaction with and Abhorrence of such Impositions, and do utterly disclaim all Legislative Power and Authority in the Church, being willing to receive one another, as Christ has received us to the Glory of God, and admit to fellowship in sacred ordinances all such as we have Grounds to believe Christ will at last admit to the Kingdom of Heaven; yet we are undoubtedly obliged to take Care that the faith once delivered to the Saints be kept pure and uncorrupt among Us, and so handed down to our Posterity.[26]

As the members of Synod expressed their approval of the Westminster Standards, they were also careful to make an important distinction between "all the essential and necessary articles," which each minister shall adopt, and liberty on articles "not essential and necessary." After the preamble, the Synod pronounced their unanimous consent that all ministers,

> . . . shall declare their agreement in and approbation of the Confession of Faith with the larger and shorter Catechisms of the assembly of Divines at Westminster, as being *in all the essential and necessary Articles*, good Forms of sound words and systems of Christian Doctrine; and do also adopt the said Confession and Catechisms as the Confession of our Faith. And we do also agree, yt all the Presbyteries within our Bounds shall always take Care not to admit any Candidate of the Ministry into the Exercise of the sacred Function, but what declares his Agreement in opinion with *all the Essential and Necessary Articles* of said Confession, either by subscribing the said Confession of Faith and Catechisms, or by a verbal Declaration of their assent thereto, as such Minister or Candidate shall think best (emphasis added).[27]

The Synod also endorsed a method whereby ministers could exercise liberty of conscience by stating scruples publicly before the brethren. These scruples, however, must "be only about articles not essential and necessary." The Synod or Presbytery shall make final judgment on these scruples and determine whether or not said scruples are about "essential and necessary articles of faith." The paragraph about exceptions states:

[26] *Minutes of the Synod*, 19 September 1729, 103.

[27] Ibid., 103, 104.

> And in Case any Minister of this Synod or any Candidate for the Ministry shall have any Scruple with respect to any Article or Articles of sd. Confession or Catechisms, he shall at the Time of his making sd. Declaration declare his Sentiments to the Presbytery or Synod, who shall notwithstanding admit him to ye Exercise of the Ministry within our Bounds and to Ministerial Communion if the Synod or Presbytery shall judge his scruple or mistake to be only about articles *not Essential and necessary* in Doctrine, Worship or Government. But if the Synod or Presbytery shall judge such Ministers or Candidates erronious in *Essential and necessary Articles of Faith*, the Synod or Presbytery shall declare them uncapable of Communion with them (emphasis added).[28]

Anticipating that there would be differences of opinion over "extra-essential and not-necessary points of doctrine" the Synod included a statement of brotherly charity toward all, and denounced prejudice between ministers who differ. The Adopting Act[29] concluded with these words: "And the Synod do solemnly agree, that none of us will traduce or use any opprobrious Terms of those yt differ from us in these *extra-essential and not-necessary points of doctrine*, but treat them with the same friendship, kindness and brotherly Love, as if they had not differed from us in such Sentiments" (emphasis added).[30]

The magnanimous spirit of the Adopting Act was embodied in Dickinson's phrase "essential and necessary," which phrase is repeated five times in the Synod's overture. Ministers could take exceptions to the Confession and Catechisms provided they are not about "essential" points of doctrine, but, it is the Synod or Presbytery that determines what is allowable not the candidate or minister. The "essentials" language of the Adopting Act was a compromise.[31] One party had desired subscription to

28 Ibid., 104.

29 While there is debate over whether the morning session (sometimes called the "Preliminary Act") or the afternoon session, or both, comprise the official "Adopting Act," the Synod minutes indicate a continuity of the day's activity. There is a direct flow into the afternoon session after a break from the long session of the morning. After having defined the foundational principles of subscription in the morning, the afternoon session was an outworking of those principles among those present at the Synod meeting. The two sessions are seamless in the original minutes.

30 *Minutes of the Synod*, 19 September 1729, 104.

31 Charles Hodge states: "It is very evident, indeed, that the act was a compromise. Both parties were desirous to avoid a schism; yet both were anxious that their own views should prevail. Their only expedient was to find some common ground on which they could stand." *Constitutional History*, Vol. I, 152. The Synod's action seemed to grant something to everyone—Thompson got his formal adoption of the Confession, Dickinson got his

all articles, another party was opposed to subscribing fallible human creeds; the 1729 compromise required that ministerial communion be based on receiving the "essential and necessary" doctrines of the Confession. The Synod adopted the Confession and Catechisms as the church's doctrinal standards, however, this was not understood to be a wooden acceptance of every article.

In the afternoon session of September 19, 1729, the Synod having previously adopted the foundational principles of subscription, proceeded to implement this Act among themselves. After reading the minutes of the morning session, which articulated the agreed upon meaning of subscription, each member of the Synod now had to personally adopt the Westminster Standards as the confession of his faith before the Synod brethren. In order to accomplish this end, each member was given the opportunity of "proposing *all* the Scruples yt any of them had to make against *any* Articles and Expressions in the Confession of Faith and larger and shorter Catechisms" (emphasis added). The afternoon minute states that after these opinions were presented, the Synod "unanimously agreed in the solution of those Scruples."[32]

After individual scruples were "unanimously agreed" to be acceptable, i.e., not about "essential and necessary" doctrines, the whole Synod "unanimously declare" exceptions to two sections of the Confession wherein every member had scruples about "some clauses"[33] that granted authority to civil magistrates in church affairs. Since these scruples were

declaration of not imposing on other men's consciences and Craighead got the "scruples" principle from the Irish Pacific Act.

32 The unanimous "solution of those scruples" should not necessarily be interpreted as uniformity in the Synod taking exception to only certain clauses in chapters 20 and 23 of the Confession. The afternoon minute states, "after proposing all the Scruples yt any of them had against any Articles and Expressions," which does not indicate how many or what kind of scruples were mentioned by all the individuals present. Limiting "scruples" to only the "unanimous" scruples of chapters 20 and 30 is not clear from the minutes. What is certain is that all of these scruples met the Synod's criteria of subscription, i.e., being scruples over "extra-essential and not-necessary points of doctrine" which principle had been established that morning. The practice of asking candidates to state "scruples" after 1729 indicates an understanding that one might take exception to articles other than the two chapters originally noted in 1729; otherwise, to ask candidates for a statement of scruples would be meaningless.

33 The Synod inscribed their universal scruple: "excepting only some Clauses in ye 20. And 23. Chapter, concerning which Clauses, the Synod do unanimously declare, yet they do not receive those Articles in any such sense as to suppose the civil Magistrate hath a controlling Power over synods with Respect to the Exercise of their ministerial Authority; or Power to persecute and for their Religion, or in any sense contrary to the Protestant succession of the Throne of Great Britain." *Minutes of the Synod*, 19 September 1729, 104.

held in common by every member present, they were recorded in the minutes. These uniform exceptions having been noted, the Synod declared the "Confession and Catechisms to be the Confession of their faith."[34]

The afternoon session thus completed the work that had begun in the morning. The Synod accomplished two purposes on September 19, 1729: principles for understanding the meaning of subscription were adopted; and members of Synod executed those principles among themselves in their adoption of the Westminster Standards individually and as an ecclesiastical body. Both individual and common scruples were voiced that day, yet, none of those scruples were judged to be about "essential and necessary articles." Having openly acknowledged every scruple before one another as the morning minute had directed, the Synod had now completed their work of adopting the Westminster Standards.

Confessional Subscription

The first Synod record of examining an individual minister according to the new 1729 directives came the next year. David Evans, who had withdrawn from the Synod three years previously, desired to reunite with his brethren. The 1730 Synod minutes record: "And having proposed all the Scruples he had to make about any articles of the Confession and Catechism &c: to the Satisfaction of the Synod, and declared his adopting the Westminster Confession of faith and Catechisms agreeable to the last years adopting Act, he was unanimously received in as a Member again."[35] Evans articulated all his scruples and then adopted the Westminster Confession and Catechisms "agreeable to last years Adopting Act." These were two separate actions: he joined in the *unanimous* exceptions of 1729 (chps. 20 and 23), one would presume, by declaring his adoption of the Westminster Standards in the same manner as the original Synod of 1729, and just prior to this declaration, he had "proposed all the scruples he had about any articles" as the Adopting Act required.

On the same day of Evans' examination, an overture was presented to the 1730 Synod requesting a clarification on the meaning of the Adopting Act:

> Whereas some Persons have been dissatisfied at the Manner of wording our last years Agreement about the Confession &c: supposing some Expressions not sufficiently obligatory upon Intrants; overture yt the Synod do now declare, that they understand those

[34] Ibid.

[35] *Minutes of the Synod*, 17 September 1730, 108.

> Clauses that respect the Admission of Intrants or Candidates in such a sense as to oblige them to receive and adopt the Confession and Catechisms at their Admission in the same Manner and as fully as the Members of the Synod did that were then present. Which overture was unanimously agree to by the Synod.[36]

It appears that questions had been raised about the "manner of wording" in the Adopting Act. Some persons had queried whether certain "expressions" or "clauses" in the Act had been misunderstood. The Synod responded by reiterating their expectation that all Intrants to the ministry must "receive and adopt the Confession and Catechisms at their Admission in the same Manner and as fully as the Members of the Synod did that were present"—referring back to the 1729 Adopting Act of the previous year.[37]

The mediating stance of the Adopting Act satisfied the present needs of the church, however, there were rumblings among conservatives jealous for a stricter form of subscription and fearful that they had given away too much. The Synod statement of 1730 addressed some initial concerns about the potential latitude latent in the Adopting Act itself. A catalyst for the strengthening of the conservative perspective was the first heresy trial in American Presbyterianism: the trial of Samuel Hemphill of Philadelphia. Hemphill was received by the Synod in 1734 from the Presbytery of Straban in Ireland where he had been ordained. Hemphill had subscribed the Confession according to the formula used in Ireland and he was recommended to the Synod with "satisfactory Certificates from the same Presbry of his Qualifications for and Ordination to the sacred Ministry." Synod minutes record simply that he was "admitted a member of this Synod."[38]

Hemphill served as an assistant to Jedidiah Andrews at the (First) Presbyterian Church in Philadelphia and quickly drew attention in the city as a fine preacher. It was soon discovered, however, that Hemphill had plagiarized a sermon from a Dr. Clarke, known openly to be an Arian,

[36] Ibid. The 1730 statement may have meant that only the universal exceptions of the 1729 afternoon minute were sanctioned by the Synod, on the other hand, the overture more likely was intended as a general restatement of 1729. One thing is indisputable, the 1730 overture with which Synod agreed, must be understood as consistent with the immediately preceding minute describing Evans' examination by the Synod. Evans stated his scruples according to the directives of the 1729 morning minute and Synod accepted Evans because his scruples were within the "essential and necessary" boundaries.

[37] *Minutes of the Synod*, 17 September 1730, 108.

[38] *Minutes of the Synod*, 21 September 1734, 121.

along with stealing several other sermons. A commission investigated the situation and charges were brought against Hemphill for Arminianism and Socinianism. The charges were sustained unanimously and Hemphill was suspended from ministerial office in 1735. An important aspect of this case was the fact that Hemphill had publicly stated no "scruples" before the American Synod when he was admitted, but his preaching had demonstrated that in fact Hemphill had serious objections to parts of the Confession.[39]

The Hemphill case sheds light on the emerging tension over understanding subscription at this point in the Synod's history. Dickinson responding to Benjamin Franklin's criticism of the Synod's disciplinary action against Hemphill, offers this explanation: "We allow of no Confession of Faith as a test of orthodoxy for others, but only as a declaration of our own sentiments; nor may this be imposed upon the members of our own society, nor their assent required to anything as a condition of their communion with us, but what we esteem essentially necessary." Appended to the reply to Franklin is a copy of the Adopting Act, morning minute.[40]

The 1735 Synod, distraught over the dangers of heresy,[41] sent an overture to the Synod of Ulster stipulating that in the future every minister coming to America from Europe would be expected to have a "firm Attachment to sd. Confession, &c., in opposition to the new Upstart Doctrines and Schemes, particularly such as we condemn'd in Mr. H-ll's Sermons." The Synod also pronounced that each minister or probationer must "subscribe or adopt the westminstr. Confessn. of Faith & Catechisms

39 For detailed information on the Hemphill affair see the essay in this volume by William S. Barker.

40 *Remarks upon a Pamphlet entitled a Letter* was Dickinson's first response to Franklin's criticism of the Commission of Synod; quoted in Briggs, *American Presbyterianism*, 232. Note the use of "essentially necessary" alluding to the Adopting Act (morning minute). In *A Vindication of Reverend Commission,* Dickinson, et.al., argued that the failure in the Hemphill case was the neglect of the Adopting Act principles, i.e., mandatory stating of scruples. If Hemphill had been honest enough to state his exceptions plainly, the crisis could have been averted. The Hemphill affair is a case study in the prudence of the 1729 Adopting Act that mandates careful scrutiny of candidates and ministers. Rather than a flippant acceptance of the Westminster Standards as a whole, individuals should be pressed to declare where they have "scruples;" in most cases there will be exceptions given the human fallibility of both the subscriber and the Westminster Divines.

41 The Synod was very concerned about false doctrine. The letter denounces ". . . the great & almost universal Deluge of pernicious Errrs. [Errors] & damnable Doctrines yt so boldly threaten to overthrow the Christian world . . . when so many Wolves in Sheeps Cloathing are invading the Flocks of Xt. Every where in the world . . ." *Minutes of the Synod,* 22 September 1735, 131.

before sd. Pry in Manner and Form as they have done."[42] Pointing back to their own action in 1729, the Synod's letter informs the Irish that ministerial trials in America will require that "scruples" be publicly stated and the Synod will judge if the essentials criteria be met or not.

Another indicator of the concern over heterodoxy and the subscription standard of 1729, are minutes from the 1735 meeting of Synod which inquire if those admitted to presbyteries since the last meeting of Synod "have adopted ye Westminster Confession of faith & Catechisms &c: according to ye adopting Act of the Synod, ..." The answer is affirmative and then the minutes state: "Mrs. Isaac Chalker and Hugh Carlisle not having seen the adopting Act, have now had the same read to them and now concur in their assent to the Terms of the Adopting Act." [43] Synod minutes of 1735 also record: "Ordered yt each Presbry have the whole adopting Act inserted in their Presbry Book" [44] By "whole" Adopting Act, one should probably understand both the morning and afternoon sessions of September 19, 1729. Which half had been neglected? Dickinson certainly kept the principle of "essentials" (the morning) before the church in his writings during this period. Perhaps some of the conservatives had been emphasizing only the afternoon session. It is difficult to determine the answer with certitude, however, given the reemphasis on the afternoon minute during the 1736 meeting of Synod, it is most likely that the morning session alone had been circulating throughout the church as "The Adopting Act" at least in some places.

There was apparently apprehension in the Synod that some presbyteries were not utilizing the Adopting Act in its examination of ministers and in at least these two cases it was true. Chalker had been ordained by East-Jersey and Carlisle admitted to New Castle in the last year, yet, neither one knew the contents of the Adopting Act. Requiring that the Adopting Act be inserted into each Presbytery Book was one way to remedy the problem.

The Controversial Synod of 1736

Concern over subscription in the wake of the Hemphill trial, the seeming neglect in a few presbyteries, and suspicions of doctrinal latitude raised the stakes for interpreting the Adopting Act. While the Adopting Act had conferred a degree of freedom for individual scruples as well as presbytery's

[42] Ibid., 132.

[43] *Minutes of the Synod*, 9 September 1735, 127.

[44] Ibid., 128.

right of judgment on "essentials," the situation was now more serious, since the Adopting Act had apparently failed to protect the church in the Hemphill case. The Adopting Act problem was a principal consideration of the Synod at its annual meeting in 1736. After the perfunctory taking of attendance and the reading of last year's minutes, the Synod heard a report from Dunagall Presbytery: "The Presbry of Dunagall report yt Mr. Alexdr Creaghead was last winter ordained to ye work of the Ministry, and at yt Time did adopt the Westminster Confession of Faith &c. And also both he and Mr. Jno. Paul lately from Ireland having now heard the several Resolutions and Acts of ye Synod in Relation to ye adopting sd. Confession &c. did before the Synod declare their Agreement thereunto."[45]

An overture was presented to the 1736 Synod from the people of Paxton and Derry that raised questions about the meaning of the Adopting Act. A Synod response was drawn up by a committee that stated in part:

> That the Synod do declare, yt inasmuch as we understand yt many Persons of our Perswasion both more lately and formerly have been offended with some Expression or distinction in the first or preliminary act of our Synod, contained in the printed Paper, relating to our receiving or adopting the westminster Confession & Catechisms &c: That in order to remove said offence and all Jealousies yt have arisen or may arise in any of our People's minds on occasion of sd. Distinctions and Expressions, the Synod doth declare, yt the Synod have adopted and still do adhere to the westminstr. Confession Catechism and Directory without the least variation or alteration, and without any Regard to sd. Distinctions. And we do further declare yt this was our meaning and true Intent in our first adopting of sd, Confession, as may particularly appear by our adopting act which is as followeth.[46]

Immediately following the above statement is the text of the 1729 afternoon minute only.[47] There is a significant shift of emphasis by highlighting the afternoon minute to the exclusion of the agreed upon principles of the morning session. Since the morning minute of 1729 had so plainly declared the Synod's own unanimous definition of confessional subscription, the apparent suppression of those principles in 1736 begs significant historical questions. It is interesting to note that Dickinson and what would become mostly the New Side party were absent from

[45] *Minutes of the Synod*, 16 September 1736, 137.

[46] *Minutes of the Synod*, 17 September 1736, 141.

[47] Ibid.

the meeting of Synod that year. The overture was unanimously approved by the twenty members present, but twenty-one members were absent in 1736.[48]

One would surmise that the 1736 "clarification" would not have been approved by Dickinson and his colleagues had they been present. The 1736 Synod asserted its adherence to the Confession and Catechisms "without any Regard to sd. Distinctions" in the "first or preliminary act." This was a brazen discountenancing of the morning minute that had been the heart and soul of the compromise. This new exclusive interpretation may well have served the purposes of the conservative party but it was not reflective of the whole Synod's point of view. It appears that a conservative majority in 1736 passed a conservative interpretation of 1729. One can appreciate the strict subscriptionist's over-reaction to the trial of Hemphill and their sincere conviction that the morning minute could potentially undermine the authority of the Confession. What made the 1736 declaration divisive is that these earnest convictions were not shared by the entire Synod (notably those absent), many of whom did not believe strict subscription was the cure.

The re-interpretation of 1736 was one of the catalysts for the eventual Old Side/New Side schism of the colonial church in 1741.[49] The Synod of New York, when it recorded the Adopting Act in its original 1745 minutes, listed only the text of the 1729 morning session as the "Adopting Act."[50] During the years of reunion negotiations, the two synods (Philadelphia and New York) addressed confessional subscription and the New Side was particularly interested is discussing "that paragraph about essentials."[51] For New Side Presbyterians, the larger of the two bodies by two to one, the original Adopting Act was a non-negotiable principle of ministerial communion. When reunion of the two synods finally occurred in 1758, the reunited body reaffirmed its attachment to the principles of 1729.[52]

[48] According to Briggs, only three of the twenty members who voted for the 1736 overture would end up in the New Side camp: William Tennent Sr, William Tennent Jr., and Richard Treat. Of the 21 absent from Synod in 1736, only two would join the Old Side: George Gillespie and Hugh Conn. *American Presbyterianism,* 237, n.

[49] See D. G. Hart's essay on the Old Side/New Side schism and reunion in this volume.

[50] See Appendix, *Minutes of the Synod of New York*, 1745, 322.

[51] See *Minutes of the Synod of New York*, 1749–1758.

[52] The 1758 Plan of Union, article two stated: "That when any Matter is determined by a Major Vote, every Mem[ber] Shall either actively concur with, or passively Submit to Such Deter[min]ation; or, if his Conscience permit him to do neither, he Shall, [after] Sufficient Liberty modestly to reason and remonstrate, peaceab[ly with]draw from our Communion, without attempting to make any Sc[hism] provided always, that this Shall

Samuel Davies officiating at the ordination service of two men just six weeks after reunion, asked the subscription question in this manner: "Do you receive the Westminster Confession of Faith as the Confession of *your faith*; that is, do you believe it contains an excellent summary of the pure doctrines of Christianity as taught in the Scriptures?...And do you propose to explain the Scriptures according to the *substance* of it? "[53] Davies speaks of the "substance" of the Confession, i.e., the central or "essential" doctrines which make up the doctrinal system of Westminster. This is consistent with Davies' explanation of American subscription to the British in 1754; he described how the ministerial candidate is allowed "to mention his objections to any articles in the Confession" and he would then be admitted to the presbytery, notwithstanding these objections, as long as the presbytery did not judge them "essential" to Christianity.[54] Davies, who was moderator of the Synod of New York at the 1758 reunion, envisioned no change whatsoever in his understanding of the practice of confessional subscription.

Reunion did not settle the subscription issue. Distortion of the Adopting Act surfaced again in the heresy trial of Samuel Harker who would eventually be deposed from office in 1763. Harker protested his expulsion and appealed to 1729 in order to justify his own position. John Blair, writing to defend the action of the Synod, reiterated the original intent of adopting the theological system of Westminster:

> He (Mr. Harker) would have it believed to be a violation of an Act of Synod, A.D. 1729, which he calls *one of the great Articles of their Union* and which he thought *sufficiently secured the right of private judgement*, wherein it is provided that *a minister or candidate shall be admitted notwithstanding scruples respecting article or articles the Synod or Presbytery shall judge* not essential or necessary in DOCTRINE, WORSHIP, AND GOVERNMENT. But in order to improve this to his purpose, he takes the words *essential or necessary* in a sense in which it is plain from the Act itself the Synod never intended they should be taken. He would have them to signify what is essential to 'Communion with Jesus Christ,' or the

be understood to extend only to [Such] Determinations, as the Body Shall Judge *indispensable* in Doct[rine] or Presbyterian Gover[n]ment" (italics mine). Note the 1729 "essential and necessary" concept in the use of the word "indispensable." *Minutes of the Synod of New York and Philadelphia*, 29 May 1758, 341. Compare *Minutes of the Synod of New York*, 18 May 1749, 270.

[53] Trinterud, *Forming of an American Tradition*, 149. The italics are Davies'.

[54] From Samuel Davies' dairy quoted in William Henry Foote, *Sketches of Virginia*, First Series (1850; reprint, Richmond: John Knox, 1966) 246.

> Being of Grace in the heart, and accordingly supposes that no error can be essential which is not of such malignity as to exclude the advocate or maintainer of it from communion with Jesus Christ. But the Synod say essential in *Doctrine, Worship and Government*—i.e., essential to the system of doctrine contained in our *Westminster Confession of Faith* considered as a system, and to the mode of worship and plan of government contained in our Directory. . . That, therefore, is an essential error in the Synod's sense, which is of such malignity as to subvert or greatly injure the system of doctrine and mode of worship and government contained in the Westminster Confession of Faith and Directory.[55]

Opposition to Harker was unanimous. Formerly Old Side as well as New Side men agreed that Harker's view was an unacceptable interpretation of the Adopting Act. Harker's appeal to the morning minute of 1729, though he misunderstood it, is evidence of the prevailing use of the Adopting Act (morning minute) among Presbyterians in the 1760s. Harker is not criticized by Blair for appealing to the "essentials" principle of the Adopting Act, rather he is condemned for distorting its original intent. While Blair and his Old Side colleagues may have had different opinions about the role of the morning minute, they were agreed that Harker's perspective was a serious distortion of the Presbyterian commitment to Westminster Calvinism.

The Ordination Vow

The movement to reorganize the American Presbyterian Church into a delegated General Assembly with a formal constitution began in 1785. After prolonged debate and amendment to draft proposals brought before the Synod of New York and Philadelphia, Presbyterians finally adopted a Plan of Government and Discipline, a revised Westminster Directory for Public Worship and an amended Westminster Confession of Faith in 1788. The altered paragraphs in the Confession included: chapter 20 (fourth paragraph), chapter 23 (third paragraph) and chapter 31 (first

[55] John Blair, *The Synod of New York and Philadelphia Vindicated*. Philadelphia, 1765, 10, 11 quoted in Briggs, *American Presbyterianism*, 321,322. Blair denies that "essentials" refers to fundamentals of the gospel only which was Harker's position. Blair, answering for the synod, declares that "essentials" is referring to the fundamentals of the *system of doctrine* contained in the Westminster Standards, i.e., essentials of Calvinism. Charles Hodge acknowledges that John Blair's equating of "essentials" with the "system of doctrine" is a valid interpretation of 1729. *Constitutional History*, Vol. I, 170; Vol. II, 273.

paragraph)—each amendment underscoring the freedom of the church from state interference.

The changes to the Confession, and a slight amendment of the Larger Catechism (Q. 109), were all discussed in detail and finally approved as part of the Constitution of the Church. Any future alterations or amendments would require that two-thirds of the presbyteries and the General Assembly approve such changes.[56] The inherent fallibility of the Form of Government and Discipline and the Confession was imbedded in the constitutional recognition that, in contrast to Holy Scripture, these documents may be altered. The Introduction to the Plan of Government declared: "God alone is Lord of the conscience, and hath left it free from the doctrines and commandments of men; which are in anything contrary to his word, or beside it in matters of faith or worship. . . . The Bible is the only rule that is infallible in matters of faith and practice. It is the only authoritative constitution, and no church may make rules binding upon men's consciences."[57]

The new constitutional ordination / subscription vow for ministers asked this question: "Do you sincerely receive and adopt the confession of faith of this church, as containing the system of doctrine taught in the holy scriptures?"[58] The phrase "system of doctrine" pointed back to the original morning minute of 1729, as well as the Old Side/New Side reunion language of 1758, and firmly grounded the new Constitution in the historic Adopting Act. The 1788 ordination question was a compromise formula upon which future generations would place a variety of interpretations. And each of the competing perspectives would claim to be the genuine heir of the 1729 heritage.

The nineteenth-century would witness continued debates among Presbyterians over confessional subscription. Conservatives would argue that the old Synod of Philadelphia was correct in interpreting 1729 in terms of the afternoon minute and the strict reinterpretation of 1736. Receiving and adopting the "system" of the Confession meant embracing the whole confession without exception since the originally scrupled chapters had been amended in 1788. A larger group of Presbyterians, recalling the original intent of the morning minute, believed the "system" referred

56 *Minutes of the Synod of New York and Philadelphia*, 28 May 1788, 636.

57 Trinterud, *Forming of an American Tradition*, 297, 298. The preface to the Plan of Government listed eight principles upon which the Presbyterian ecclesiology would be established. These citations are from points I and VII.

58 *The Constitution of the Presbyterian Church in the United States of America* (Philadelphia: Thomas Bradford, 1792) 158.

to the Confession's Calvinistic doctrines; this group advocated the distinction between doctrines "essential" to the system and those that were not. The spirit of Dickinson and the old Synod of New York would be alive and well in the nineteenth century.

And there was a third small party who held that "system of doctrine" referred to the fundamental doctrines shared in common with all Christian churches. This minority expression drew inspiration from the 1729 language "systems of *Christian* doctrine." Some of the early pre-1729 discussions about subscription had advocated this opinion, however, it ultimately had been rejected in the compromise of 1729. Nonetheless, this perspective still had its eighteenth-century advocates in such men as Hemphill and Harker. Even in the nineteenth century, a few voices would continue to herald a loose view of subscription that favored mere assent to catholic Christianity as the "substance" of Westminster doctrines.

The issue of subscription unfortunately was not laid to rest in either the 1758 reunion or the establishment of the General Assembly in 1789. The Westminster Confession and Catechisms were unanimously adopted as constitutional documents of the Presbyterian Church, but there was no consensus on the degree of confessional attachment required for ministerial communion. Continual tension over subscription in the nineteenth-century became so potent that it would be one of the primary factors creating the Old School/New School Presbyterian schism (1838–1869).

Despite the ongoing struggle over confessional subscription, the colonial spirit of compromise for the sake of union, which had produced the original Adopting Act of 1729, would also prevail in later times. When the Old School/New School denominations reunited in 1864 (South) and 1869 (North), Presbyterian groups again reunited based upon the subscription principles from 1729.[59] The original Adopting Act has repeatedly proven itself, even into the twentieth century and beyond, to be the most prudent path for peace among Presbyterians that take ordination vows "to receive and adopt the system of doctrine" in the Confession.

Publicly stating exceptions to the Confession and then formally adopting the Westminster Standards as the confession of one's faith have been the two primary elements of confessional subscription for almost three hundred years. Although presbyteries may differ in the details of what may constitute the "essential and necessary articles," historically there has been a rather broad consensus about what it means to adopt the

[59] For an overview of Old School/New School debates on the meaning of the Adopting Act, see S. Donald Fortson III, "The Presbyterian Creed: Old School/New School Reunion and Confessional Subscription" (Ph.D. diss., Westminster Theological Seminary, 2003).

Calvinistic "system of doctrine" found in the Confession. As long as any Presbyterian debate has continued about Westminster and the doctrinal affirmations expected of ministers and elders, the original Adopting Act of 1729 always seems to surface as a trustworthy model for setting appropriate boundaries. The ultimate wisdom of the Adopting Act stems from its nature as a compromise that held the church together through a common pledge to maintain unity in the essentials and liberty in non-essentials.

5

The Heresy Trial of Samuel Hemphill (1735)[1]

William S. Barker

Introduction

THE Presbyterian Church in Scotland, from its beginning affirmed three notes or marks of the true church: ". . . first, the trew preaching of the Worde of God. . . . Secondly, the right administration of the Sacraments of Christ Jesus. . . . Last, Ecclesiastical discipline uprightlie ministred, as Goddis Worde prescribes. . . ." (*The Scotch Confession of Faith*, Article XVIII). John Calvin in his 1559 edition of the *Institutes* makes only the first two explicit: "Wherever we see the Word of God purely preached and heard, and the sacraments administered according to Christ's institution, there it is not to be doubted, a church of God exists" (IV.i.9).[2] Twenty years earlier, in his *Reply to Cardinal Sadoleto*, Calvin had said, ". . . there are three things on which the safety of the church is founded, viz., doctrine, discipline, and the sacraments. . . ."[3] Later on in the *Institutes* Calvin described discipline as the sinews of the body:

> Accordingly, as the saving doctrine of Christ is the soul of the church, so does discipline serve as its sinews, through which the members of the body hold together, each in its own place. Therefore, all who desire to remove discipline or to hinder its resto-

[1] Material in this article has appeared earlier in *American Presbyterians* 69 (1991) 243–56, and in *The Practice of Confessional Subscription*, ed. David W. Hall (Lanham, MD: University Press of America, 1995) 149–69.

[2] Calvin, *Institutes of the Christian Religion*, rev. ed., trans. Ford Lewis Battles, ed. John T. McNeill (Grand Rapids: Eerdmans, 1986).

[3] John C. Olin, ed., *A Reformation Debate* (New York: Harper & Row, 1966) 63.

> ration—whether they do this deliberately or out of ignorance—are surely contributing to the ultimate dissolution of the church. (IV. xii.1)

It is apparent that for Calvin, if the Word of God is purely preached and heard and the sacraments are administered according to Christ's institution, then church discipline will naturally follow. The Belgic Confession of 1561, like the Scotch Confession, includes three marks of the true church: ". . . the pure doctrine of the gospel is preached therein; . . . she maintains the pure administration of the sacraments as instituted by Christ; . . . church discipline is exercised in punishing of sin . . ." (Article XXIX). Discipline is also implied by reference to subjection to the Word in the Gallican, or French, Confession of 1559: ". . . properly speaking, there can be no Church where the Word of God is not received, nor profession made of subjection to it, nor use of the sacraments" (Article XXVIII).

The exercise of church discipline was thus a well-established part of the Reformed tradition as members of various strands of that tradition migrated to America in the 17th and 18th centuries. Illustrative of the early American Presbyterian church's exercise of discipline with regard to doctrinal truth is its first heresy trial, that of Samuel Hemphill in 1735.

The Hemphill Case

On Monday morning, September 22, 1735, the Synod of the Presbyterian Church, meeting in Philadelphia, received the following letter:

> To the Revd. Members of ye Synod,
>
> By way of Answer to ye Notification which I received Saturday last, I have only to observe, yt ye Dispute between the Synod and me being made publick in the World, which was first begun by the Commission, what I have at present to offer to the Synod, is contained in an Answr. to the Vindication of the Revd. Commission now in the Press and will be speedily published, and yt I despise the Synod's claim of Authority.
>
> Your humble Servt.
>
> Sam: Hemphill
>
> Monday morning
>
> P.S. I shall think you'll do me a deal of Honour if you entirely exommunicate me.[4]

[4] Guy S. Klett, ed., *Minutes of the Presbyterian Church in America, 1706–1788* (Philadelphia: Presbyterian Historical Society, 1976) 130.

When the promised publication appeared on October 30, it included this "Postscript":

> Since the Writing of this, Mr. *Hemphil* has been inform'd that the Rev. Synod has with great Formality, Gravity and Solemnity, excommunicated him entirely out of their Society. As Gratitude is a Debt always due for a Favour bestow'd, and as expelling the said *Hemphil* out of so bad Company, was the greatest Favour and Honour these Rev. Gentlemen were capable of doing him, he takes this publick Opportunity of thanking them very heartily for it.[5]

Such was the ultimately bitter tenor of the controversy surrounding the first heresy trial in American Presbyterian history. Samuel Hemphill himself appears on the scene for only about a year, but because his trial and the ensuing literary debate involved such significant figures as the young Benjamin Franklin and Jonathan Dickinson, the Hemphill case has attracted some attention from scholars.[6] What has been only casually noticed, however, is the light this controversy sheds on the understanding of subscription to the Westminster Confession and Catechisms only six years after the Adopting Act of 1729.[7]

[5] [Benjamin Franklin], *A Defence Of the Rev. Mr. Hemphill's Observations: or, An Answer to the Vindication of the Reverend Commission* (Philadelphia: B. Franklin, 1735) 48. Franklin's four published writings on behalf of Hemphill can also be found in *The Papers of Benjamin Franklin*, ed. Leonard W. Labaree *et al.*, 24 vols. (New Haven: Yale U. Press, 1959-) II: 28–33, 37–65, 66–88, and 90–126.

[6] The following all deal with the Hemphill case primarily out of interest in Franklin: Merton A. Christensen, "Franklin on the Hemphill Trial: Deism Versus Presbyterian Orthodoxy," *Wm. & Mary Q.*, Third Series, 10 (July 1953) 422–40; Alfred Owen Aldridge, *Benjamin Franklin and Nature's God* (Durham, N.C.: Duke University Press, 1967) 86–98; Melvin H. Buxbaum, *Benjamin Franklin and the Zealous Presbyterians* (University Park and London: Pennsylvania State U. Press, 1975) 76–115; and Elizabeth E. Dunn, "From a Bold Youth to a Reflective Sage: A Revelation of Benjamin Franklin's Religion," *Penn. Mag. Hist. Biog.*, 111 (1987) 501–524.

[7] Charles Augustus Briggs gave it some attention in connection with subscription in *American Presbyterianism: Its Origin and Early History* (New York: Charles Scribner's Sons, 1885) 230–35. Leonard J. Trinterud, *The Forming of an American Tradition: A Re-examination of Colonial Presbyterianism* (Philadelphia: Westminster Press, 1949) 62–63, discusses it only briefly. Details on Hemphill and the case can be found in Richard Webster, *A History of the Presbyterian church in America, From Its Origin Until the Year 1760, with Biographical Sketches of Its Early Ministers* (Philadelphia: Joseph M. Wilson, 1857) 416–20 and 110–15. Most recently the trial has been discussed by Marilyn J. Westerkamp, *Triumph of the Laity: Scots-Irish Piety and the Great Awakening, 1625–1760* (New York: Oxford University Press, 1988) 158–61.

From nearly the very beginning the significance of the Adopting Act has been variously understood. On the one hand strict subscriptionists have emphasized the Synod's action of the afternoon of September 19, 1729 in which the ministers declared the Westminster Confession and Catechisms to be the confession of their faith, excepting only some clauses in the 20th and 23rd chapters pertaining to the civil magistrate.[8] On the other hand there are those who have emphasized the action of the morning of that same day in which there was repeated reference to "essential and necessary" articles of faith and the possibility of expressing scruples with regard to "extra-essential and not-necessary points" of doctrine.[9] The Synod of 1730 sought to clear up some contemporary misunderstanding of the Adopting Act by passing unanimously the following:

> Whereas some Persons have been dissatisfied at the Manner of wording our last years Agreement about the Confession & c: supposing some Expressions not sufficiently obligatory upon Intrants; overtured yt the Synod do now declare, that they understand those Clauses that respect the Admission of Intrants or Candidates in such a sense as to oblige them to receive and adopt the Confession

[8] Klett, *Minutes*, 104. Old School Presbyterian theologians have generally taken this view. The views of Charles Hodge are discussed in William S. Barker, "Subscription to the Westminster Confession and Catechisms," *Presbuterion: The Covenant Seminary Review*, 10 (1984) 11–14. For James Henley Thornwell, see his *Collected Writings* (Edinburgh: Banner of Truth, 1974) 4:313, 366–67, 442–43, and 493–94. More recent examples would be Morton H. Smith, *How the Gold Is Become Dim: The Decline of the Presbyterian Church U.S., as Reflected in Its Assembly Actions*, 2d ed. (Jackson, MS: Steering Committee for a Continuing Presbyterian Church, 1973) 38–39; and George W. Knight III, "Subscription to the Westminster Confession of Faith and Catechisms," *Presbuterion: The Covenant Seminary Review* 10 (1984) 21–23.

[9] Klett, *Minutes*, 103–4. Those who understand the Adopting Act in this way would include Frederick W. Loetscher, "The Adopting Act," *JtPHS* 13 (Dec. 1929) 337–55; Trinterud, *Forming*, 48–49, 66–67; James Hastings Nichols, "Colonial Presbyterianism Adopts Its Standards, " *JPHS* 34 (March 1956) 53–66, and Thomas A. Schafer, "The Beginnings of Confessional Subscription in the Presbyterian Church," *McCQ* 19 (Jan. 1966) 102–119. James R. Payton Jr., "Background and Significance of the Adopting Act of 1729," in *Pressing Toward the Mark: Essays Commemorating Fifty Years of the Orthodox Presbyterian Church*, ed. Charles G. Dennison and Richard C. Gamble (Philadelphia: Committee for the Historian of the Orthodox Presbyterian Church, 1986) 131–45 agrees with this interpretation of the Adopting Act but deplores it, whereas the other writers praise it. A nineteenth-century view similar to that of Payton is given by Ashbel Green in his extended review of Samuel Miller's *Letters to Presbyterians on the Present Crisis in the Presbyterian Church in the United States* (Philadelphia: A. Finley, 1833) that ran in the *Christian Advocate* from July, 1833 to April, 1834; cf. 11: (Aug. 1833) 364–66, (Sept. 1833) 411–13.

> and Catechisms at their Admission in the same Manner and as fully as the Members of the Synod did that were then present.[10]

This action makes it clear that a minister seeking to join the Presbyterian Church in America must adopt the Westminster Confession and Catechisms. What remains unclear is whether he may express scruples only with regard to the passages concerning the civil magistrate or that he may express whatever differences he may have and let the Synod or a presbytery determine if such a difference is acceptable, being not essential or necessary.

Such was the situation when Samuel Hemphill was received by the Synod in 1734. In the year following his trial the Synod of 1736 sought to tighten up the matter of confessional subscription by adopting without dissent the following overture:

> That the Synod do declare, yt inasmuch as we understand yt many Persons of our Perswasion both more lately and formerly have been offended with some Expressions or Distinctions in the first or preliminary act of our Synod, contained in the printed Paper, relating to our receiving or adopting the westminster Confession and Catechisms & c: That in order to remove said offence and all Jealousies yt have arisen or may arise in any of our People's minds on occasion of sd. Distinctions and Expressions, the Synod doth declare, yt the Synod have adopted and still do adhere to the westminster. Confession Catechisms and Directory without the least variation or alteration, and without any Regard to sd. Distinctions. And we do further declare yt this was our meaning and true Intent in our first adopting of sd. Confession, as may particularly appear by our adopting act which is as followeth.[11]

And then the afternoon action of September 19, 1729 is quoted without the morning's preliminary action referring to essential and necessary articles. Charles Augustus Briggs comments, "This act does not antagonize the Adopting Act, but it points in the direction of strict subscription," and he shows in a lengthy footnote how those in attendance at the 1736 Synod were predominately of the stricter subscription viewpoint.[12] James Hastings Nichols, however, says that this 1736 action "in effect consti-

[10] Klett, *Minutes*, 108.

[11] Ibid., 141.

[12] Briggs, *American Presbyterianism*, 235–38.

tuted a substitute constitution,"[13] and Thomas Schafer concludes that in "1736 the subscriptionists had scuttled the 1729 agreement . . . ."[14]

Is there a way to harmonize the actions of 1736 and of 1730 with the whole Adopting Act of 1729, indeed of harmonizing the morning and the afternoon actions of 1729? Exponents of a broad or looser style of subscription have tended to champion the preliminary action of the 1729 Synod as representing the church's spirit of genuine compromise and to see the 1736 action as a one-sided decision engineered by a momentarily dominant minority faction. On the other hand, exponents of a very strict style of subscription have tended to emphasize the 1736 action as consistent with the afternoon adopting action of 1729, thus neglecting the morning's preliminary action as representing the sentiments of those like Jonathan Dickinson, architect of compromise, who had earlier opposed subscription.

It seems strange, however, that the unanimous actions of church courts within a short span of time, or indeed on the morning and afternoon of the same day, should be contradictory of each other. There were differing convictions about confessional subscription within the Synod, but there was a larger measure of unity than has usually been recognized. This unity revolved around the method of subscription. The controversy over Hemphill shows the particular procedure of subscription that evidently satisfied both sides at the time.

Because it is critical to a proper understanding of early American Presbyterian confessional subscription to see that the view ascribed to Dickinson was not merely his own but became the expression of the entire Synod, and because some of the authorities on Franklin have not fully understood the Presbyterian Church's procedure in the controversy, the sequence of events and the authorship of the documents relevant to the Hemphill case are here laid out in great detail in the first section. Then in the second section, the specific role of the Westminster Confession in the controversy is described.

The Sequence of Events

It is important, first of all, to identify the main figures in the controversy and to place the documents properly in the sequence of events. Who was Samuel Hemphill? Precious little is known about him, and no one seems to know what became of him after 1735. Franklin says simply, in

[13] Nichols, "Colonial Presbyterianism," 61–62.

[14] Schafer, "The Beginnings," 188.

his *Autobiography*, "On our Defeat he left us, in search elsewhere of better Fortune. . . ."[15] Franklin does furnish some further information about his age, style, and origins:

> About the Year 1734. there arrived among us from Ireland, a young Presbyterian Preacher named Hemphill, who delivered with a good Voice, & apparently extempore, most excellent Discourses, which drew together considerable Numbers of different Persuasions, who join'd in admiring them. Among the rest I became one of his constant Hearers, his Sermons pleasing me, as they had little of the dogmaticall kind, but inculcated strongly the Practice of Virtue, or what in the religious Stile are called good works.[16]

A similar version of the facts, from quite a different angle, is provided by the senior pastor of the (First) Presbyterian Church of Philadelphia, Jedidiah Andrews:

> There came from Ireland one Mr. Hemphill at yt Time to sojourn in Town for the winter, as was pretended, till he could fall into Business among some People in the Country (tho' some think he had other views at first, considering the Infidel disposition of too many here). Some desiring I shd have assistance and some leading Men not disaffected to the way of Deism so much as they shd be, yt Man was imposed upon me and the Congregatn. Most of the best of the People were soon so dissatisfied yt they would not come to meeting. Free-thinkers, Deists and Nothings getting a scout of him flocked to hear. I attended all winter, but making Complaint brought the Ministrs together, who acted as is shown in the books I send you. Never was there such a Tryal known in the American world.[17]

Records of the Irish Presbyterian Church show that Hemphill, having studied at Glasgow, was received by the Presbytery of Strabane "on first tryals" by June of 1729, was licensed and had "subscribed according to order" by June of 1730. On June 18, 1734 Strabane Presbytery reported to the General Synod at Londonderry that "they have in tryals for ordi-

[15] *The Autobiography of Benjamin Franklin: A Genetic Text*, ed. J. A. Leo Lemay and P. M. Zall (Knoxville: University of Tennessee Press, 1981) 97.

[16] Ibid., 96.

[17] Letter of June 14, 1735, from Jedidiah Andrews to "Reverend and Dear Sir" (a clergyman in the Boston area, but not Benjamin Colman or Thomas Prince since they are both referred to in the final sentence); photocopy in the Presbyterian Historical Society, Philadelphia.

nation Mr Saml Hemphill, who designs to pass into the Plantations in America."[18]

The minutes of the Synod of Philadelphia show that he was present in September of 1734 and "being recommended by the Presbry of Straban in Ireland, to all their Revnd. Brethren where the Providence of God shall call him; and he also bringing ample and satisfactory Certificates from the same Presbry of his Qualifications for and Ordination to the sacred Ministry, he is, upon his Desire, admitted a member of this Synod, and recommended to the Regards and Assistance of which so ever of our Presbry's his Abode shall be fixed among." At that same meeting Hemphill and three others "declared for and adopted the Westminster Confession Catechisms and Directory commonly annexed, the former as the Confession of their faith and the latter as the Guide of their Practice in Matters of Discipline as far as may be agreeable to the Rules of Prudence & c: as in the adopting Acts of this Synod is directed."[19] But Hemphill was accompanied not only by satisfactory certification. An Irish minister named Patrick Vance had also sent word to his brother-in-law in America, a Mr. J. Kilpatrick, that Hemphill's doctrine was not sound.[20] When Hemphill preached two sermons to the people of New London in Chester County, he was summoned before the Presbytery of New Castle but was cleared.[21] By November of 1734 he was serving as Jedidiah Andrews' assistant in the (First) Presbyterian Church of Philadelphia and attracting people such as Franklin. Other than his role in the trial itself and the following literary debate little else is known about him.[22]

[18] *Records of the General Synod of Ulster, From 1691 to 1820*, 3 vols. (Belfast, 1890–98) II:140, 149, 189. Cf. Briggs, *American Presbyterianism*, 230 footnote: "He subscribed . . . according to the Synodical formula: 'I believe the Westminster Confession of Faith to be agreeable to the Scriptures of the Old and New Testaments and founded thereupon and as such I own it to be the confession of my faith. Subscribed Sam. Hemphill.' (See *MS. Minutes Presbytery of Strabane*, McGee College Library, Londonderry.)"

[19] Klett, *Minutes*, 121.

[20] [Benjamin Franklin], *Some Observations on the Proceedings Against the Rev. Mr. Hemphill; With a Vindication of His Sermons*, 2d ed. (Philadelphia: B. Franklin, 1735) 3–4. The Irish church subsequently heard charges against Vance for having "written to the prejudice of Mr Hemphill's character" (*Records of the General Synod of Ulster*, 2:208–9, 215, 223). Vance defended himself as having evidence, and eventually he was vindicated by the Sub-Synod of Derry and the General Synod (Westerkamp, *Triumph*, 158).

[21] [Franklin], *Some Observations*, 5. Cf. Webster, *A History of the Presbyterian Church*, 111.

[22] There is a Samuel Hemphill in the *Dictionary of National Biography*, who is a contemporary but somewhat older. He received an M.A. from Glasgow College on April 30, 1716, just eight weeks after the date that Briggs reports our Samuel Hemphill entered there.

Benjamin Franklin was twenty-nine years old at the time of the Hemphill trial, but was already well established in Philadelphia with a successful printing business. He was a leading member of the Junto club, founder of the Philadelphia Library Company, owner of the *Pennsylvania Gazette* and of his *Poor Richard's Almanac,* and a grand master of the Masons.[23] He had previously attended the Presbyterian Church, once for five Sundays in a row, but found the preaching of Andrews doctrinal and unedifying. The arrival of Hemphill in the pulpit kindled his interest, and it is in accord with the evidence to see him as the ringleader of those in support of Hemphill. He reports on events at the trial as though present,[24] and it is easy to imagine him as practically the counsel for the defense. Many years later he would write in his *Autobiography*: "I became his zealous Paritsan, and contributed all I could to raise a Party in his Favour; and we combated for him a while with some Hopes of Success. There was much Scribbling pro & con upon the Occasion; and finding that tho' an elegant Preacher he was but a poor Writer, I lent him my Pen and wrote for him two or three Pamphlets. . . ."[25] Experts on Franklin are agreed that the writings on Hemphill's side are properly to be ascribed to Franklin, in large part if not in toto.[26] The characteristic Franklin wit shines throughout the pamphlets, but there is a strident tone, particularly in his final piece, *A Defence of the Rev. Mr. Hemphill's Observations*, that is quite different from the persona portrayed in his *Autobiography*, written between 1771 and 1790, of a benevolent Deist who is above the hairsplitting of religious controversy.[27]

He was ordained on December 24, 1718, by Augher Presbytery, served congregations in Castleblayney and Antrim, and died on March 28, 1741. Ironically, he engaged in the controversy over subscription in the Irish church, opposing the anti-subscriptionists.

23 Buxbaum, *Benjamin Franklin*, 76–77.

24 [Franklin], *Some Observations*, 10.

25 *Autobiography*, 96.

26 See the editorial comments in Volume II of *The Papers of Benjamin Franklin*; Buxbaum, *Benjamin Franklin*, 234 n. 140; Christensen, "Franklin on the Hemphill Trial," 434.

27 This is the contention throughout Buxbaum's *Benjamin Franklin*. Elizabeth Dunn comments: "Ethics often occupied his thoughts, and he believed Hemphill's preaching to be more useful than the teaching of religious dogma for inculcating virtue in the populace. At the same time, he carefully avoided directly challenging the religious establishment of Philadelphia" ("From a Bold Youth," 516), but that last sentence hardly accords with *A Defence of the Rev. Mr. Hemphill's Observations*. H.W. Brands, *The First American: The Life and Times of Benjamin Franklin* (New York: Doubleday, 2000), says, "He was not proud of his performance in the Hemphill case; in his autobiography he glossed it over almost to the point of prevarication." (145). Edmund S. Morgan, *Benjamin Franklin* (New Haven: Yale University Press, 2002), says, "Franklin's articles [on the Hemphill case] are the clear-

The other main actor in the Hemphill case is the Commission of Synod. Several misunderstandings about the Commission contribute to Melvin Buxbaum's regarding it as unfair in its treatment of Hemphill.[28] The Commission of Synod, from 1720 on, was a standing body designed to act with the authority of Synod between the annual meetings of the General Synod.[29] Each year a number of ministers would be chosen to serve in this capacity during the intervening months. On September 19, 1734, the following were appointed to be the Commission for the year ensuing: Jedidiah Andrews, James Anderson, John Thomson, George Gillespie, Robert Cross, Jonathan Dickinson, John Pierson, Thomas Creaghead, and the moderator of Synod, who that year was Ebenezer Pemberton.[30] When Andrews brought charges against his younger associate Hemphill, he himself did not serve on the Commission—in fact, having presented the charge he "left all to the Ministrs and meddled no more," describing himself as "weary of these things."[31]

Another significant thing to note about the Commission is that Jonathan Dickinson was not present to participate in the trial. The seven remaining regular members of the Commission were joined, however, by thirteen correspondents who participated in voting upon the verdict. These included William Tennent Sr., David Evans (who served as Clerk), Richard Treat, Adam Boyd, Joseph Houston, Andrew Archbold, Robert Jamison, Thomas Evans, Alexander Hutchison, Robert Cathcart, Nathaniel Hubbel, Gilbert Tennent, and William Tennent Jr.[32] These twenty ministers were more than half of the thirty-nine who were then members of the Synod, and they represent a fair balance of whatever factions may have existed at that time. In view of what the Commission would subsequently say about subscription, it is significant that John Thomson, the original proposer of subscription, was a member. When the Commission decided to suspend

est statements he ever made about Christianity as he thought it ought to be" (21). Walter Isaacson, *Benjamin Franklin: An American Life* (New York: Simon and Schuster, 2003), says, "His resentment of the entrenched, pious clerical establishment seemed to get the better of his temper" (109).

28 Buxbaum, *Benjamin Franklin*, 95, 102, 111, 115, and 233 n. 81.

29 Charles Hodge, *The Constitutional History of the Presbyterian Church in the United States of America*, 2 vols. in 1 (Philadelphia: Presbyterian Board of Publication, 1851) 1:112. Klett, *Minutes*, 47.

30 Klett, *Minutes*, 119, 118.

31 Andrews, Letter of June 14, 1735.

32 *An Extract of the Minutes of the Commission of the Synod, Relating to the Affair of the Reverend Mr. Hemphil* (Philadelphia: Andrew Bradford, 1735) 3. (Webster, *A History of the Presbyterian Church*, 417, fails to include William Tennent Jr.)

Hemphill, the minutes note: "This is the unanimous Determination of the whole Commission and all the Correspondents," and they gave thanks "that in the whole Transaction we have not had one dissenting Vote."[33]

It is important at this point to put the documents pertaining to the Hemphill affair in proper logical order. First is Franklin's *Dialogue between Two Presbyterians*, printed in *The Pennsylvania Gazette* on April 10, 1735, just one week before the Commission meeting concerning Hemphill was to begin. In it Mr. S. discusses with Mr. T. whether the Synod "are going to persecute, silence and condemn a good Preacher [Mr. H.], for exhorting them to be honest and charitable to one another and the rest of Mankind."[34] The Commission began its sessions on Thursday, April 17 and continued to Saturday, April 26 except for Sunday, April 20, when Robert Cross and Ebenezer Pemberton preached before the Commission "and a very numerous audience, the Person accus'd being likewise present. . . ."[35] *An Extract of the Minutes of the Commission of the Synod, Relating to the Affair of The Reverend Mr. Samuel Hemphil* was published in the first week of May, with the reason given as follows: "The late Tryal of the Reverend Mr. Samuel Hemphil, before the Commission of the Synod, being the Subject of much Discourse; we thought it necessary to publish our Minutes upon that Affair, to prevent any Misrepresentations, and unjust Aspersions that might be cast upon us, and to give the World a View of the Grounds which we went upon in the Censure we have passed upon him."[36] The verdict agreed upon was "That Mr. Hemphill be suspended from all the parts of his ministerial Office until the next meeting of our Synod, and that it be referred to the Synod to judge, when met, whether the Suspension shall be continued or taken off, or whatever else shall be judged needful to be done, according as things shall then appear: And accordingly we do suspend the said Mr. Samuel Hemphill as above."[37]

On June 14, as already mentioned, Jedidiah Andrews wrote a letter to a fellow clergyman in the Boston area, sending three copies of a book—evidently *An Extract of the Minutes of the Commission*—one each for his recipient, Benjamin Colman, and Thomas Prince, commenting that "It has been, since last November, the most trying Time with me yt ever I met

[33] *An Extract*, 13.

[34] *The Papers of Benjamin Franklin*, 2:31.

[35] Robert Cross, *The Danger of perverting the Gospel of Christ, Represented in a Sermon preach'd before the Commission of Synod at Philadelphia. April 20th, 1735* (New York: John Peter Zenger, 1735) 30.

[36] *An Extract*, 2.

[37] Ibid., 13.

with in all my Life," and indicating that: "There is in the Press an Answr to the *Abstract* and a *Vindication of his sermons*. What it will be I know not; there are men appointed to defend what is done."[38]

The work anticipated by Andrews, and no doubt expected by the Commission since a committee was set up to defend its actions, appeared on July 17 as *Some Observations on the Proceedings Against the Rev. Mr. Hemphill; With a Vindication of His Sermons*. This work, published anonymously but now ascribed to Franklin, was printed by Franklin after an illness of six or seven weeks and proved so popular that a second edition was required in August.[39]

Meanwhile the sermons of Robert Cross and of Ebenezer Pemberton, preached before the Commission on April 20, were published because they had been claimed by Hemphill to be prejudicial to his case, Franklin stating that he was willing to surrender his sermon notes to the Commission only after these sermons were preached.[40] These were published prior to September 4, when appeared the most important document for our understanding of confessional subscription, *A Vindication of the Reverend Commission of the Synod In Answer to Some Observations On their Proceedings against the Reverend Mr. Hemphill*. This work of sixty-three pages (the last fifteen of which are an "Appendix" with fuller extracts from Hemphill's seven sermons that were considered) is often ascribed to Jonathan Dickinson, but is clearly not by Dickinson alone since at least parts of it bear the stamp of an eye-witness to the events of the trial, and Dickinson, though a member of the Commission for that year, was not listed as present for the Hemphill case.[41] The authorship of *A Vindication*

[38] Andrews, Letter of June 14, 1735 to "Reverend and Dear Sir."

[39] [Benjamin Franklin], *Some Observations on the Proceedings Against the Rev. Mr. Hemphill; With a Vindication of His Sermons*, 2d ed. (Philadelphia: B. Franklin, 1735) 2.

[40] Cross, *The Danger of perverting the Gospel* (the text was Galatians 1:7–9); Ebenezer Pemberton, *Sermon Preach'd before the Commission of the Synod, at Philadelphia. April 20th, 1735* (New York: John Peter Zenger, 1735) (the text was Luke 7:35); [Franklin], *Some Observations*, 13.

[41] *A Vindication of the Reverend Commission of the Synod In Answer to Some Observations On their Proceedings against the Reverend Mr. Hemphill* (Philadelphia: Andrew Bradford, 1735). On page 12 concerning the sermons of Cross and Pemberton, by then published, it says: "What convictions these Sermons afforded Mr. *H–ll*, we cannot tell; but the next Morning he offered to read his Notes before *The Commission*, which proposal we readily accepted of, esteeming it the likeliest Way to prevent our being mistaken in the Principles he maintained; and the surest Method of obtaining a just and impartial View of the Doctrines he had Propagated." On page 6 of this document is the first hint that Hemphill's sermons were plagiarized.

of the Reverend Commission should rather be ascribed to the committee that was assigned (as shown by Andrews' letter) "to defend what is done." The Synod met in Philadelphia within two weeks of this work's publication, September 17–25, and after unanimously confirming the Commission's verdict by declaring Hemphill "unqualified for any future Exercise of his Ministry within our Bounds," took this action: "The Brethren appointed to justify the Commission against any Complaints from Mr. Hemphill if he should publish any such, having complied with the Commisions order in yt Matter, are desired by the Synod to continue to answr. any further Publications of Mr. Hemphill's or his Friends in yt Cause if they shall think it necessary."[42]

While the Synod was meeting, there appeared *A Letter to a Friend in the Country, Containing the Substance of a Sermon Preach'd at Philadelphia, in the Congregation of the Rev. Mr. Hemphill, Concerning the Terms of Christian and Ministerial Communion.* This forty-page work includes a three-page preface, "The Publisher to His Lay-Reader," signed by "A LAYMAN," who clearly is Franklin. The body of it purports to be a letter dated August 30, 1735, describing to an outsider the good qualities of a sermon preached on Hemphill's behalf. It is most likely that the entire work is Franklin's.[43]

By November 27 the answer appeared in *Remarks Upon a Pamphlet, Entitled, A LETTER to a Friend in the Country, containing the Substance of a SERMON preached at Philadelphia, in the Congregation of the Rev. Mr. Hemphill.* This work is almost universally ascribed to Jonathan Dickinson although the title page does not include an author. It does contain the characteristically Dickinsonian position: "We can't too often declare, that the Door of *Christian Communion*, should stand as wide open as the *Gates of Heaven*; and each Christian Society, have a right to judge for themselves how wide that is."[44] It should rather be regarded, however, as by the committee established by the Commission and mentioned by the Synod's minutes.

42 Klett, *Minutes*, 130–31. The dates for the publication of these several documents are given in the editorial comments in *The Papers of Benjamin Franklin* as derived from contemporary announcements in Franklin's *Pennsylvania Gazette* or Andrew Bradford's *American Weekly Mercury*. Some of Christensen's dating, 432–33, is incorrect.

43 Buxbaum, *Benjamin Franklin*, 234 n. 140.

44 [Jonathan Dickinson?], *Remarks upon a Pamphlet, Entitled, A Letter to a Friend in the Country, containing the Substance of a Sermon preached at Philadelphia, in the Congregation of the Rev. Mr. Hemphill* (Philadelphia: Andrew Bradford, 1735) 21.

Next in the sequence of responses, although it actually appeared on October 30, four weeks earlier than *Remarks upon a Pamphlet*, is Franklin's bitterest piece, *A Defence Of the Rev. Mr. Hemphill's Observations: or, An Answer to the Vindication of the Reverend Commission*. Sometime during the summer it had become clear that Hemphill not only advocated a deistic theology, but he had plagiarized his sermons from Samuel Clarke, Benjamin Ibbot, and James Foster, British preachers known for their Arian views. Franklin describes this embarrassment in his *Autobiography*:

> During the Contest an unlucky Occurrence hurt his Cause exceedingly. One of our Adversaries having heard him preach a Sermon that was much admired, thought he had somewhere read that Sermon before, or at least a part of it. On Search he found that Part quoted at length in one of the British Reviews from a Discourse of Dr. Forster's. This Detection gave many of our Party Disgust, who accordingly abandoned his Cause, and occasion'd our more speedy Discomfiture in the Synod. I stuck by him, however, as I rather approv'd his giving us good Sermons compos'd by others, than bad ones of his own Manufacture; tho' the latter was the Practice of our common Teachers. He afterwards acknowledg'd to me that none of those he preach'd were his own; adding that his Memory was such as enabled him to retain and repeat any Sermon after one reading only.[45]

In *A Defence* Franklin employed a Swiftean analogy: "Thus the Difference between him and most of his Brethren, in this part of the World, is the same with that between the *Bee* and the *Fly* in a Garden. The one wanders from Flower to Flower, and for the use of others collects from the whole the most delightful Honey; while the other (of a quite different Taste) places her Happiness entirely in Filth, Corruption, and Ordure."[46]

A Defence clearly is the work that Hemphill had rudely informed the Synod, in his letter of September 22, was "now in the Press and will be speedily published." In it Franklin names names, identifying Robert Cross, pastor of the church in Jamaica on Long Island, as the person previously described as "one of the chief managers of the whole affair" on the Commission.[47] The final answer from the Synod's committee, appearing by January 6, 1736, was issued under the pseudonym of "Obadiah Jenkins" and was entitled *Remarks upon the Defence of the Reverend Mr. Hemphill's*

[45] Franklin, *Autobiography*, 96–97.

[46] Franklin, *A Defence*, 10.

[47] Ibid., 18.

Observations: In a Letter to a Friend. It claims to be a letter dated November 24, 1735 from a gentleman in New York who has followed the controversy thus far and states to his correspondent: "I am fully of your Mind, that the *Commission* will not undertake a Reply. I hope those Reverend Gentlemen will find better Employment than to rake the Kennels. They will doubtless esteem such a scurrilous Paper below their Notice."[48] The editors of *The Papers of Benjamin Franklin* base their judgment that "Obadiah Jenkins" is a pseudonym, and that Jonathan Dickinson was probably the author, on a contemporary note on the copy in the Historical Society of Pennsylvania.[49] This copy is bound together (in third place) with *A Vindication of the Reverend Commission* and *Remarks upon a Pamphlet.* A contemporary hand has written on top of page 1 of *A Vindication* "By Mr. Dickinson" and on the title page of Obadiah Jenkins' *Remarks upon the Defence* the initial "J. D." above "Obadiah" and "Nomenfictum" after "Jenkins."[50]

A more specific handwritten note appears, however, on the microfilmed copy in the Speer Library of Princeton Theological Seminary. Opposite the first page of Jenkins' *Remarks upon the Defence*, a contemporary hand has written "Chiefly by Mr. D_____ to p. 15" and "Partly by Mr. P_____ from p. 16_____." Most likely this refers to Jonathan Dickinson and Ebenezer Pemberton as main members of the committee assigned to respond to the publications of Hemphill or his supporters. Clearly the authors of Obadiah Jenkins' *Remarks* desired at this point to mask the fact that they were here responding officially for the Synod. For one thing, they descended to Franklin's level of argument, specifically indicating which sermons Hemphill had stolen from whom, and picking up the Swiftean analogy: ". . . instead of imitating the *Bee*, in collecting Honey from every Flower, he has but acted the *Drone*, in stealing other Men's Labours."[51] They also wanted it to appear that Hemphill's latest defense did not really merit a reply: ". . . I can't but think that the Commission have sufficiently vindicated themselves, from all his scurrilous Imputations of out-doing

48 Obadiah Jenkins, *Remarks upon the Defence of the Reverend Mr. Hemphill's Observations: In a Letter to a Friend* (Philadelphia: Andrew Bradford, 1735) 2.

49 *The Papers of Benjamin Franklin*, 2:91 n. 4.

50 This volume is actually stored for the Historical Society of Pennsylvania in the next-door Library Company of Philadelphia. There is no indication of authorship for *Remarks upon a Pamphlet*, but the reverse of the title page has written in a similar hand "S. Horton's Book." Perhaps all three works belonged to Simeon (or Simon) Horton, who joined the East Jersey Presbytery prior to the Synod of 1735, but was not present at the Synod meeting.

51 Jenkins, *Remarks upon the Defence*, 18.

the Jesuits in *Subterfuge, Distinction and Evasion. . . .*"[52] By this point neither side had more to say.

The Role of the Confession in the Controversy

Franklin had rejoiced in Hemphill's sermons because they expressed the sort of deistic religion that he had come to hold. The six articles that the Commission framed against the preacher included his teaching of a religion based on the Law of Nature, of no necessity of conversion for those born to Christian parents in a Christian society, of a Socinian Christ whose death was not a satisfaction of God's justice, of a faith involving persuasion of the mind upon rational grounds and producing suitable affects but not mentioning receiving of Christ in the terms of the gospel, of salvation through the Light of Nature apart from divine revelation, and of justification by faith as not necessary for "those who have been educated and instructed in the knowledge of the Christian Religion."[53] But Franklin recognized that the obstacle standing in the way of acceptance of such views in the Presbyterian Church was the Westminster Confession of Faith. From the very beginning much of the literary debate revolved around the role of the Confession.

Franklin first argued against the finality of any creed or confession. *In the Dialogue between Two Presbyterians*, after Mr. T. says, "We ought to abide by the Westminster Confession of Faith; and he that does not, ought not to preach in our Meetings," Mr. S. responds, "But has not a Synod that meets in King George the Second's Reign, as much Right to interpret Scripture, as one that met in Oliver's Time? . . . why must we be forever confin'd to that, or to any, Confession?"[54] In his climactic speech Mr S. concedes that Hemphill's doctrine may not be entirely in accord with all of the church's standard: ". . . he does not perhaps zealously propagate all the Doctrines of an old Confession."[55] Pursuing this line further in *Some Observations on the Proceedings*, Franklin makes a telling distinction: "And if these Reverend Gentlemen were as well acquainted with what they call their *well known* Confession of Faith as they pretend to be, they would not have found Hemphill's Sermons inconsistent with it; he will undertake to prove that all his Discourses are agreeable to the *fundamental* Articles of it, which was all he declared to at his Admittance into the Synod: And

[52] Ibid., 19.

[53] *An Extract of the Minutes*, 7–11.

[54] *The Papers of Benjamin Franklin*, 2:31–32.

[55] Ibid., 2:32.

surely they would not offer to condemn him for differing with them about extra-essentials."[56] At the conclusion he charges, ". . . it seems very hard that they should make this Book the Standard and Test, when at the same time they own'd to him, that *they knew not how many fundamental Articles were in it.*" Franklin was well aware of the discussions surrounding the Adopting Act of 1729:

> I shall only add, that many of these reverend Gentlemen, who are now so zealous for the Confession, that they seem to give it the Preference to the Holy Scriptures, were of late years more indifferent than Hemphill has yet appear'd to be; and altho' they then agreed, that there were some Articles in it of no great Moment whether Men believed 'em or not, nay some publickly declared they did not understand many of 'em, (which I sincerely believe was very true) yet they would now make 'em all Fundamentals, in order to serve a Turn.[57]

In *A Letter to a Friend,* he merely questions the necessity or usefulness of framing long confessions of faith if neither Christ nor his Apostles did so.[58] By the time of *A Defence,* however, Franklin sees no point in hiding his true colors and, through Hemphill, renounces any allegiance to the Confession: "Whether Hemphill's Notions of Christianity be or be not inconsistent with the darling *Confession of Faith,* he is not at all concern'd to enquire; whatever Notions he might have formerly entertain'd of this idol Confession, he now declares it to be no more *his* Confession, & c."[59] Franklin goes on to term the doctrines of the imputation of Adam's guilt and of the imputed righteousness of Christ as ridiculous and reveals that for him the final authority in religion is not even Scripture: "And if there was such a Text of Scripture, for my own Part, I should not in the least hesitate to say, that it could not be genuine, being so evidently contrary to Reason and the Nature of Things."[60]

Over against this onslaught, the committee appointed by the Commission, and subsequently the Synod, to respond to Hemphill and his friends labored to show how the Westminster Confession functioned in the Presbyterian Church. In their final response, Obadiah Jenkins' *Remarks upon the Defence,* they testify to their respect for the authority

[56] Franklin, *Some Observations,* 18.

[57] Ibid., 30.

[58] Franklin, *A Letter to a Friend,* 11.

[59] Franklin, *A Defence,* 28.

[60] Ibid., 32.

of the Confession: ". . . if renouncing as an Idol, the Confession of Faith, received by the Presbyterian Churches in *England, Scotland,* and *Ireland,* as well as by our Synod, and subscribed by himself as the Confession of his Faith, are just reasons for refusing him Ministerial Communion, the Censure of the Synod is justified by his own Pen."[61] In the second response, *Remarks Upon a Pamphlet,* it is made clear that Presbyterians are not imposing their beliefs on any but themselves: "We allow of no *Confession of Faith,* as a *Test of Orthodoxy* for others, but only as a Declaration of our own Sentiments; nor may this be imposed upon the Members of our own Society, nor their Assent required to any Thing as the Condition of their Communion with us; but what we esteem essentially necessary. If others differ from us, they have *Liberty* to think for themselves, if they will but allow us the same *Liberty.*"[62] This work concludes with a quotation from "the acute and ingenious Mr. *Lock,* in his *Letter concerning Toleration*":

> This is the fundamental and immutable Right of a spontaneous Society, that it has Power to remove any of its Members, who transgress the Rules of its Institution. But it cannot by the Accession of any new Members, acquire any Jurisdiction over those, that are not joined with it. And therefore Peace, Equity, and Friendship, are always mutually to be observed, by particular Churches, in the same Manner, as by private Persons, without any Pretence of Superiority or Jurisdiction over one another.[63]

Then as an appendix to prove that the Presbyterian Church operates in such a fashion there is added verbatim the preliminary part of the Adopting Act from the morning of September 19, 1729.[64]

For clarification of the way confessional subscription was intended to work, however, a crucial passage from the first response by the committee, *A Vindication of the Reverend Commission,* deserves to be quoted fully:

> But we cannot overlook without some Remarks, this surprising Narrative here given, and elsewhere repeated, that *all he declared to at his Admission into the Synod, were the fundamental Articles of the Confession of Faith.* When it is certainly true, and can be attested by above Forty Members of the Synod then present, that he solemnly Declared his Assent to every Article in the *Westminster Confession of Faith,* and in the Larger and Shorter *Catechisms* with-

[61] Jenkins, *Remarks upon the Defense,* 22.

[62] *Remarks Upon a Pamphlet,* 26.

[63] Ibid., 29–30.

[64] Ibid., 31–32.

out one Exception; and assured us, he had before Subscribed the same in *Ireland*.

That we may once for all give the Reader a just View of this Case, and obviate all further Complaints about this matter, it will be proper to observe, that in the Year 1729, the Synod came to an unanimous Agreement about a Test of Orthodoxy, and of our Union in the essential Articles of Christianity, in the following method. It was agreed that all of the Ministers in this Synod, do Declare their Agreement in and Approbation of the *Confession of Faith*, with the Larger and Shorter *Catechisms* of the Assembly of Divines at *Westminster*, as being in all the essential and necessary Articles, good Forms of sound Words, and Systems of Christian Doctrine; and do adopt them as the Confession of their Faith, & c. And in Case any Minister of this Synod, or any Candidate of the Ministry, shall have any Scruple with respect to any Article or Articles of the said *Confession* or *Catechisms*, he shall at the Time of his making said Declaration, declare his Scruples to the Presbytery or Synod, who shall notwithstanding admit him to the Exercise of the Ministry within their Bounds, and to ministerial Communion; if the Synod or Presbytery shall judge his Scruple or Mistake to be only about Articles not essential or necessary, in Doctrine, Worship or Government. By which it appears, that if Mr. *H–ll* had any Objection to make, against any Thing in the *Confession* or *Catechisms*, he should have particularly offered his Objections, and submitted it to the Judgment of the Synod, whether the Articles objected against, were essential and necessary, or not: And accordingly at the Time of his adopting the *Confession* and *Catechisms*, he was called upon to propose his Objections, if he had any; but he replied, he had none to make, and that he had before subscribed the same in *Ireland*, as before hinted. And now the World must Judge, whether it would not have been more to Mr. *H–ll's* Reputation, to have past over this whole Affair in Silence, than to have thus expos'd himself to the just Censure of all those that see the Repugnancy of this Confession of Faith to his Sermons; and that know how to value Sincerity. Nor is it any Excuse, that the Synod have not defined how many fundamental Articles there are in the *Confession*; since they have reserved to themselves the Liberty to judge upon each Occasion, what are, and what are not Fundamental.[65]

[65] *A Vindication of the Reverend Commission*, 22–24. Briggs, *American Presbyterianism*, 232–33, quotes a substantial portion of this, but it is important to have the full context.

Here we have again the preliminary part of the Adopting Act from the morning of September 19, 1729 with two very significant aspects included. First, five years after the Confession was adopted, with exceptions acknowledged only with regard to clauses in the 20th and 23rd chapters concerning the civil magistrate, the procedure was followed of asking Hemphill whether he had *any* exceptions to declare, not just to these portions of the Confession. Second, it is stated that the Synod has not defined which articles are fundamental but has reserved that judgment to itself.

It has been argued that this procedure, of operating according to the "Preliminary Act" of the Synod of 1729, reflects simply the position of Jonathan Dickinson, who had after all opposed confessional subscription prior to 1729.[66] It must be remembered, however, that *A Vindication of the Reverend Commission* was published only two weeks before the Synod of 1735 met to approve the Commission's suspension of Hemphill and to exclude him from the ministry. There is no evidence that anyone in the Synod disapproved of the language of *A Vindication*, which surely would have been "must" reading for every member. Secondly, *A Vindication* spoke for the whole Commission, which included the original proposer of confessional subscription, John Thomson, and several others who were known to favor strict subscription. Thirdly, as we have seen, the authorship of *A Vindication* could not have been Dickinson's alone since it bears the marks of an eye-witness to the trial and Dickinson himself was not present. Once again a handwritten note on the microfilm copy in the Speer Library of Princeton Seminary may provide the answer concerning authorship. Opposite the first page there appears in a contemporary hand: "Written from p. 1 to p. 14 by Mr. *Pemberton* of N.Y. The rest by Mr. *Dickinson* of Eliza. Town Except.g p. 37, & 38. which were inserted by Mr. *Cross* of Jamaica in Vindicã. of himself."[67] Most probably Ebenezer

66 George W. Knight III, "A Response to Dr. William Barker's Article 'Subscription to the Westminster Confession of Faith and Catechisms,'" *Presbuterion* 10 (1984) 58. On Jonathan Dickinson and subscription see Keith J. Hardman, *Jonathan Dickinson and the Course of American Presbyterianism* (Ph.D. diss., U. of Pennsylvania, 1971) 48–65 and Bryan F. Le Beau, "The Subscription Controversy and Jonathan Dickinson," *JPH* 54 (1976) 317–35. For a revision of Trinterud's analysis of factions in the church see Elizabeth I. Nybakken, "New Light on the Old Side: Irish Influences in Colonial Presbyterianism," *JAH* 68 (1982) 813–32.

67 I am grateful to Herbert L. Samworth, author of *Those Astonishing Wonders of His Grace: Jonathan Dickinson and the Great Awakening* (Ph.D. diss., Westminster Theological Seminary, 1988), for calling my attention to this handwritten note. Ms. Jean Preston of the Special Collections, Van Pelt Library, University of Pennsylvania terms it mid-eighteenth century handwriting. This handwritten note is not in the copy in Yale's Beinecke Library

Pemberton (who as Moderator of the Synod of 1734 served as Moderator of the Commission for Hemphill's trial,[68]) and Jonathan Dickinson were the committee to which the task of responding to Hemphill and his friends was assigned, with the possible addition of Robert Cross, whom Franklin identified as "one of the chief managers of the whole Affair."[69] In any case, Cross, who was one of the strongest advocates for strict subscription, had a hand in the production of *A Vindication* and no doubt would have objected if this publication did not accurately describe the method of subscription from 1729 to 1735.

The conclusion to be drawn from the evidence in the Hemphill case is that, whatever differences of emphasis may have existed among the members of the Synod concerning the "Preliminary Act" of the morning or the "Adopting Act" of the afternoon of September 19, 1729, both were regarded as of continuing validity. The Synod had in fact adopted all of the Westminster Confession and Catechisms as its doctrinal standard, and the method of subscribing was for a candidate to declare any exception that he might have, upon which the appropriate judicatory would decide if the exception was to an essential or necessary article, as it had decided concerning the parts about the civil magistrate in 1729. To be sure some, like Thomson, would tend to emphasize the adoption of the Confession and Catechisms as the church's doctrinal standards, and some, like Dickinson, would tend to emphasize the method of subscription; and these differences in emphasis would contribute to tension leading to the division of 1741.

The immediate reaction of the Synod of 1735 to its experience with Hemphill was to adopt a lengthy overture from an unidentified source concerning future ministers from the north of Ireland, "seeing it is too

nor is it in the copy at the Massachusetts Historical Society, the two copies listed in Charles Evans' *American Bibliography*.

68 *An Extract of the Minutes*, 3.

69 Franklin, *A Defence*, 18. On the same day as the Commission's committee was continued by the Synod, the following motion "made by a Member" was adopted: ". . . the Synod do agree yt if any of our members shall see Cause to prepare any Thing for the Press upon any Controversy in religious Matters, yt before such Member publish what he hath thus prepared, he shall submit the same to be perused by Persons to be appointed for yt Purpose, and yt Messrs. Andrews, Dickinson, Robt. Cross, Pemberton and Pierson northward of Philada. and Messrs. Anderson, Thomas Evans, Cathcart, Stevenson and Thomson in the Bounds of ye Synod southward of Philada.—Any three of each Committee to be a Quorum." (Klett, *Minutes*, 131.) This may represent a response to George Gillespie's *A Treatise against the Deists or Free-Thinkers, proving the Necessity of Revealed Religion*, announced as "Just Published" in the *American Weekly Mercury* for July 31–August 7, 1735.

evident to be denied and called in Question, yt we are in great Danger of being imposed upon by Ministrs. and Preachers from thence, tho' sufficiently furnished with all Formalities of Presbyterial Credentials, as in the Case of Mr. H–ll. . . ." The first of five points had to do with subscription:

> . . . That no Ministr. or Probationer coming in among us from Europe be allowed to preach in vacant Congregations until first his Credentials and Recommendations be seen & approven by the Pry unto which such Congregatn. doth most properly belong, and until he preach with approbation before sd. Pry and subscribe or adopt the westminster Confessn. of Faith & Catechisms before sd. Pry in Manner and Form as they have done; and yt no Ministr. employ such to preach in his Pulpit until he see his Credentials & be satisfied, as far as may be, of his firm Attachment to sd. Confession & c: in opposition to the new upstart Doctrines & Schemes, particularly such as we condemn'd in Mr. H–ll's Sermons.[70]

The remaining points required that no congregation present a call to such a minister until he had preached within the bounds of the Synod for a full six months, nor until members of the presbytery concur, that a student under care become well known to most of the ministers of the presbytery, and "That the Synod would bear Testimony agst the late too common, and now altogether unneccessary Practice of some Presbrys in the north of Ireland viz. Their ordaining men to the Ministry *sine Titulo*, immediately before they come over hither. . . ." Besides their presbyterial credentials, such candidates are to bring also private letters of recommendation "from some Brethren there who are well known to some of our Brethren here to be firmly attached to our good old Principles and Schemes, inasmuch as the instance of Mr. H–ll and some other Considerations to the same Purpose make us afraid lest we may again be imposed upon by men of his stamp, tho' furnished with all the Formalities of Presbyterial Credentials."[71] Robert Cross, John Thomson, and Joseph Houston were assigned to communicate this action properly to the General Synod of Ireland.

The apparently stricter subscription described in the action of the Synod of 1736, no doubt influenced by the experience with Hemphill, refers to offence "with some Expressions or Distinctions in the first or preliminary act of our Synod, contained in the printed Paper, relating to our

[70] Klett, *Minutes*, 132.

[71] Ibid., 132–33.

receiving or adopting the westminster Confession & Catechisms & c."[72] The printed paper referred to may indicate a version of the Adopting Act of 1729 which, like *A Vindication of the Reverend Commission* and *Remarks upon a Pamphlet*, contained only the morning or preliminary part of the action of September 19. The Synod of 1735 had ordered "yt each Presbry have the whole adopting Act inserted in their Presbry Book," perhaps indicating that what had been commonly circulated was only the morning or preliminary part of the Adopting Act. Hence the Synod of 1736 felt the need to emphasize "our firm attachment to our good old received doctrines contained in sd. Confession without the least variation or alteration,"[73] as indeed the Westminster doctrinal standards had been adopted in 1729.

But this did not change the method of subscribing, which must have remained as described in *A Vindication of the Reverend Commission*, with a minister or candidate declaring any exceptions and the judicatory rendering its judgment.[74] Such a principle was, after all, embodied in the original overture of 1727 from John Thomson that led to the Adopting Act: "Fifthly, to enact, that if any minister within our bounds shall take upon him to teach or preach any thing contrary to any of the said articles, unless, first, he propose the said point to the Presbytery or Synod to be discussed by them, he shall be censured so and so."[75] Such a procedure of declaring any exceptions would require serious study of the Westminster standards and would compel a candidate to be open about his differences. Thus Thomson and Dickinson, Cross and Andrews, could all join in screening out a deist like Hemphill, whose sermons "were all of them as to their general Scope, opposed to the Necessity of our Interest in Christ's

[72] Ibid., 141.

[73] Ibid., 142. Trinterud (*Forming*, 66) and Briggs (*American Presbyterianism*, 237–38) correctly point out that the stricter subscriptionists were disproportionately predominant in the attendance at the 1736 Synod. See the analysis in Barker, "Subscription to the Westminster Confession," 7–8. No doubt the lopsided representation contributed to the emphasis on the latter part of the Adopting Act by the Synod of 1736.

[74] There is one clear instance in the Synod Minutes where a minister "Proposed all the Scruples he had to make about any articles of the Confession and Catechisms &c: to the Satisfaction of the Synod" in his subscribing to the Westminster Standards. This was David Evans in 1730 (Klett, *Minutes*, 108). We do not know what Evans's scruples were. It was not difficult for the Synod to unite against the deistical convictions of Hemphill. Whether it would have agreed in opposing some lesser deviations from the Confession in an area other than that of the civil magistrate is not clear.

[75] Quoted in Charles Hodge, *Constitutional History*, Vol. 1, 141. See also Webster, *A History of the Presbyterian Church*, 103.

Satisfaction, and to our Justification thro' Faith in his Blood,"[76] and whose doctrines "we are obliged to declare Unsound and Dangerous, contrary to the sacred Scriptures and our excellent Confession and Catechisms, having an unhappy tendency to corrupt the Faith once delivered to the Saints. . . ."[77]

Conclusion

Presbyterianism in colonial America was thus able to exercise discipline with regard to doctrine in a way that proved difficult in contemporary Congregational circles. Jonathan Edwards, then the young pastor in Northampton, Massachusetts, was involved in an unsuccessful effort to block the ordination of Robert Breck for Arminian views in 1734–36, exactly the same time as the Hemphill case in Philadelphia.[78] George Marsden describes some of the dynamics of the controversy over discipline in Massachusetts Congregationalism:

> The eastern Massachusetts clerical establishment was unhappy with the "Presbyterian" manner in which the Hampshire Association was controlling the western side of the province. . . . Further, the western clergy were wielding subscription to the Westminster Confession of Faith like the strictest Presbyterians.[79]

In contrast to colonial American Presbyterianism's concern for doctrinal discipline is the attitude of the recent *Dictionary of Heresy Trials in American Christianity*, in which the editor in his "unscientific Postscript" revels in the contributions of the heretics and decries the opposition of the orthodox: "The tradition of the heretics offers one of the finest opportunities of renewal that the churches have. . . . Dissenting heretics should be welcomed *and* heard. . . . The far greater threat to free inquiry is illustrated in the cocksureness of the orthodox position rather than that of the dissenter."[80] Such postmodern sentiments may share the viewpoint of the young Benjamin Franklin and the cocksure Samuel Hemphill, but they are a far cry from the spirit and concern of John Calvin and the Reformed tradition.

[76] *A Vindication of the Reverend Commission*, 36.

[77] *An Extract of the Minutes*, 12.

[78] The Breck case is described in George M. Marsden, *Jonathan Edwards: A Life* (New Haven: Yale University Press, 2003) 176–82.

[79] Ibid., 178. Cf. 316 for Edwards's attraction to Presbyterian forms of discipline.

[80] George H. Shriver, ed., *Dictionary of Heresy Trials in American Christianity* (Westport, CT: Greenwood, 1997) 487.

Calvin in the *Institutes* described the three ends in view in church discipline. First is the honor of God and to keep the church as the body of Christ from disgrace. Second is "that the good be not corrupted by the constant company of the wicked, as commonly happens." And third is "that those overcome by shame for their baseness begin to repent" (*Institutes*, IV.xii.5). The Westminster Confession of Faith gives the same three purposes of church censures in reverse order:

> Church censures are necessary, for the reclaiming and gaining of offending brethren, for deterring of others from the like offences, for purging out of that leaven which might infect the whole lump, for vindicating the honour of Christ, and the holy profession of the Gospel, and for preventing the wrath of God, which might justly fall upon the Church, if they should suffer His covenant, and the seals thereof, to be profaned by notorious and obstinate offenders. (XXX, 3)

In the Hemphill case, with regard to reclaiming and gaining of the offending brother, seeing him begin to repent, it is not known what became of Samuel Hemphill, as Benjamin Franklin indicated. There is a reference to a Samuel Hemphill receiving payment for services in Virginia in 1758.[81] Perhaps he modified his doctrinal views and repented of his plagiarism subsequent to his 1735 trial, or at least found a more compatible ecclesiastical context.

With regard to the other two purposes of church discipline, however, there can be little doubt that the removal of Hemphill from the ministry was for the health of the membership of the Presbyterian church and for the honor of Christ. The measures taken for serious yet flexible, good faith subscription to the Westminster Confession and Catechisms, as set forth in *A Vindication of the Reverend Commission*, provided appropriate safeguards of doctrinal orthodoxy as the church grew and candidates for the ministry came from a variety of backgrounds. The Presbyterian Church would divide in 1741 over some of the effects of the Great Awakening, but would reunite in 1758 with renewed commitment to the Westminster Standards as a doctrinal norm. From that point well into the Federal period it would enjoy a period of stability, peace, and influence upon the new republic.

[81] Virginia. *Session Laws 1758 Sept.* (Williamsburg: William Hunter, 1758) 9. Retrieved from Readex database Early American Imprints, Series I: Evans, Record No. 0F2F81FDD080BB40.

6

Jonathan Dickinson and the Reasonableness of Christianity

Bryan F. LeBeau

JONATHAN Dickinson was not present at the creation of the first presbytery in America. Nevertheless, he would become a leader in what has been called the formative years of American Presbyterianism. As such he merits inclusion in this anniversary volume and will no doubt be mentioned several times in passing. Jonathan Dickinson was of that New England/English Puritan branch of American Presbyterianism that, along with Northern Ireland/Scotch-Irish immigrants, helped mold the church's identify. As Leonard Trinterud has argued, the encounter of these two groups led first to "a fiery ordeal of ecclesiastical controversy" and then to a spiritual awakening and to a blending of that diversity into a new order, American Presbyterianism.[1] Among Dickinson's several contributions to that new order was his defense of the reasonableness of Calvinist Christianity against its "enlightened" detractors.

The Early Years

Jonathan Dickinson was born on April 22, 1688, in Hatfield, Massachusetts. His grandfather, Nathaniel, had come to America from England as part of the Great Migration of 1630. He and his son, Hezekiah, moved to the Connecticut River Valley of western Massachusetts over the course of a few decades before the latter landed in Hatfield shortly before Jonathan's birth. Both of the first generations of the Dickinson family were prosperous and prominent. Perhaps most interesting in terms of Jonathan's future

[1] Leonard J. Trinterud, *The Forming of an American Tradition: A Re-examination of Colonial Presbyterianism* (Freeport, NY: Books for Libraries Press, 1949) 7.

in the church, his grandfather—along with twenty-one other families—moved from Wethersfield, Connecticut, where he was among the town's first settlers and wealthiest and most prominent residents, to Hadley, Massachusetts in protest against Wethersfield's adoption of the Half-way Covenant and a Presbyterian scheme of church polity.[2]

Jonathan's mother, Abigail, was the daughter of Samuel Blackman of Stratford, Connecticut, and the granddaughter of the Reverend Adam Blackman, Stratford's first minister. As a young man, he spent time in Stratford visiting his maternal grandparents and likely came into contact with the Reverend Israel Chauncy, one of the founders of Yale College, or the Collegiate School as it was known until 1718. Dickinson enrolled in the college in 1702, one year after its founding and took up residence with the Reverend Abraham Pierson, the college's first president, or rector, in Killingworth (later Clinton) the college's first home.

That all three of the Dickinson's Class of 1706 entered the ministry reflects the college's purpose. Erected by a general synod of the consociated church of Connecticut and chartered by the Connecticut General Assembly, the school was committed to "the grand errand" of propagating "the blessed reformed Protestant religion in the wilderness." Its founders confessed that, as the posterity of the founders of the colony, they had been negligent in carrying out that errand, but that the anticipated "religious and liberal education of suitable youth" would be "the most probably expedient" in its renewal. It is also the case, however, that the Collegiate School was established in response to what was perceived by its founders as Harvard's defection from orthodoxy, as represented by the so-called liberal forces of latitudinarianism under the leadership of Thomas Brattle and John Leverett. Cotton Mather opposed Brattle and Leverett. He also joined the movement for the erection of the Connecticut college, authoring the "Proposals for Erecting an University," wherein he called upon the Collegiate School to become a "preserver of religious orthodoxy" in New England.[3]

[2] John Putnam Demos, *Entertaining Satan: Witchcraft and the Culture of Early New England* (New York: Oxford University Press, 1986) 349–51; Richard B. Sewall, *The Life of Emily Dickinson* (New York: Farrar, Straus and Giroux, 1987) 17.

[3] Richard Warch, *School of the Prophets: Yale College, 1701–1740* (New Haven: Yale University Press, 1973) 12–14, 34, 48; Roland H. Bainton, *Yale and the Ministry: A History of Education for the Christian Ministry at Yale from the Founding in 1701* (New York: Harper, 1957) x, 1; Ebenezer Baldwin, *Annals of Yale College* (New Haven: Hezekiah Howe, 1831) 10, 12, 19–20.

Dickinson graduated from the Collegiate School in 1706 and returned to take his master of arts in divinity three years later. While studying for his bachelor's degree, however, Jonathan quite likely met Joanna Melyen, a frequent visitor to Killingworth and her cousins the Hubbards and the Fowles. Joanna was the sister of Samuel Melyen, the minister of Elizabeth Town, New Jersey. If indeed they knew one another, Joanna may well have acquainted Dickinson with her home town and led the way for his aspiring to that town's pulpit when Samuel abruptly left his position after only four trouble-laden years. It is also possible, however, that Dickinson gained knowledge of the northern New Jersey communities that had been heavily settled by New Englanders from Rector Pierson, who had officiated in Newark for over twenty years before moving to Killingworth.

In either event, Dickinson began officiating in Elizabeth Town in 1708. Within months he married Joanna, and on September 29, 1709, he was ordained and installed in the Elizabeth Town church, where he would remain for the rest of his life, by the consociated ministers of Fairfield Country, Connecticut. As previously noted, Elizabeth Town, like other northern New Jersey communities—Newark, Middletown, Shrewsbury, Woodbridge, and Piscataway—had been settled by New Englanders. They had been enticed there by the colony's proprietors and governors, who offered generous land grants and large measure of religious and civil freedoms, whereby the New Englanders hoped to erect "New Zions in the New Jersey wilderness." They were mostly Independents, or Congregationalists, but by that point in time the "bifurcation of New England," as it has been titled, had begun. They had begun to adopt various Presbyterian ways, most notably in the manner of, or requirements for, church membership and admission to the sacraments. They placed less emphasis on visible signs of "God's renewing graces" and greater preference for ministerial associations and, later, presbyteries and synods, as opposed to autonomous congregations.[4]

[4] Nicholas Murray, *Notes, Historical and Biographical, Concerning Elizabeth Town, Its Eminent Men, Churches, and Ministers* (Elizabeth Town, NJ: E. Sanderson, 1844) 45; Everard Kempshall, *The Centennial of the Anniversary of the Burning of the Church Edifice of the First Church of Elizabeth, New Jersey* (Elizabeth: Elizabeth Daily Journal, 1881) 13–14; William T. Hanzsche, "New Jersey Molders of the American Presbyterian Church," *Journal of the Presbyterian Historical Society* 24 (June 1946) 71; Douglas Jacobsen, *An Unprov'd Experiment: Religious Pluralism in Colonial New Jersey* (Brooklyn: Carlson, 1991) 252–26; Theodore Thayer, *As We Were: The Story of Old Elizabethtown* (Elizabeth: Grassmann, 1964); Trinterud, *The Forming of an American Tradition,* 7, 15–16, 19; Warch, *School of the Prophets,* 57.

Dickinson's grandfather's protest notwithstanding, this tendency toward Presbyterianism was particularly strong in the Connecticut River Valley, where Dickinson was raised, and in the colony of Connecticut, where he was educated for the ministry. Those tendencies were incorporated into the Saybrook Platform at about the time Dickinson was preparing for the ministry, which provided Connecticut with what Leonard Trinterud has called "a sort of halfway house" between Congregationalism and Presbyterianism.[5] It was that Platform that led to the establishment of county consociations with the power of oversight over local congregations, one of which—the Fairfield Consociation—ordained Dickinson at Elizabeth Town.

Nevertheless, Dickinson did not immediately join the Presbytery of Philadelphia, which had been established only two years before he moved to Elizabeth Town. In fact, none of the New England derived churches of northern New Jersey were represented, but that would soon change. Over the next decade those churches modified their Presbyterianized Congregationalism to the point where they could join the Presbytery, where they would join forces—or perhaps come into conflict—with the Scots, Ulster Scots, and others from which American Presbyterianism would be born, but not without considerable labor. By 1716, the Presbytery numbered twenty-five ministers: eight were Scots, seven were Irish, three were Welch, and seven were New Englanders. In that year, the Presbyteries of New Castle, Long Island, and Snow Hill were created and joined with the original Presbytery to form the Synod of Philadelphia. The next year, Dickinson joined the Presbytery and Synod of Philadelphia.[6]

Upon his joining, Dickinson was the youngest member of the presbytery and synod. Nevertheless, he rapidly rose to prominence in both. He assumed a series of progressively more responsible positions of leadership, and in 1721 published the first of his several major publications that established him as a trusted and authoritative spokesman for the church: *Remarks upon Mr. Gale's Reflections on Mr. Wall's History of Infant Baptism.* As would be the case with several of his theological disputations, Dickinson's *Remarks* would be only the initial salvo in his defense of Presbyterianism against its Baptist challengers. To be more specific, he would defend infant baptism against those who found it unscriptural, which in turn led the Baptists to call into question the very legitimacy of the Presbyterian Church.

[5] Trinterud, *The Forming of an American Tradition,* 16, 18, 29.

[6] Ibid., 34.

The Path of Leadership: The Moderate Reformer

In 1722 the Synod of Philadelphia elected Dickinson its moderator for the first time. It was an honor, but one that led him into his first crisis. For Dickinson, the Subscription Controversy, which led to the Adopting Act of 1729, provided the controversy in which the still new ministerial member of the Synod staked out his territory of being moderate reformer—one who championed the cause of liberty of conscience, largely reflecting his New England theological heritage, but who did so in a moderate manner so as not only to avoid schism but also to establish limits on liberty of conscience thereby protecting the church from heresy and external attack. It began with the Reverend George Gillespie's overture to the Synod of 1721 and ended not with the Adopting Act of 1729 but with Dickinson defense of the church in the Samuel Hemphill case. Given Don Fortson's detailed coverage of this event, as well as Will Barker's essay on Samuel Hemphill, I will only summarize Dickinson's involvement in the matter, as it helps set the stage for his writings on the reasonableness of Christianity.

The Westminster Confession had been central to the church since its adoption by Parliament in 1648. But its proper role in the church had proved controversial in England, Scotland, and Northern Ireland, as it would in the British colonies. The Subscription Controversy in the Presbyterian Church in American arose when Gillespie, on behalf of several ministers who had grown concerned over the Synod's attracting a number of ministers they considered confessionally unorthodox, proposed to make subscription to the Westminster Confession a prerequisite for ministerial ordination. The overture was adopted, but Dickinson and other New England ministers entered a formal protest. New Englanders accepted the Westminster Confession, but like their English counterparts they objected to any requirement by which they were to subscribe to the confession, or any part therein as a doctrinal standard. Those tied to the Synod of Ireland or the General Assembly of Scotland thought differently, and therein lay the roots of conflict.

When the Synod of Philadelphia met in 1722, Dickinson, as moderator, preached the opening sermon, and in that sermon he attacked Gillespie's overture. The sermon identified him with the cause of British nonsubscriptionists; of individual conscience as opposed to the imposition of human creeds and dogmas; of the primacy of Scripture in relation to unscriptural doctrines, especially of an exclusionary nature; and of evangelism in the midst of the growing tide of formalism. The sermon, subsequently published, was descriptively titled: *A Sermon Preached at the Opening of the Synod at Philadelphia, September 19, 1722. Wherein Is Considered the Character of the Man of God, and his Furniture for the Exercise both of Doctrine and Discipline, With the True Boundaries of the Church's Power.*[7]

The debate continued for several years until any resolution could be reached. In 1728, another overture for the measure as "an expedient for preventing the ingress and spread of errors among either ourselves or the flocks committed to our care" was presented to the Synod.[8] And, once again, Dickinson responded. He restated his earlier objection. He explained that he, too, was committed to maintaining and defending the Presbyterian community, or union. He agreed that it was incumbent on the Synod to maintain and defend the truths of the Gospel. But he disagreed with those who insisted that subscription to the Westminster Confession was the "most reasonable" means to those ends. Dickinson argued that such an imposition would cause confusion, instead, among its members, be an obstruction to "spiritual edification," and "procure rents and divisions" in the church.[9]

When the Synod met in 1729, it appointed a committee composed of individuals from both sides to resolve the impasse. Dickinson was not only appointed to that committee, but he also quite likely drafted the compromise that became the Adopting Act of 1729. The document began by reaffirming the proposition that the Synod did not claim any authority to impose its faith on the consciences of other men, but, it continued, its authors nevertheless felt obliged to take care that their faith be kept pure and uncorrupt. Therefore, they agreed that all current ministers of the synod, as well as those who might wish to be admitted in the future, "declare their agreement in, and appropriation of, the Confession of Faith ... as being in all the essential and necessary articles, good forms of sound words and systems of Christine doctrine." The Synod voted its approval,[10]

[7] David C. Harlan, "The Travail of Religious Moderation: Jonathan Dickinson and the Great Awakening," *Journal of Presbyterian History* 61 (1983) 412.

[8] "Records of the Presbytery of New Castle upon Delaware," pt. 5. *Journal of the Presbyterian Historical Society* 15 (December 1932) 178.

[9] Jonathan Dickinson, *Remarks upon a Discourse Intitled An Overture Presented to the Reverend Synod of Dissenting Ministers Sitting in Philadelphia, in the Month of September, 1728* (New York: J. Peter Zenger, 1729).

[10] Keith Jordan Hardman, "Jonathan Dickinson and the Course of American Presbyterianism, 1717–1747" (Ph.D. diss., University of Pennsylvania, 1971) 67; *Records of the Presbyterian Church in the United States of America*, ed. William H. Roberts (Philadelphia: Presbyterian Board of Publication and Sabbath School Work, 1904) 94–95.

but that did not settle the matter as various presbyteries as well as the Synod persisted in debating the exact meaning of its words.

The Adopting Act need not detain us further except to point to that event in which Dickinson, the primary spokesman for freedom of conscience stepped forward to defend the limits of that freedom in the case of the Reverend Samuel Hemphill, which began in 1735. Hemphill, who had recently arrived from Scotland, and who had subscribed to the Westminster Confession both in Ireland and Philadelphia, took a post as ministerial assistant to the Reverend Jedediah Andrews in Philadelphia. Within a year, Hemphill stood accused of preaching sermons of unsound doctrine (e.g., Arian and Deist) and of plagiarizing his sermons from proponents of both despite orders to desist. The matter might have gone unnoticed except within the church, if Hemphill's case had not been publicly championed by Benjamin Franklin. Franklin praised Hemphill's sermons for their "usefulness," by which he meant their emphasizing good words, and he defended his freedom of speech against the challenges of his fellow ministers. Franklin also pointed out that some in the Synod who had once opposed subscription had since become its most ardent defenders—read Jonathan Dickinson, among others.[11] The Synod had little choice but to defend itself against Franklin's charges, and in its defense stepped forward Jonathan Dickinson.

In his *A Vindication of the Reverend Commission of the Synod in Answer to Some Observations on Their Proceedings against the Reverend Mr. Hemphill,* Dickinson, no doubt in response to Franklin's pointed charge against him, pointed out that the nature of the debate concerning ministerial subscription had changed since 1729. Whereas he continued to oppose any imposition of human creeds on individual conscience, "the prodigious growth of errors and infidelity" as of late threatened "to undermine the great doctrines of the gospel," thereby obliging him and others to appear in its defense—"to resist the torrent of irreligion that seems to

[11] Benjamin Franklin, *Some Observations on the Proceedings against the Reverend Mr. Hemphill; with a Vindication of His Sermons, in vol. 2 of The Papers of Benjamin Franklin*, ed. Leonard W. Labaree (New Haven: Yale University Press, 1960) 38–40; Benjamin Franklin, "Dialogue between Two of the Presbyterians Meeting in This City," ibid., 27 and editor's note; Merton A. Christensen, "Franklin on the Hemphill Trial: Deism versus Presbyterian Orthodoxy," *William and Mary Quarterly*, 3rd ser., 10 (July 1953) 424, 426–27 n. 13; Melvin H. Buxbaum, *Benjamin Franklin and the Zealous Presbyterians* (University Park: Pennsylvania State University Press, 1975) 82, 94; William S. Barker "The Hemphill Case, Benjamin Franklin, and Subscription to the Westminster Confession," *American Presbyterians* 69 (Winter 1991) 246.

threaten the destruction of the Christian world."[12] Several exchanges followed, but within a year, Hemphill disappeared, and Franklin desisted in his attacks.

Earlier I mentioned Dickinson's role as defender of the faith against the Baptists. He played a more significant role in defending the church against its Anglican critics, with whom relations had never been good. To Anglicans, Presbyterians were a constant reminder of the attraction of nonconformity in Britain and in the colonies. To Presbyterians, Anglicans embodied charges of illegitimacy and memories of persecution in Britain and the colonies—as well as, of course, the constant threat of Anglican establishment beyond the few colonies where it already existed (Virginia, Maryland, the Carolinas, Georgia, and four counties in New York).

Dickinson was the principal Dissenter in the Presbyterian-Anglican debates for over twenty years. He spoke from the perspective of the Middle Colonies, but the debates transcended regional boundaries. Presbyterian-Anglican relations were especially strained in the Middle Colonies, where Presbyterians existed in sufficiently large numbers to pose a threat to the Church of England, but where Anglicans were often closely linked to proprietors and royal governors. The threat of establishment existed in New England as well, however, where Dickinson's defense of Presbyterianism against Anglican attacks were widely published and read. The debate usually focused on specific issues—by way of example, the legitimacy of Presbyterian ordination. Dickinson weighed in on this topic in 1724 with *A Defense of Presbyterian Ordination,* engaging in a public debate that did not end until he had gone to press a dozen times and that included some of Dickinson's most widely read publications, like *The Scripture Bishop* (1732) and *The Vanity of Human Institutions in the Worship of God* (1736).[13]

And then there was the role Dickinson played in the Great Awakening. Once again, as the Great Awakening will be discussed elsewhere in this collection of essays, it will suffice to summarize Dickinson position in this watershed event. In brief, Dickinson was not only a major player in the Great Awakening, he was a proponent. He defended it against its Old Side critics, but he also opposed its divisive tendencies, thereby becoming a leader of the what has come to be known as the moderate New Side. Charles Maxson and Leonard Trinterud have suggested that Dickinson was second only to Jonathan Edwards in his leadership of the Awakening.

[12] Jonathan Dickinson, *A Vindication of the Reverend Commission of the Synod in Answer to Some Observations on Their Proceedings against the Reverend Mr. Hemphill* (Philadelphia: Andrew Bradford, 1735) 1–2.

[13] Hardman, "Jonathan Dickinson," 90.

Leigh Eric Schmidt has called him a distant second to Edwards, but added: "By dint of perseverance, consistency, and long preparation, Jonathan Dickinson held firm against foes at the extremes—Old Side and New, infidels and enthusiasts, Arminians and Antinomians—and eventually, within colonial Presbyterianism at least, won out over them."[14]

David Harlan has suggested that Dickinson did not see the alternatives of New and Old Side as mutually exclusive. Rather, he saw them as mutually compelling allegiances, and in the end he responded not by aligning himself with one side or the other, but "by trying to reconcile their multiple commitments." This, Harlan pointed out, stands in contrast to the uncompromising Edwards and Gilbert Tennent, who argued that there was "no such thing . . . as being of neither party; all must be on one side or the other, either for or against." Harlan and others have suggested that Dickinson steered a middle course, but in doing so "lurched from one side to the other, leaving behind . . . a series of zig-zag trails that through the Great Awakening epitomized the experiences of scores of ministers who tried to steer between extremes of enthusiasm and formalism, between Calvinism and Arminianism, between New Lights and Old Lights. . . ."[15]

I agree that Dickinson seized the middle ground. Elsewhere, however, I argued that that middle ground represented neither the final step in a retreat from the rampant enthusiasm of the Awakening nor an erratic ambivalence. Rather, as Schmidt has written, it represented the staking-out of a moderate New Side position, consistent with Dickinson's preexisting "vision of a renewed social and religious order." And his vision became that of most New Side Presbyterians. When others of the Awakening sought the middle ground, they found Dickinson was already there, that he had been there from the start, and that he had served to define it.[16]

Among all of Dickinson's published commentaries on the Great Awakening, perhaps the most definitive in outlining his moderate posi-

[14] Charles Hartshorn Maxson, *The Great Awakening in the Middle Colonies* (Gloucester, MA: Peter Smith, 1958) 24; Trinterud, *The Forming of an American Tradition,* 42; Leigh Eric Schmidt, "Jonathan Dickinson and the Making of the Moderate Awakening," *American Presbyterians* 63 (winter 1985) 351.

[15] Harlan, "Travail of Religious Moderation," 411–12; J. M. Bumsted and John E. Van de Wetering, *What Must I Do to be Saved? The Great Awakening in Colonial America* (Hinsdale, IL: Dryden, 1976) 115; Martin E. Lodge, "The Great Awakening in the Middle Colonies" (Ph.D. diss., University of California at Berkeley, 1964) 275.

[16] Bryan F. Le Beau, *Jonathan Dickinson and the Formative Years of American Presbyterianism* (Lexington: University Press of Kentucky, 1997) chap. 6; Schmidt, "Jonathan Dickinson," 341–42.

tion was his *Witness of the Spirit,* which he delivered as a sermon to his Elizabeth Town congregation on May 7, 1740, nine days after George Whitefield's second visit to Elizabeth Town. Whitefield had been accompanied by Gilbert Tennent, who the previous March had delivered his blistering, and divisive, Nottingham sermon, *The Dangers of an Unconverted Ministry.* Where he had been enthusiastic in his report on Whitefield's first visit six months earlier and its impact on his congregation, Dickinson was now more cautious. While continuing to champion the Awakening and its impact on the souls of the converted, he also addressed voices of censoriousness and opposition.

Alan Heimert and Perry Miller called *Witness of the Spirit* the "first sustained analysis of the psychology of conversation" of the Awakening—earlier even than Jonathan Edwards' better known *Distinguishing Marks of a Work of the Spirit of God,* published one year later. Similarly, it was also an earlier and less complex statement on the same subject as Edwards' *Treatise Concerning Religious Affections,* written during the winter of 1742/43, arguably the best explanation of religious psychology in early American literature.[17] Keith Hardman concluded that in *Witness of the Spirit* Dickinson was the first to offer a compromise between evangelical demands for sudden conversion and the long-standing Calvinist emphasis on preparation. While Leonard Trinterud argued that with its publication, Dickinson not only aligned himself with the revival and against its opponents, but also, as he did so from a moderate position, that he charted the future of American Presbyterianism.[18]

Dickinson's efforts at moderation notwithstanding, the Great Awakening divided the Synod of Philadelphia and in 1741 led to its disunion. At that meeting, Robert Cross, on behalf of the Old Siders, declared that the more radical proponents of the revival, the New Brunswick men in particular, with their "unscriptural, antipresbyterial, uncharitable, [and] divisive practices," were responsible for the "dreadful divisions, distractions, and convulsions" that threatened the "infant church," whereupon he questioned their right to remain members of the Synod. No formal vote was taken. Confusion reigned, but in the end the New Brunswick men left, creating the first schism in the church's brief history.[19]

[17] Alan Heimert and Perry Miller, ed., *The Great Awakening: Documents Illustrating the Crisis and Its Consequences* (Indianapolis: Bobbs-Merrill, 1967) x, 101.

[18] Trinterud, *The Forming of an American Tradition,* 93; Hardman, "Jonathan Dickinson," 339.

[19] *Records of the Church,* 157.

Dickinson and the other members of the Presbytery of New York were absent from the Synod of 1741, but they would go on record as concluding that the Synod had ejected the New Brunswick men illegally.[20] Soon they would leave that body to form the Synod of New York, but they remained committed to healing that breach that had occurred. And as early as February 1742, that reconciliation was advanced one large step when Dickinson received a written retraction from Gilbert Tennent, wherein Tennent admitted that he had mismanaged his affair in the Awakening and that he could not justify the "excessive heat of temper" he had sometimes shown. He wrote that it was a time of "great spiritual desertion" for him, and that he hoped that the breach between the Old and New Side could be healed. The letter was recognition of the role Dickinson had come to play in the church—that of someone who held and would continue to defend a middle ground upon which both sides could, and would, stand.[21] Dickinson's efforts at reconciliation would take time, however, and in 1745 the ministers of the New York Presbytery received the consent of the other members of the Synod of Philadelphia to withdraw. On September 19, Dickinson presided as moderator over the first meeting of the Synod of New York in Elizabeth Town. The new Synod included those who had been expelled from the Synod of Philadelphia, reorganized into the Presbyteries of New Brunswick and Londonderry.

On the Reasonableness of Christianity

With all of this as prelude, addressing Jonathan Dickinson's response to the Enlightenment is made much easier, as it is consistent with his role in all other ways as the moderate reformer. Sydney Ahlstrom has referred to it as the "quiet revolution," wherein American culture embarked upon a spiritual transition from its largely medieval outlook to one of distinctly modern religious ideas.[22] Dickinson played a leading role in that revolu-

20 George Gillespie, *A Letter to the Reverend Brethren of the Presbytery of New York, or of Elizabeth Town. In Which Is Shown the Unjustness of the Synod's Protest, Entered Last May at Philadelphia, Against Some of the Reverend Brethren* (Philadelphia: Benjamin Franklin, 1742); Milton J. Coalter Jr., *Gilbert Tennent, Son of Thunder: A Case Study of Continental Pietism's Impact of the First Great Awakening in the Middle Colonies* (Westport, CT: Greenwood Press, 1986) 83; Hardman, "Jonathan Dickinson," 235–36; Trinterud, *The Forming of an American Tradition,* 114; Lodge, 216.

21 The complete text of Tennent's letter is in Richard Webster, *A History of the Presbyterian Church in America, from Its Origin until the Year 1760* (Philadelphia: Joseph M. Wilson, 1857) 189–91.

22 Sydney E. Ahlstrom, *A Religious History of the American People* (New Haven: Yale Uni-

tion. Once again, he was not as thorough in his consideration of the issues raised by the Enlightenment, but, at least on the issue of free will, Dickinson's work both preceded and influenced that of Edwards. Jon Pahl has written that by the time Edwards entered the fray, due in large part to Dickinson the question had already been decided or at least a consensus, or "harmony in discord," had been reached.[23]

The Enlightenment was a significant influence on Dickinson and helped determine the position he took in the Subscription Controversy, the Samuel Hemphill Affair, Dickinson's Anglican debates, and the Great Awakening and his many publications in those matters. But two other publications are commonly cited as those wherein Dickinson addressed the ideas of the Enlightenment without reference to any other precipitating event. They will be the focus of this section of my essay: *The Reasonableness of Christianity* (1732) and *Familiar Letters to a Gentleman* (1745). The reader will note that the first appeared at the start of the Great Awakening, the latter at the end.

Central to the challenge posed by the Enlightenment to Calvinism was the apparent conflict between the former's insistence on man's free will and the latter's doctrine of God's sovereign free grace. Moreover, although it began as an issue of intellectual debate, especially among theologians, by the end of the colonial period it encompassed political ideology, or the search for an acceptable line between absolute freedom and tyranny. The case has been made that American Revolutionary ideology had its roots in the debate over free will, and that the debate over free will peaked during the Great Awakening. Jonathan Dickinson was among the first to address the matter.

As Norman Fiering has written, there were three parts to the problem of reconciling the doctrines of God's sovereign free grace and free will: predestination by free grace and man's inability to effect his own salvation; development of a determinist hypothesis based on the concept of natural law; and the question of whether will and intellect are separate or inseparable. Jon Pahl has described the responses to this problem as points on a continuum. At the extremes stood the determinists, or those who precluded any human agency and those who insisted that man was entirely a free agent. But the more commonly held positions resided somewhere in between those extremes, commonly sharing varying portions of the two. Some allowed man only a limited degree of personal liberty or what they

versity Press, 1972) 350–51.

[23] Jon Pahl, *Paradox Lost: Free Will and Political Liberty in American Culure, 1630–1760* (Baltimore: Johns Hopkins University Press, 1992) 119.

called an "inclining necessity," while others placed greater emphasis on free will, or "innate liberty," while retaining elements of God's sovereign free grace.[24]

It is important to note that by this time, if ever, Calvinists did not deny man sufficient freedom, moral autonomy, or even free will, to be held responsible for his sins. Where the debate raged was over how free will was employed, what choices were possible, and whether freedom was an act of the will or of the intellect and the will inseparably bound. In brief, Dickinson, as would Edwards, concluded that the will (or affections) and the intellect (or rational soul) were two powers of the mind, but that they should not be seen as distinct agents with difference provinces and authorities capable of performing separate action.[25]

John Locke provoked many involved in the debate over free will. In Dickinson's case it was Locke's *Reasonableness of Christianity*(1695) in particular that drew him into the debate and provided him with the title of his first foray. Sydney Ahlstrom has written that in the eighteenth century, "there gradually came to prevail among educated classes a climate of opinion in which moderate common-sense prevailed." Locke's *Reasonableness* helped create that climate. To Dickinson, however, in its attempt to bring theology in line with the new psychological empiricism, it was latitudinarian, perhaps Deistic, and quite likely a contributor to rationalistic Christianity and even natural religion. That Dickinson chose to employ the same title was intentional, if only to pose an alternative to what Locke had defined as "reasonable." Dickinson sought to define and defend a Christian doctrine that included "a simultaneous commitment to faith and reason."[26]

Dickinson's *Reasonableness* consisted of a series of sermons, or essays, on the subject of free will. He began by addressing the being and attributes of God, with the following passage:

> Reason is the dignifying and distinguishing property of human nature, whereby man, above the rest of the lower creation, is qualified to know, obey, and enjoy his creator; by which alone he is capable of that faith, without which it is impossible to please God, and even of believing that first article, that God is, as well as that He

[24] Norman S. Fiering, "Will and Intellect in the New England Mind," *William and Mary Quarterly,* 3rd ser. 29 (October 1972) 516–17; Pahl, *Paradox Lost*, xi–xii, 6, 12–13.

[25] Fiering, "Will and Intellect," 516–17, 553.

[26] Ahlstrom, *A Religious History,* 353; Harlan, "Travail of Religious Moderation," 412; John Frederick Woolverton, *Colonial Anglicanism in North America* (Detroit: Wayne State University Press, 1984) 103; Hardman, "Jonathan Dickinson," 280.

> is a rewarder of those that diligently seek him. Whence it follows, that He who had made us rational creatures, expects from us a reasonable service, and cannot be pleased with that faith, practice, or hope, that is grounded on education, or common opinion, and not the result of rational reflection, or enquiry.[27]

With this as his understanding of the importance of rational reflection, Dickinson set out to offer "some rational evidence of the truth of Christianity" and, thereby, the reasonableness of its truths, rather than relying on our receiving them on trust (1–2).

Dickinson wrote that although God's sublime nature and perfection are beyond even "the most exalted understanding," God has provided man with demonstrative evidence of both, as well as of his holiness, justice, goodness, and truth, in the works of his creation (3–4). Put another way, we can see the cause by the effect—in effect, a cosmological proof of God's existence. Dickinson insisted that the world, in all of its "amazing magnificence," including man and "such noble, immaterial thinking substances as our souls," could neither be its own efficient cause, nor the product of chance. It had to have proceeded not only from an author, but from an author equal to the work—or an infinitely wise and powerful being (4–8).

Dickinson identified those attributes of God, which we are able to discern from nature or from God's creation. To begin with, it is clear that God is eternal, spiritual, and perfect. We know this because what has not eternally existed, namely the world God created, had to have had a beginning, and what has had a beginning must have been produced by something else. As there cannot have been a time when there was absolutely nothing, the cause of all things must be an eternal, uncaused, and independent being. Further, we can determine that the cause of all things must be a spiritual being, because we are thinking beings and, as such, could not be derived from mater incapable of thought. And we know that the cause of all things must be perfect, because that being must have "all the perfections of all the innumerable intelligent beings that now are or ever have been in the world" (13–16). Dickinson argued that we know from nature that God, the first cause of things, is infinite and, because God is infinite, there must be only one God, two infinite beings being a contradiction.

[27] Jonathan Dickinson, *The Reasonableness of Christianity, in Four Sermons, Wherein the Being and Attributes of God, the Apostasy of Man, and the Credibility of the Christian Religion Are Demonstrated by Rational Considerations. And the Divine Mission of Our Blessed Savior Proved by Scripture Arguments, Both from the Old Testament and the New; and Vindicated Against the Most Important Objections, Whether of Ancient or Modern Infidels* (Boston: S. Kneeland and T. Green, 1732).

Because the world was created out of nothing, with all of its many perfections, we can conclude that God is omnipotent and infinitely wise (17, 19, 21–22, 24–25). And because the creator of such a world must have all things of the present and future in mind at once, we know that God is omniscient (29).

Dickinson offered that in a similar manner he could show as well that God is infinitely good, just, merciful, and loving, among other things, but that he preferred to offer some "practical inferences" from what he had already written. He argued that, given such attributes, man should worship God in a similarly glorious rationalism—namely a worship that grows out of a "deep impression of our own nothingness," of our "natural unworthiness," of our "moral pollution," and of our being "vile worms and indigent creatures." This would constitute a "rational acknowledgment," Dickinson insisted, of our dependence on God for our very life and breath and for all that we hope and treasure (30–32).

Dickinson provided "rational evidence" of our apostasy from God and of our recovery through Christ as mediator. To begin with, as it would be inconsistent with God's merciful nature to have created man in a state of corruption and pollution, such a state must have been the result of the rebellion and apostasy of our first parents, of whom we are the corrupt stock. For similar reasons, namely God's divine compassion, it also follows that we were rescued or delivered from our fallen state by the blood of Christ, and thereby, Christ is entitled to our complete subjection and obedience (39–42, 56–57).

As it is also "agreeable to the very dictates of reason" that there are such things in nature as virtue and right, vice and wrong, Dickinson continued, and that, given our fallen state, our "leading affections and passions . . . are manifestly irregular and vicious," it is our first inclination to accept the latter, or that which is repugnant to the holiness of God. God rightfully expects better of us, however, and "we face destruction if we fail in the engagement between reason and passion" in our attempt to regulate our appetites which provide us with such inclinations (44–46). When our nature is polluted and our faculties depraved, however, our reason is nonplussed, and our best rational inquiries fruitless and in vain. "Here let the Deist try his skill," Dickinson concluded. "Let him without the assistance of revelation, draw up a perfect system of the laws of nature. Let him consult the means of restoring our lost innocency and of keeping our affections and passions under the government of religion and reason. . . . And in the conclusion, he'll have but his labor for his pains and continue in the same inextricable labyrinth" (46, 54).

Fortunately for man, Dickinson wrote, God has provided that revelation, whereby, with the application of his reason and passion, we may be saved. Why else would God have created so noble a being as man, if not for some higher purpose than that of his earthly existence. Why else would God have endowed man with a rational and immortal soul, if we are not candidates for another world where we will meet the rewards of our life on earth (49–50, 53). In sum, Christ, the eternal Son of God, "beholding our apostate and perishing state," out of divine compassion died for us. He purchased with his own blood our deliverance or provided our ransom so that God might be just in pardoning and justifying us though we be sinner (62–66, 68, 74). All God asks in return is that we follow two rules: First, all must labor to ensure "a true and lively faith in Jesus Christ," without which no one will be saved; and second, all must demonstrate the truth and sincerity of their faith "by a holy and heavenly life." Faith without holiness, Dickinson reminded us, "is as a carcass without breath" (164–73).

Familiar Letters to a Gentleman, upon a Variety of Seasonable and Important Subjects in Religion appeared in 1745. It was Dickinson's most widely read publication, going through some six editions in America and five in Scotland by 1842. It consisted of nineteen "letters" that improved upon a number of positions that he had taken in *The Reasonableness of Christianity* on the Enlightenment and its relationship to Christianity, to Presbyterian Calvinism in particular. By 1745, however, Dickinson wrote from a post-Awakening perspective. And, as Leigh Eric Schmidt has put it, whereas before the Awakening, Dickinson defended Christianity against a rationalism that threatened to destroy it, in the wake of the Awakening he felt compelled to defend Christianity against "a religion that would destroy rationalism."[28]

Dickinson made his intentions clear at the start when he wrote that the extravagances of some "late pretenders to extraordinary attainments in religion" had cast such a blemish on the Great Awakening that many were in danger of questioning not only the Awakening but Christianity itself, rather than merely inquiring into "the manifestly false pretenses and enthusiastic flights" of those who had claimed such attainments. More specifically he noted that such extreme behavior had raised serious questions among some concerning the doctrine of special grace and experimental piety. He described such doubts as "one of the darkest symptoms upon this

[28] Jonathan Dickinson, *Familiar Letters to a Gentleman, upon a Variety of Seasonable and Important Subjects in Religion* (Boston: Rogers and Fowle, 1745); Schmidt, "Jonathan Dickinson," 248, 353 n. 39.

land," as it led people to question not only the validity of the Awakening, but also "the experiences of vital religion, which are necessary to constitute them Christians" (i–iii).

Although perhaps not intended, Dickinson provided a bridge from his *Reasonableness of Christianity* to his *Familiar Letters* by pointing to the danger of infidelity posed by those who while railing against "priestcraft, cant, and enthusiasm," ridiculed "all pretenses to vital piety" and all gospel doctrines regarding future rewards and punishments as "unreasonable or unintelligible dreams and fiction." In response, he restated the position he had taken thirteen years earlier, that "faith must be built upon evidences that will reach the understanding, as well as foster passions of the soul." And, once again, he insisted that such evidence could be found in Christianity and in the world around them. That evidence, he argued, should be sufficient not only for Deists to allow that Christianity is worthy of God and agreeable to his glorious perfection, but also for all men to allow that Christianity is suitable for the perfection of man's nature. Directing his remarks to criticisms raised concerning the Awakening and the behavior of the "awakened," he added that the evidence for this can be seen in Christianity's influence upon the hearts and lives of those who sincerely profess it, whereby they are "distinguished from the rest of the world" (6, 11–19).

Pursuing this new direction, or application, of his defense of the reasonableness of Christianity, Dickinson discussed what he and other defenders of the Great Awakening considered to be the internal evidence of the "real" Christian or the marks by which those who have been chosen by God can be distinguished from others. The first such mark was the passing away of "old things," as the "spirit of the mind" is renewed and a new man created "in righteousness and true holiness." This is reflected in the person's new "thoughts and disposition," "desires and affections," "views and apprehensions," and "joys and satisfactions" (62–65). That was followed by spiritual warfare between the chosen and his remaining corruptions. The chosen remains imperfect, despite his new spiritual state, but his new affections cry out against the imperfections that remain in his heart and in his outward conduct. Whereas others submit to such imperfections, "as all careless and secure sinners do into the hands of sin and satan," the chosen commit themselves to continuous battle against such failings (65–67).

Dickinson allowed that those who have been chosen by God cannot doubt their change of state. However, in response to those who pretended to "extraordinary attainments of religion," and/or were being criticized for undue confidence or airs of self-righteous, Dickinson pointed out that rather than being comfortable with their change of state, the truly chosen remain apprehensive. They continue to fight against their failings, and are comforted only by the thought that they are being continually led to victory over their imperfect states by God (65, 67–68). That the chosen also experience "comfort, peace, and joy" in their newfound state, as promised them by Christ in Scripture, Dickinson does not see as contradictory. What doubt can remain in the heart of a Christian, he asked, when he feels such promises fulfilled in him and when he has been comforted by Christ (69)?

Dickinson explained that there is a vast difference in the various methods of divine operation that turn the power of Satan to God, but that in every case the change is verified by the recipient's change of heart and behavior. Where he was once "careless and secure" in "pursuit of his lusts" and "hardened against all [of God's] solemn warnings," he is thoroughly awakened out of his security and "put upon a serious and lasting inquiry as to how he might be saved. His conscience can no longer be quieted by "imperfect performances," which will continue despite his new found state, as Christ never promised even the chosen that they would be infallible in all of their conduct. And he realizes that he is at Christ's mercy and that he must come to Christ with unqualified faith in, and dependence on, him (72–73, 80–82).

Once again in response to critics of the Awakening, Dickinson allowed that there are some "convinced sinners" whose religious impressions wear off and whose efforts fall short of the effects he has described. But in all those "whose convictions are abiding and effectual" his internal evidences apply. The result is a thorough and lasting change both of heart and life that cannot be imputed to the "irregular sallies of an over-heated imagination," as critics charged. Put another way, if sanctified men, though zealous in their efforts to serve God, through "heated imaginations or erroneous apprehensions of their duty" should err in their ways or act counter to the "true interests of Christ's kingdom," their error is in their opinion, not in their will. They have been misled by their heads, not by their hearts. Thus, although they may have had real experiences in true and vital piety, at any given time, their imaginations may still be imposed upon by "enthusiasms and delusion" (74–75, 77, 80–82).

Dickinson returned to his defense of the doctrine of God's sovereign free grace that he had begun in *Reasonableness of Christianity.* This time he focused on defending the doctrine of preparation, which had been a focal point of the Awakening and come under fire by Anglicans, Arminians, Deists, and the like. He posed the question as follows: "If we are of ourselves capable of no qualifying conditions of the divine favor, or . . . if we must feel that we lie at [God's feet in] mercy, and that all our refuges, and all our endeavors in our own strength to relieve our distressed souls, are fruitless and vain, you can't tell to what purpose any of our endeavors are, or what good it will do us to use any means for our salvation" (92).

Dickinson established that the "lost, impotent, [and] deplorable state" he just described was the case for every unrenewed sinner, or "natural man." In that state, man is so corrupt and defiled that he cannot atone for his sins employing his own powers, and that remains the case as long as he is in an unrenewed state with a corrupt heart and affections, and as long as he continues to live by the natural dispositions of his soul. We can expect no more than "impure streams from a corrupt fountain" (92–95, 97). Nevertheless, it is not hopeless. Scripture makes clear, Dickinson insisted, that "he who seeks shall find," or, put another way, he who seeks shall find even though he seeks amiss, as long as he does so in faith and sincerely. Dickinson acknowledged that this begs the question of man's inability to act in faith and sincerity, but it did pose an alternative to doing nothing—which his critics argued followed from their understanding of the doctrine of God's sovereign free grace. Dickinson's response was that they who make no attempt to receive Christ, even though that attempt is necessarily flawed, can claim no interest in him or in any of his saving benefits (96–98). If it be argued that if God "in sovereignty designs mercy for us," and we shall obtain it whether we seek it or not, or that, if not, it is vain to strive, once again Dickinson insisted that God "never does in sovereignty appoint salvation for any" who neglect the gospel means (106–7).

Finally, with this having been said, Dickinson took up what he considered to be Antinomian abuses of the doctrine of the nature and necessity of a believer's "union to God." He explained that a believer's "union to God" should be considered a mystical union that admits of "no clear and full illustration" in this imperfect world and thus beyond our complete comprehension. Nevertheless, the reality and certainty of this union is not beyond our knowledge. Both are clearly revealed, he argued, as are the blessed effects of the union that are experienced by the children of God (353–54). And true repentance is the most genuine effect, leading—in contrast to what Antinomians might suggest in their word and deed—to "a life of continued self-abasement and self-judging, and a life of repeated and renewed mourning after pardon of and victory over our remaining corruptions" (375, 377, 379–80).

The Reasonableness of Christianity and *Familiar Letters to a Gentleman*, though written some thirteen years apart, both shed light on Dickinson's response to those ideas of the Enlightenment that challenged basic Calvinist doctrines. Those intervening years, however, are crucial to our understanding of the different approaches taken in each document. Taken together, they provide an important Calvinist commentary on the Enlightenment. *Familiar Letters*, however, written after the Great Awakening, in the midst of the turmoil surrounding that event, also served as Dickinson's final defense of the Great Awakening and attempt to secure what came to be known as the moderate awakening.

Founding the College of New Jersey

Jonathan Dickinson spent the final years of his life establishing what may be his greatest legacy to the church and nation, the founding of the College of New Jersey, which became Princeton University. Ironically that development came out of the controversy of the Great Awakening about which we have been speaking. Calls for the founding of a college to train ministers for the Presbyterian Church in the Middle Colonies could be heard during the 1730s—most noticeably during the Subscription Controversy and Samuel Hemphill Affair—in attempt to fill vacant pulpits with orthodox ministers. But the final call was sounded by those New Siders who separated from the Synod of Philadelphia during the Great Awakening. Dickinson was the acknowledged leader of that group.

The final push for the establishment of a college began in 1738, precipitated by growing concern in the Synod of Philadelphia over what was being taught by William Tennent, Sr. at the Log College—as it was derisively known by its critics—in Neshaminy, Pennsylvania. Its graduates provided leadership for the radical Awakening among the Presbyterians in the Middle Colonies. In that year the Synod acknowledged that it had been laboring "under a grievous disadvantage for want of the opportunities of universities and professors skilled in the several branches of useful learning."[29] Most prospective ministers lacked the resources necessary to attend colleges in Europe or even New England. In 1739 the Synod adopted an overture calling for the erection of a school or seminary. The Tennents and other supporters of the Log College protested on the grounds that they saw the Synod's actions as an attempt to suppress the Log College, but,

[29] *Records of the Church*, 141; Collins, *Princeton*, 7; Thomas Clinton Pears Jr., "Colonial Education among Presbyterians," *Journal of the Presbyterian Historical Society*, pt. 1, 30 (June 1952) 124; and pt. 2, 30 (Sept. 1952) 165–66.

in their absence, the measure was adopted and a committee appointed to pursue it that included Jonathan Dickinson.[30]

For various reasons that need not detain us here, nothing was accomplished in pursuit of the overture of 1739 until 1743, when the Synod of Philadelphia revived the matter. Once again it proposed establishing a seminary within its jurisdiction and soon thereafter a school was established at New London, Pennsylvania under Francis Alison. That school, however, never secured adequate financial support. In 1752 Alison left to accept a position at the newly organized College of Philadelphia (University of Pennsylvania), and the school was moved to Newark, Delaware. It never became a college.[31] Next to take up the charge were members of the Synod of New York, or of the New York Presbytery to be more specific.

In March 1745 Dickinson and a group of ministers and laymen of the New York Presbytery—independent of the Presbytery—drew up plans for a college. Sometime in late 1745 or early 1746 they applied to New Jersey Royal Governor Lewis Morris for a charter but their application was rejected. Lewis explained that he did not believe that he had the authority to grant such a charter without permission from London, but it was also quite likely the case that he, a "zealous Anglican," as one critic put it, was not willing to grant the charter to a group of Presbyterians, even if they were acting independent of any official church body.[32]

Morris died shortly thereafter, and he was succeeded on an interim basis by John Hamilton. Although also an Anglican, Hamilton granted the college charter, dated October 22, 1746. In that Hamilton did not secure the approval of either the Provincial Council or the Crown, the charter was swept up in controversy, but plans for the college moved forward. Adequate funds were raised and on April 20, 1747, an article in the *New York Weekly Post Boy* announced that the College of New Jersey had appointed Jonathan Dickinson president of the college, which would open during the fourth week in May at Elizabeth Town.[33] The location,

[30] Thomas J. Wertenbaker, "The College of New Jersey and the Presbyterians," *Journal of the Presbyterian Historical Society* 36 (Dec. 1958) 210; *Records of the Church*, 148; Trinterud, *The Forming of an American Tradition,* 84.

[31] Trinterud, *The Forming of an American Tradition,* 138–39; Webster, *A History of the Presbyterian Church in America,* 256–57; Charles Hodge, *The Constitutional History of the Presbyterian Church in the United States of America* (Philadelphia: William S. Martien, 1840) 2:265.

[32] Collins, *Princeton,* 10–12; Wertenbaker, "The College of New Jersey," 21.

[33] Henry Clay Cameron, *Jonathan Dickinson and the College of New Jersey* (Princeton: C. S. Robinson, 1880) 26; Collins, 13–14.

in Dickinson's home, was intended to be temporary. Soon thereafter, new names appeared among those listed as trustees, including the Reverends Gilbert Tennent, William Tennent Jr., Samuel Blair, and Samuel Finley. They had closed the Log College and switched their allegiance—with Dickinson's blessing—to the College of New Jersey.[34]

The next year the new Governor of New Jersey, Jonathan Belcher, with his Provincial Council's approval, granted the college a second, and more secure, charter and provided for its relocation to Princeton. On October 8, 1748, Belcher wrote to Dickinson stating his intention of supporting the infant college. "I say our infant college," Belcher explained, "because I am determined to adopt it for a child and to do everything in my power to promote and establish so noble an undertaking." Belcher had no way of knowing that before he could rejoice in Belcher's support, Dickinson had died on October 7. When he learned of Dickinson's death, Belcher wrote to Dickinson's friend and ministerial colleague, Ebenezer Pemberton: "The death of that eminent servant of God, the learned and pious Dickinson, is a considerable rebuke of Providence, and is to remind us that we have such precious treasure in earthen vessels, and that our eyes and hearts must be lifted to the great head of the church, who holds the stars in his right hand. Then let us not despond or murmur."[35]

[34] Collins, *Princeton,* 14–15; Wertenbaker, "The College of New Jersey," 16–17; Jonathan Dickinson to [unknown], 3 March 1747, General Manuscripts, Firestone Library, Princeton University.

[35] David C. Humphrey, "The Struggle for Sectarian Control of Princeton, 1745–1760," *New Jersey History* 91 (Summer 1973) 85; Collins, *Princeton,* 22–23; John DeWitt, "Historical Sketch of Princeton University," in *Memorial Book of the Sesquicentennial Celebration of the Founding Fathers of the College of New Jersey and of the Ceremonies Inaugurating Princeton University* (New York: Scribner, 1898) 342; John MacLean, *History of the College of New Jersey, 1746–1854* (Philadelphia: Lippincott, 1887) 81–83.

7

Gilbert Tennent—
Pietist, Preacher, and Presbyterian

C. N. Wilborn

THE Great Awakening landed two men in the Colonial Hall of Fame—George Whitefield and Jonathan Edwards. One can almost say the Great Awakening produced these men and, so, it is hard to speak of the eighteenth-century Awakening without these names rolling across the lips. Whitefield is known for his popular preaching to masses and Edwards for his weighty treatises on any number of subjects. There are other men who probably deserve equal billing or, at least, "co-star" status when it comes to any account of the Great Awakening. One of those oft-overlooked men is Gilbert Tennent. According to Milton Coalter, "Tennent was certainly not the theological equal of Edwards" and, for that reason, "scholars have overlooked the fact that one genius did not an Awakening leadership make."[1]

While Tennent may have been overlooked as an Awakening leader, in Colonial Presbyterianism there are few figures that gain a more peculiar interest than Gilbert Tennent. He is memorialized in some of the most unusual places. For example, Old School Presbyterians since the days of Archibald Alexander have lauded his evangelistic zeal. This can be explained because he was, after all, a Presbyterian and Presbyterians, even of the strictest brand, are evangelistic. His Presbyterianism, however, cannot explain why he is memorialized in a mural at Bob Jones University, which is hardly a bastion of Presbyterianism! What accounts for his diverse following? What explains his popularity?

His popularity certainly does not emanate from reprint editions of his sermons or books. Although Tennent "published more than any oth-

[1] Milton J. Coalter Jr., *Gilbert Tennent, Son of Thunder* (Westport, CT: Greenwood, 1986) xvi.

er clergyman of the middle colonies"[2] prior to the Revolution, today his works enjoy antiquarian interest rather than popular sales. Milton Coalter, Tennent's biographer, is certainly correct when he suggests that the answer to Tennent's popularity lies in the subtle (or not so subtle) effect of Continental pietism upon our subject.[3] Pietism stressed the subjective side of religion and the subjective elements of Christianity have, since the Great Awakening, found greater audiences than the objective elements. Coalter's thesis is opposed to that of the widely followed twentieth century work of Leonard Trinterud, who missed or misinterpreted the affects of pietism upon the colonial Presbyterians and makes Tennent out to be a representative Scotch-Irish Presbyterian.[4] In the following pages, it will be argued that Tennent's preaching, pastoral model, and revivalistic emphases all substantiate the thesis that pietism shaped Tennent and through his influence continues to mold generations of Presbyterians and Protestants of all brands.

Origins and Influences

Gilbert Tennent was born in County Armaugh, Ireland, in 1703. The eldest son of William Tennent, Sr. and Katherine Kennedy Tennent, his family immigrated to colonial America in 1718. His father had been educated at Edinburgh, receiving his Master of Arts in 1693 from Edinburgh.[5] Sometime after graduation, William Tennent was licensed by one of the Scottish presbyteries and later he was received as a probationer by the historic Presbyterian Synod of Ulster in Northern Ireland. During this time he married a daughter of a prominent and staunch Presbyterian min-

[2] Ibid, xvi. Indeed, outside of selected Tennent sermons published in Archibald Alexander, *Sermons of the Log College,* one would be hard pressed to find any Tennent publications in reprint today.

[3] Ibid., xix. While the term piety refers to godliness and has a rightful place in the Christian vocabulary, pietism refers to the subjectivistic response to a perceived spiritual lethargy, believed to be integrally united to creedal orthodoxy.

[4] Leonard J. Trinterud, *The Forming of an American Tradition* (Philadelphia: Westminster, 1949) 54–56. In these three pages Trinterud distances both Frelinghuysen and Tennent from any pietistic influences and associations and credits their "kindred spirit" to "their common Calvinism, their common Puritan heritage, and their common religious outlook." He seems to make no connection between Continental pietism of the period and "their common religious outlook."

[5] Ibid., 35; Archibald Alexander, *The Log College* (1851; reprint, Edinburgh: Banner of Truth Trust, 1968) 14, suggests that Tennent, being in the Established Church of Ireland, would have been educated at Trinity College, Dublin. The evidence weighs against Alexander in favor of the Edinburgh education.

ister Gilbert Kennedy. Despite having married a committed Presbyterian and having an outspoken dissenting father-in-law, William Tennent transferred his ecclesiastical membership to the Church of Ireland just two years after his marriage to Katherine. Soon thereafter Tennent was ordained a presbyter by the Bishop of Down. His ecclesiastical shift is probably best understood against the backdrop of the persecution imposed by the Irish Parliament against any dissenting Christians (which included Presbyterians) in Northern Ireland.

In 1718, two years after having arrived in North America, the Scotsman applied to the Synod of Philadelphia to be received as a minister in the budding Presbyterian Church. Not surprisingly, the Synod moved slowly and deliberately on this request. After being thoroughly examined on his knowledge and views of doctrine, polity, and sacraments, and after submitting a written explanation of the reasons for preferring the Presbyterian Church to the Episcopal Church, he was solemnly received. Once approved for the gospel ministry by the Synod of Philadelphia, the Synod instructed the moderator to seriously exhort Tennent to remain steadfast in his new position—quite reasonable considering his windblown past.

After a tumultuous period as a parish minister in East Chester (1718-20) and Bedford (1720–25), New York, Tennent sold his New York property and moved his burgeoning family to Bucks County, Pennsylvania. There he ministered for some time near Neshaminy Creek.[6] It is in this region that the Tennent clan gained early attention, in connection with the founding of the Log College.

The Log College, named for its rugged frontier-like appearance and used derisively by some, was William Tennent's attempt to meet the growing need for education in the New World. While it provided a classical education it did not provide what Presbyterians from the Old World deemed sufficient; in other words, it was not Edinburgh, Glasgow, or St. Andrews. It was in the Log College setting that the younger sons of William Tennent were educated along with a handful of other men who desired an education spiked with pietistic fervor. The Log College and the name Tennent eventually stood at the center of a major division in Colonial Presbyterianism.

While Gilbert was not educated within the walls of the Log College, he was educated by his father in the same classical manner, with the same

[6] Tennent eventually moved to Northampton Township where his cousin, James Logan, sold him fifty acres. From Northampton he finally settled on one hundred acres in Warminster Township in 1735.

pietistic emphasis. He probably spent many hours studying aboard the ship as the family immigrated to the Americas during his thirteenth or fourteenth year. From what little is known the younger Tennent apparently had been on a track for the gospel ministry (no doubt, a dream of his father).[7] About this time, however, young Tennent began to wrestle with his own salvation and, consequently, his vocational calling. With the onset of this "law work," Tennent began to struggle with an acute awareness of God's moral law and his personal sinfulness. His personal doubts grew so great that he jettisoned his ministerial pursuits and entered upon the study of medicine. In the midst of his medical studies, "Gilbert experienced conversion, however, and this led him to resume his studies for the ministry."[8]

In 1725 Tennent was awarded the Master of Arts degree from Yale College. He next was licensed for the gospel ministry by the Presbytery of Philadelphia before being received into the Presbytery of New Castle as a probationer. Subsequently, the Presbyterian Church in New Castle, Delaware, extended him a call to be their pastor, which call Tennent apparently accepted. After accepting the call to the New Castle church, however, he was offered another opportunity from a group of people in New Brunswick, New Jersey, which apparently he found more appealing. This double-mindedness on Tennent's part sparked an investigation of the situation by the New Castle Presbytery and earned him a formal rebuke from the Synod on September 23, 1726. They exhorted him, *in absentia*, to "more caution and deliberation in his future proceedings" since he had acted "too hasty and unadvised" in several matters. Thomas Craighead, the moderator of Synod, publicly rebuked Tennent at his next appearance before presbytery. Sadly, Tennent did not heed the wise words of Synod and his ministry for the next several years was marked by hasty words, little respect for others, and an independent spirit.

In the end, the young Tennent had a very active 1726 during which he reneged on his call to New Castle, accepted a call to organize a church in New Brunswick, received a reprimanded from Synod and presbytery, and, finally, he was ordained in New Brunswick. It deserves noting also that the group in New Brunswick desired a new church and new minister because they were *dissatisfied* with their minister in the nearby town of

[7] One of the difficulties in writing biographically about Gilbert Tennent is the lack of information. See Milton Coalter, *Gilbert Tennent,* 9. Here we read, "It is impossible to describe what sort of pupil or son Gilbert was, since his childhood is practically a historical blank."

[8] Coalter, *Gilbert Tennent,* 9.

Freehold. To the local minister's credit, he did not allow the situation to fester into something unhealthy and even participated in Tennent's ordination service. On the other hand, the situation does foreshadow Tennent's propensity toward siding against the ordained ministry and with the disgruntled laity.

From this inauspicious beginning Tennent went on to gain fame as a leading revivalistic preacher, friend of George Whitefield, and an active party in the division of the young colonial Presbyterian Church. His activity and associations mark him as the most widely recognized American Presbyterian of the Great Awakening.

By the beginning of 1727 Gilbert Tennent was settled in New Jersey on the south bank of the Raritan River between Elizabethtown and Trenton. Alexander suggests that Tennent's preaching "was very popular and attractive with all classes of hearers." His popular approach was complemented by his uncommon height, his grave expression, and his clear voice. "No one could hear him," wrote Alexander, "without being convinced that he was deeply earnest."[9] Yet, with all the native ability, he found his first months of ministry in New Brunswick to be disappointing in affect.[10] His faithfulness in administering the office of word and sacrament was not enough for this pietist-trained minister. The lack of apparent spiritual results led Tennent into self-doubt, inordinate introspection, and physical illness. "I had done so little for God," he bemoaned. He asked God to spare him, with the promise that he would do more for the "conversion of souls" if allowed to live just six more months! While his lamentation is commendable, it reveals a one-sided view of the ministry. He had been engineered for visible results which equated with remarkable, time-oriented events in the individual life. When he did not see outward expressions of the new birth, he counted himself a failure.

In the midst of his fears, doubts, and illness, Tennent found Theodore Frelinghuysen as a balm in Gilead. Frelinghuysen, a German-born, Dutch Reformed, pietistic revivalist, was his nearest ministerial contact and proved not only to be an unguent for the Presbyterian's troubled soul, but also the possessor of answers to his ineffectual ministry. With the purported answers to his unimpressive ministry came a number of other in-

[9] Alexander, *The Log College,* 25.

[10] Tennent cited in Coalter, *Gilbert Tennent,* 17. See also, Thomas Prince, ed., *The Christian History Containing Accounts of the Revival and Propagation of Religion in Great Britain and America for the Year 1744* (Boston: S. Kneeland and T. Green, 1745) 5:293.

fluences that "altered the theology, preaching, and quite likely even the personality of the Presbyterian."[11]

Gilbert had been nurtured in a home environment that challenged the motives and basis for sacramental participation, opposed the idea of conversion apart from a crisis encounter with Satan, self, and the Savior, and discounted ordinary means of grace for a singular experience through the preached word of God. The theology and practice he learned at his father's feet found complementation and, in some ways, supplementation with that of his new paragon, Theodore Frelinghuysen. For these men it was not enough to say, "I come to the communion table because I believe in Christ Jesus for the forgiveness of sins and desire to commune with Him through this sacrament by faith." No, Tennent's model for table participation was a carefully described crisis-oriented, conversion experience. Furthermore, it was not enough to say, "I trust in Jesus for forgiveness of sins and stand right before God because of the imputed righteous of Christ my Savior." Again, one must detail a crisis experience along the Damascus Road model and the Tennent experience. Finally, it was not enough to come to the ordinary means of grace out of loving obedience to the Savior through a simple faith. No, one must exhibit the *Gefühl* (emotion or feeling) appropriate to the persona of one having been born again.[12]

There is perhaps one final ingredient or influence that aids in understanding Gilbert Tennent—his maternal grandfather. Gilbert's mother was Katherine Kennedy. Katherine's father was "a thoroughgoing Presbyterian dissenter"[13] who had lost his pulpit in Scotland at the Great Ejection of 1662. Upon being ejected for nonconformity to the Anglo-Catholicizing of English and Scottish Churches under Charles II, Gilbert Kennedy removed his family to Ireland only to find the situation much the same as Scotland. Rather than compromise, as his future son-in-law would do in 1704, Kennedy pursued a different route. He moved to the open air and preached wherever there was need or desire of the people. This covert ministry ended in 1670 when he was called to the parish church in Dundonald. The similarity between his grandfather's activities and Gilbert's proclivity for itineration among those he deemed neglected and lacking is stunning and may suggest at least one other influence upon his dissenter-styled methodology.

[11] Coalter, *Gilbert Tennent,* 18.

[12] *Gefühl* is chosen here because it seems best to fit the existential laden emphasis employed by Tennent and the pietistic revivalists. The term would find popularity in the eighteenth-century pietistic relativist Frederich Schleiermacher.

[13] Coalter, *Gilbert Tennent,* 2.

Standards and Subjectivity

Tennent's pastoral ministry was marked by controversy. Sometimes he was actively involved in the controversy, other times he was passively related. Perhaps no single issue better illustrates Tennent's passive relationship to controversy than the issue of confessional subscription. From 1720 to 1737, colonial Presbyterians discussed doctrinal stability and the proper means for maintaining doctrinal integrity in the church. In 1728 a formal overture was presented to the Synod, recommending the Westminster Confession and Catechisms for Synod-wide subscription. Every Scottish and Scotch-Irish member of Synod recommended the overture to be adopted by the next (1729) Synod. During the next year John Thomson of New Castle Presbytery published a pastoral letter to the entire Synod exhorting the church to embrace the subscription measures for the good of the church. Jonathan Dickinson of New Jersey quickly responded with his own public letter begging the nascent church to reject the ploy of subscription. At the heart of Dickinson's argument was a plea for individual conscience. Dickinson did not believe it to be in the best interest of the church to manage membership through codification of belief. The debate between Thomson and Dickinson was not over the substance of the Confessional documents but over the utility of the documents. So far as one can discern, both men believed the articles of faith as set forth in the creedal summary. The men differed over the propriety of imposing these man-crafted summaries upon the conscience of individual men.

In the end, the Synod of Philadelphia unanimously subscribed to the Westminster Standards with scruples being expressed by some over "certain clauses" in the twenty and twenty-third chapters of the Confession of Faith.[14] The clauses of concern had to do with the relationship of the civil magistrate to the church. Thus, that to which the Synod subscribed was the entire Confession of Faith, with allowance made for scruples to be held toward the "certain clauses." Correspondingly, Charles Hodge understood subscription among the early men "to require every new member to receive the whole of the Confession, except the clauses relating to the power of the civil magistrates in matters of religion." It was the "whole of

[14] Charles Hodge, *The Constitutional History of the Presbyterian Church in America,* 2 vols. (Philadelphia: Presbyterian Board of Publication, 1851) 1:155–56. Interestingly, Milton Coalter carelessly says, "The twentieth and twenty-third chapters of the Westminster Confession were renounced by the entire Synod." It was "certain clauses" rather than entire chapters. This is further evinced by the amendments to the Westminster Confession at the inaugural General Assembly of the Presbyterian Church in the United States of America in 1789.

the Confession" that the 1729 Synod adopted as its own public doctrinal statement of belief. Hodge continues by saying "that at no period of our history and in no section of our Church has assent to the essential doctrines of the gospel been made the condition of ministerial communion."[15] Hodge's plain reading of the early synodical renderings on confessional subscription was against subscription only to the essentials or gospel elements of the Standards. It was instead, the "whole of the Confession" to which those colonial Fathers subscribed. "Such," concludes Hodge, "was the latitudinarianism of those days!"[16]

While Gilbert Tennent and his family did subscribe without stated qualification to the Standards at one time or another between 1729 and 1737,[17] he provides a good historical example of the exercise of individual conscience in regards to the matter. While saluting the doctrines of the Confession and Catechisms, he crossed his fingers in terms of commitment to the purpose of subscription. Subscription, however, was not only to be a way to judge a man's suitability or qualification for Presbyterian ministry, but a way to unify the church from its local expression to its broadest expression. In other words, subscription to the Westminster Standards was designed to give a unified public face to the Presbyterian Church whether it be in Philadelphia, New York, Neshaminy, or Lewes. While Tennent saw the Standards as "a norm for orthodoxy," he was fully committed to pietistic freedom of expression. Again, the emphasis for Tennent was common conversion experience. Thus, his concern was not so much for a Presbyterian Church homogenous in belief and practice, but one having a common experience. The subjective knowledge of God; the experience of God trumped the objective knowledge in a pietist paradigm.[18]

The Popular Pietist

Pietism, it should be remembered, was a reaction against a perceived deadness in churches that were committed to creedal orthodoxy.[19] Applied orthodoxy was feared by pietists as having a deadening affect upon the

[15] Hodge, *Constitutional History*, 1:170–72.

[16] Ibid., 154.

[17] We find Tennent's name recorded among those voting in favor of confessional subscription in Guy Klett, ed., *Minutes of the Presbyterian Church in America, 1706–1788* (Philadelphia: Philadelphia Historical Society, 1976) 104, 141–42.

[18] Coalter, *Gilbert Tennent*, 38.

[19] In saying this, it is not to suggest that pietists were altogether wrong. There were, no doubt, spiritual problems among some of the orthodox; but their mistake was to intimate a direct correlation between the two.

church through its emphasis upon the objective elements of belief and practice. Thus, emphasis was shifted from the objective and propositional to the subjective and experiential in the lives and works of men like Phillip Jacob Spener (1635–1705) of Germany. A result of the pietistic emphasis on individual change was a growing dissatisfaction with the church, a forming of churches within churches, and eventually division of ecclesiastical communions. The basis for communion was no longer a common faith[20] but common experience and a general suspicion of those who emphasized the objective truth of confessional orthodoxy.

Germany was not the only source of the pietistic movement. It had filtered into other parts of the Continent as well and was being felt as far away as colonial America. In the mid-Atlantic region, Scottish and Scotch-Irish Presbyterians lived among a smorgasbord of European immigrants—the Dutch, English Quakers, German and Swedish Lutherans, and a host of other sects populated the region in which Tennent was reared and in which he ministered. There were, indeed, any number of opportunities for the impressionable, young Tennent to imbibe the rudimentary elements of pietism—a lively godliness that shared a common conversion experience (emotion) and common distrust of the creedally orthodox.

One of those opportunities and sources of pietism was without a doubt, William Tennent, Sr., Gilbert's father. While Archibald Alexander lamented the scarcity of information about the elder Tennent, he admitted that there was enough information available to determine that he was suspicious of men who stressed creedal orthodoxy. At the time in which Tennent moved from Ireland to the colonies, Alexander reckons, "the state of vital piety was very low in the Presbyterian church in America."[21] The elder Tennent, therefore, stressed the subjective nature of religion as an antidote to a dry and lifeless orthodoxy.

Upon entering the ministry, Gilbert Tennent found himself in close geographical proximity to only one other minister, Theodore Frelinghuysen, a Dutch Reformed evangelist. Frelinghuysen was a product of two strands of Dutch influence—Herman Witsius' covenant theology and Jacobus Koelman's critical spirit. Thus, Frelinghuysen was orthodox in theology, but suspicious and critical of anyone who did not agree with or act like himself. For example, upon his arrival in New York in 1720, he openly

[20] Ephesians 4:5—". . . one faith"; Hebrews 10:23—"Let us hold fast the confession of our hope without wavering. . . ." Unless otherwise noted Scripture is from the English Standard Version (ESV).

[21] Alexander, *The Log College*, 17.

criticized Pastor DuBois "for possessing a huge wall mirror in his home."[22] Apparently the mirror betrayed a vain heart in the pastor!

Frelinghuysen was also a practitioner of a conversion-based Christianity. He placed every Christian testimony under the scrutiny of his pietistic conversion paradigm. First, there had to be the testimony of a "law work" in the individual. Here the individual Christian recounted his misery at the consciousness of his violation of God's law. Second, the individual testified of his conscious experience of the new birth, which freed him from the misery of the "law work." Finally, the pietistic conversion resulted in the pious acts of a truly converted soul. One had to possess this testimony in order to be considered credible and communing. In other words, the testimony of a covenant child, having grown up loving the Lord Jesus Christ, trusting Him alone for salvation, and having never known a day when he did not believe in Christ, could not pass the pietists' three-step conversion gauntlet.

A final characteristic of Frelinghuysen's pietism, which Tennent imbibed, was that of fellowship by association. The Dutch evangelist chose his allies first according to their common experience of conversion, and *second,* a Reformed confession.[23] Their practice had to conform to his pietistic paradigm. This accounts for Tennent's later association with the itinerating evangelist George Whitefield and an inordinate emphasis on the three-step conversion process.

The pietism upon which Tennent gorged himself led his ministerial emphases to be centered upon preaching for conversions. Techniques were employed to best affect the audience. Everything centered on the rhetoric of preaching. While preaching is to be held as central in worship, it is not the exclusive act of worship. For the revivalist, however, church life consisted in preaching the dead to life. Perhaps no one did it better in Presbyterian life than Gilbert Tennent.

With all Presbyterians of all times, Gilbert Tennent held the preaching of the word of God as one of the indispensable marks of the Church. Alongside this belief he held to the centrality and primacy of the preached word in worship and life. During 1734, he introduced two overtures before Synod in hopes of reversing the lamentable decline of godliness in the church. The second overture specifically addressed the preaching of the nascent church's ministers. Every minister's preaching was to be reviewed regularly to ascertain whether certain elements were present. It was im-

[22] Coalter, *Gilbert Tennent,* 14.

[23] Ibid., 22.

portant, argued Tennent, that Presbyterian sermons insist upon the "great articles of Christianity." Furthermore, the preacher must "recommend a crucified Savior to his hearers," with emphasis upon the sinner's dependence upon the "omnipotent influences of the Divine grace."[24]

There can be no doubt that Gilbert Tennent desired to "preach Christ crucified," and "Christ the power of God and the wisdom of God," (1 Corinthians 1:23–24). Whether he was preaching on the attributes of God or the nature of saving grace, Tennent managed to call sinners to repentance and holiness.[25] His content in the early years was lighter but highly rhetorical, with application plied to the consciences of men. His Philadelphia years (1743–64) were more logically formulated and ordered, with heavier content. In all phases of his preaching, he favored the Scoto-Puritan "plain style" of preaching which so exemplified the period.[26] Thomas Prince described his preaching as having "no regard to please the eyes of his hearers with agreeable gestures, or their ears with delivery, nor their fancy with language, but aim directly at their hearts and conscience."[27]

Tennent, like his independent evangelist friend George Whitefield, also utilized an "adversarial style," which promoted his revivalist cause.[28] The adversarial style seemed to exude from the pietism Tennent imbibed from Frelinghuysen and witnessed in Whitefield. Indeed, "Frelinghuysen was known by many and hated by some for his untempered [sic], almost combative candor both in and out of the pulpit." In answer to his critics, he had a poem painted on the back of his buggy. Thus the last witness of the revivalist as he departed a location was

> No one's tongue, and no one's pen
> Can make me other than I am.
> Speak, evil-speaker, without end;
> In vain you all your slanders spend.[29]

[24] Ibid., 41.

[25] For examples see Tennent, *Sermons of the Log College*, 9–96. Here we have a series of textual-topical sermons on the attributes of God, which probably originated post-1743.

[26] For a good discussion of "plain style" preaching see Perry Miller, *The New England Mind: The Seventeenth Century* (1939; reprint, Cambridge: Belknap, 1982) 331–64.

[27] Prince quoted in Harry Stout, *The New England Soul* (Oxford: Oxford University Press, 1986) 198. It should be noted that Tennent utilized extempore preaching early, only to change to manuscript preaching after 1743.

[28] Stout, in *The New England Soul*, on page 199, enters into discussion of this "adversarial style."

[29] Coalter, *Gilbert Tennent*, 18.

Controversy and Conciliation

While genuine Christian piety is marked by humility, pietism is marked by a judgmental quality. This latter quality and the adversarial-styled preaching find no better example than Tennent's famous sermon preached at Nottingham, Pennsylvania on March 8, 1740. *The Danger of an Unconverted Ministry* "served as a primer and party platform for itinerant preachers who believed the greatest enemy was not popular apathy and declension but 'blind, unregenerate, carnal, lukewarm, and unskilled guides.'"[30] Taking his starting point from Mark 6:34—"When he went ashore he saw a great crowd, and he had compassion on them, because they were like sheep without a shepherd"—Tennent pronounced his judgment upon ministers who opposed the activities of the revivalists. According to Tennent, those who opposed Awakening practices did not give proper care to their own souls and were "enemies of the spiritual kingdom of Christ."[31] Therefore, he urged parishioners not to trust their souls to such men. If they needed to go elsewhere than to their parish minister for spiritual nurture, then go they should.[32] Archibald Alexander generously described the Nottingham Sermon as "one of the most severely abusive sermons which was ever penned."[33] Evidence for Alexander's assessment is ample.

Tennent's controversial nature is revealed in numerous places but especially in his Nottingham Sermon and his protests against Synod actions. In each case, his writings reveal two characteristics, according to Charles Hodge. First, Tennent always appealed to first principles. It was not enough for Tennent to object to "the thing in debate." Rather, he was compelled by some sense of urgency "to attack the hypothesis" upon which *he thought* the debate was founded. For example, he would not debate the Old Side men with reference to their criticisms of extra-ecclesiastical activities in the Awakening. Rather he wished to criticize their piety (or lack thereof in his estimation) or even their gospel and Christianity. As Hodge says, this led him into all sorts of inconsistencies and contradictions. He was apparently "neither discriminating nor logical." The second characteristic of Tennent the controversialist was "a fondness for exaggeration."[34] A perfect illustration of this quality is seen in his response to Synod's ability to address

[30] Ibid.

[31] Alexander, *The Log College,* 35.

[32] See Tennent, "The Danger of an Unconverted Ministry," in *Sermons of the Log College,* 394–95.

[33] Ibid.

[34] Hodge, *Constitutional History,* 2:108.

ordination qualifications or activities of itinerants' evangelistic activities. Given his penchant for exaggeration, he found it practically impossible to deny Synod's authority to determine its membership, without denying all authority of Synod over any member.

As can easily be imagined, the censorious tenor of his adversarial sermons and writings proved divisive in the colonial Presbyterian church, driving a wedge between fellow ministers who professed to believe the same concerning doctrine, practice, and worship, and contributing to the 1741 Old Side-New Side division in the Presbyterian Church.[35] The sermon not only drove a wedge between New Side men like Tennent and Samuel Blair and Old Side men like John Thomson and Francis Alison, but it engendered a suspicious and disrespectful attitude in many parishioners toward their pastors.

Tennent's reputation as a controversialist did not reside within the colonial Presbyterian Church alone, nor was it limited to the Awakening period. In 1754, Tennent and Samuel Davies were in Great Britain raising funds for the nascent College of New Jersey. Among the many obstacles in their path was the attitude of various British ministers toward Tennent. His Nottingham Sermon had found circulation throughout the Kingdom and left a sour taste in many a mouth. "According to all reports," wrote George Pilcher, "Tennent was almost overwhelmed when confronted in England with copies of his highly emotional and vitriolic Nottingham sermon."[36] Everywhere the tandem went opposition confronted them, chiefly over the "famous intemperate" and sectarian sermon. Tennent was forced to express regrets for his misrepresentations and criticisms of Old Side ministers. Having found that a considerable number of men in England were offended by his 1741 tirade and that his reputation was harming his fundraising for the College of New Jersey, he "made honest concessions with regard to the Nottingham sermon."[37]

Here it is seen that Tennent, by 1754, was turning away from his earlier pietistic prattle. Indeed, his critical and intemperate zeal of the early 1740s was being tempered with knowledge as early as 1742 when he expressed

[35] For more on the Old Side-New Side Division see the essay by D. G. Hart in this volume.

[36] George Pilcher, *Samuel Davies: Apostle of Dissent in Colonial Virginia* (Knoxville, TN: The University of Tennessee Press, 1971) 142.

[37] From Samuel Davies' diary entry for January 23, 1754 as found in George William Pilcher, ed., *The Reverend Samuel Davies Abroad* (Urbana: University of Illinois Press, 1967) 60.

his own "excessive heat of temper" and "mismanaged" actions.[38] In addition to his own misgivings about his role in the schism of the Presbyterian church, his backpedaling was further propelled by the Moravian invasion of the colonies. Count Nicholaus von Zinzendorf arrived in the middle colonies in 1741 promoting his German-brand of pietism and encouraging his followers in his skewed theology. If the New Side Presbyterians had been critical and sectarian, and they had, the Moravians exceeded them in almost every way. Moravian pietists had no time or respect for any minister who did not expertly apply the revivalistic measures. They spurned enemies of the revival, and sloppy practitioners, and even *supporters* of the revival, "if he did not actively provoke the correct response."[39]

In addition to the wild-eyed fanaticism of the Moravians, there was the proselytizing method of the Moravians. The disruption brought about by their active proselytizing had deleterious affect not only in the German bodies and among the German ministers, but within the Presbyterian community as well. This provoked numerous responses from Presbyterians aligned with or sympathetic to the New Side. Concern over Moravian theology found numerous expressions, such as Samuel Blair's *Persuasive to Repentance* (1743) and Tennent's *Account of the Principles of the Moravians* (1743). Jonathan Dickinson, a moderate proponent of the revival, spent over four hundred pages explaining the injurious doctrine and practice of the Moravians in his *Familiar Letters to a Gentleman* (1745).

The disruption Moravian practice and theology was causing within the middle colonies dealt a convicting blow to Tennent's pride and revivalistic practice. As early as 1742 he expressed to Dickinson of having "a clear view of the danger of everything which tends to enthusiasm and division in the visible church."[40] Not only was the theology and practice of the Moravians paramount in Tennent's return to rationality, but his interaction with Whitefield on the topic was also illuminating. In the past, Tennent and Whitefield had been kindred spirits in the application of revivalistic methodology to the region and in the promotion of an ecumenical program. Indeed, Whitefield had hand-picked Tennent to follow-up his own "whirl-wind" tour of Boston in 1740. With Tennent's return

[38] Gilbert Tennent to Jonathan Dickinson, 12 February 1742 in Richard Webster, *A History of the Presbyterian Church in America, from its Origin until the Year 1760* (Philadelphia: Joseph M. Wilson, 1857; reprint, Stoke-on-Trent, UK: Tentmaker, 2004) 189.

[39] Marilyn J. Westerkamp, *The Triumph of the Laity* (Oxford: Oxford University Press, 1988) 207.

[40] Gilbert Tennent to Jonathan Dickinson in Webster, *A History of the Presbyterian Church*, 189–91.

to sobriety, however, the zeal that sealed the friendship was giving way to knowledge.

Whitefield had left the colonies in 1742 and returned to London. At the time of his exit, Whitefield was involved in an ecumenical board which promoted a house of worship and charity in Philadelphia. Discussion soon surfaced as to the likelihood of a Moravian filling the pulpit of the "new building" in Philadelphia and Tennent entered the fray. In response to Tennent's query about the situation, Whitefield plied his ecumenical convictions to the situation and chose to "further the kingdom" through peaceful coexistence with the unorthodox. Thus, revealing to Tennent Whitefield's low-church views and lack of discernment and respect for theological matters. Indeed, Whitefield found Tennent's 1742 concerns unacceptable and, as Coalter puts it, "chided his colonial friend for being too confined by his Presbyterian principles." As for Whitefield, he made it clear that he would preach with the expectation that people will believe in Christ and "let them join with such Congregations as they upon due urging deemed to be nearest the mind of Jesus Christ."[41] Such was Whitefield's ecumenism and it was ecumenism enough to send Tennent back toward his biblical Presbyterianism. Tennent's response is revealing as he expressed shock and horror at the revivalist's low views. "Your high opinion of the Moravians," wrote Tennent, "and attempts to join them shocks me exceedingly and opens a scene of terror and distress."[42] For Tennent, compromise on cardinal points of doctrine could not be tolerated and could not be the foundation for genuine revival and certainly not for the visible church of Christ. Although Whitefield leaned toward Tennent's Calvinism, "his heart was fundamentally in sympathy with Zinzendorf's ecumenism."[43] Thus, the call for Whitefield's repentance on this matter went unheeded.

While Tennent was politicking and preaching against the unorthodox Moravians, he was preaching a new message to his congregation and colleagues in the Presbyterian Church. Even before the founding of the Synod of New York in 1745, Tennent preached *The Danger of Spiritual Pride* (1744) in which he warned against self-righteousness and arrogance. Other notable sermons within this genre are *The Necessity of Studying to be Quiet, and doing our own Business* (1744) and *Brotherly Love Recommended* (1748). Gilbert Tennent had become acutely aware that many of his ac-

[41] Quoted in Coalter, *Gilbert Tennent,* 111. The Billy Graham approach to ecumenism is seen clearly in Whitefield.

[42] Ibid.

[43] Ibid., 112.

tions, especially from 1738 to 1741, were wrong-headed and dishonoring to Christ. Due to his shift in sentiment, he had been accused and publicly exposed in print for his hypocrisy in 1743. Tennent responded to this public humiliation, not with an outburst or tirade against the author, but with a reasoned response which "offered a careful modification of Tennent's earlier views based on the concept of balance."[44]

By this time, Tennent knew that his revivalistic zeal had been wrong. "I would to God," he wrote, "the breach were healed . . . I have mismanaged in doing what I did."[45] His efforts to heal the breach continued throughout the 1740s, reaching a pinnacle in 1749 with his lengthy *Irenicum; or, a Plea for the Peace of Jerusalem.* While this sermon did not affect an immediate reunion of the two bodies, it set the tone for future deliberations which concluded in 1758 with the rejoining of the Old Side Synod of Philadelphia and the New Side Synod of New York. While many men labored for the reunification, it is worth noting that Old Sider Francis Alison said, "Gilbert Tennent . . . has written more and suffered more for his writings, to promote peace and union, than any member of this divided church."[46] For fifteen years the Son of Thunder, who almost single-handedly divided Colonial Presbyterianism, labored for the peace and purity of the church. For his labors, Tennent was rewarded by being elected the first Moderator of the reunited Synod of New York and Philadelphia.

At the 1759 Synod of the reunited church, as retiring Moderator, Tennent delivered two sermons on the topic of peace and persecution. In those sermons he pled for just and honest dealing with brothers, humility, courtesy, candor, charitableness in speech and conduct. He derided rashness, extra-biblical terms of communion, and judgmental and divisive attitudes and speech. His desire for peace was apparently genuine and his willingness to promote it obvious. Unfortunately, the years following the formation of the joint Synod and preceding Tennent's death were marked by anything but peace.[47]

[44] In the winter of 1743, John Hancock anonymously published an article entitled *The Examiner; Or Gilbert against Tennent.* In this side by side analysis of Tennent's writings against the Old Side and against the Moravians, Hancock showed Tennent to be inconsistent and hypocritical. See a discussion of this in Coalter, *Gilbert Tennent,* 113–21.

[45] Tennent quoted in Webster, *A History of the Presbyterian Church in America,* 189.

[46] Alison quoted in Coalter, *Gilbert Tennent,* 156.

[47] For a thorough discussion of the turmoil within the post-1758 Colonial Presbyterian Church see Leonard Trinterud, *The Forming of An American Tradition,* 152–65.

Extracurricular Affairs

From brief dictionary sketches that one might read and popular treatments of Gilbert Tennent, it would appear that his life was consumed by little more than revivalism and controversy. A representative article, however, should provide some insight into his other interests, as uninteresting as they may be. One of those more mundane areas of his involvement was institutional education. While Tennent defended the education offered through the Log College and discounted the Old Side insistence on European or New England liberal arts education, we find him supporting a new institution, the College of New Jersey. By the time of his father's death (May 6, 1746), the Log College had ceased to exist although the need for an educated ministry had not. Both parties in the colonial Presbyterian Church recognized the need for education. Demand was greater than supply when it came to educated ministers. The young nation was growing at an accelerated pace and this produced "a sense of urgency for the creation of an institution for ministerial education closer to home."[48]

The united Synod of Philadelphia put the ball in play in 1739 when she voted unanimously for the establishment of a school. Among those appointed to the study committee for the schools erection was the moderate proponent for revival, Jonathan Dickinson. For several reasons the Synod did not return to the issue until 1743 and then, on November 24, 1743, a synod school was begun at New London, Pennsylvania under the direction of Francis Alison of the Old Side. The school never gained ascendancy and Alison departed for the College of Philadelphia in 1752.

By now the Synod of New York had formed and with Dickinson's leadership was actively pursuing the establishment of a college that would "prove as well a seminary of vital piety as of good literature."[49] Plans were drawn up for the college as early as March 1745 and, after some obstacles were providentially removed, the charter for the college was granted on October 22, 1746. The charter, which was ground breaking in colonial history, provided "equal liberties and privileges . . . to every denomination of Christians, any different religious sentiments notwithstanding."[50] The charter allowed for a self-perpetuating board of trustees and among the first added was Gilbert Tennent.

[48] Bryan F. Le Beau, *Jonathan Dickinson and the Formative Years of American Presbyterianism* (Lexington: The University Press of Kentucky, 1997) 166.

[49] Ibid., 177–78.

[50] Ibid., 178. Le Beau provides a good overview of the political context of the time and the establishment of the college on pages 165–86.

As a trustee and friend of the college, Tennent embarked upon a tour of the British Isles to raise operating funds for the new college. He was partnered on this trip with his junior ministerial colleague from Virginia, Samuel Davies. Davies referred to Tennent as "my Father and Friend" and leaned upon him during the sea travel for "social comfort."[51] While knowledge of Tennent's intemperate dealings with his Old Side brethren preceded him to Britain, he did find some comfort in a friendly, though private, reunion with George Whitefield in London.[52] Although Tennent's association with Whitefield and his Awakening demeanor harmed his fund-raising efforts in England and Scotland, he was successful in Ireland. Early on Tennent proved to be more of a liability to the cause among Scottish Presbyterians and, so, for several reasons departed for Ireland where his reputation was less publicized. According to Coalter, "Tennent's decision paid off richly." No doubt the payoff was due to Davies' considerable success once freed from Tennent's reputation as well as Tennent's labors in a less hostile Ireland. The figures suggest that Davies secured nearly £3000 in England and Scotland while Tennent gathered another £500 in Ireland. Thus, in the words of Pilcher, "The infant institution was placed on a sound financial basis."[53]

Another aspect of Tennent's life which is often overlooked due to his Awakening activism is his pastoral life. From 1726, Tennent served his original congregation at New Brunswick, New Jersey; however, by 1743 there are indications that his welcome in New Brunswick was greatly diminished.[54] All parties welcomed a move and in the fall of 1743 arrangements were made for the New Side controversialist turned conciliator to move to Philadelphia, the heart of the Old Side. He was taking up a call from a New Side congregation meeting in the building constructed by and for Whitefield. Later the congregation would leave the "Whitefield tabernacle" for a new building on Arch Street, where they assumed the street's name.[55]

As a pastor, Tennent apparently did not wear well on the parishioners. He was regarded as austere and proud, lacking in affection for the people. It appears that his adversarial style of preaching and politicking carried

[51] Pilcher, *The Reverend Samuel Davies* Abroad, 28.

[52] Ibid., 43–44.

[53] Pilcher, *Samuel Davies,* 157.

[54] Trinterud, *The Forming of an American Tradition,* 119; 332, n. 27.

[55] Tennent and his congregation were forced to leave the "New Building," as Whitefield's building was called, when Whitefield and his board revoked the original plan which prohibited Moravians from preaching in the building. Coalter, *Gilbert Tennent,* 126–27.

over into his shepherding, if indeed he exercised much pastoral care to his New Brunswick congregation. "By sending Tennent to the City of Brotherly Love," argues Milton Coalter, "the Conjunct Presbyteries hoped this pattern would not be repeated."[56]

Whatever pastoral improvements Tennent may have experienced in his early years in Philadelphia, by the end of his life, the congregation was not willing to follow his leadership. Indeed, Tennent did not seem to know the mind of his congregation of twenty years. He was caught off guard when a persuasive group in the church supported the call of George Duffield to come as the assistant to the aging revivalist. Tennent opposed the call, but the congregation proceeded to execute the call. The sickly pastor was shocked: "I was very far from expecting such . . . as had happened, the sight of which astonished and distressed me, for it look'd like burying me while I was alive in a House under which God I had built."[57] The only thing that kept Duffield from coming to the Arch Street Church was doubts on his part and his Presbytery of Donegal.

Facts from the life of Gilbert Tennent are many when it comes to his exploits as a churchman, revivalist, and controversialist. They are less numerous concerning his pastoral labors, but when it comes to his family life even fewer details are available. We know he was married sometime before 1740, but to whom and for how long is not known. This unknown first wife died in 1740 and he preached her funeral. Within the next couple years, Tennent married Cornelia Banker de Pyster Clarkson, a widow, ten years his senior with several children from a previous marriage. Both Cornelia and Tennent's mother, Katherine, died in the spring of 1753, prior to his junket to Great Britain with Samuel Davies. Sometime after his return to the colonies in 1755 Tennent married one last time. This time the object of his affections was Sarah Spofford, a widow with one daughter. Over the next nine years, Sarah gave birth to Gilbert's first biological children—Gilbert, Cornelia, and Elizabeth. Gilbert died at sea as a young man, Elizabeth died as a young girl, and Cornelia lived to marry a Philadelphia medical doctor. The only information pertaining to his fatherly ways comes from the marble slab over his tomb: "as a husband, brother, father, and friend, among the most excellent."[58] Gilbert Tennent died on July 23, 1764 in Philadelphia.

[56] Ibid., 119.

[57] Ibid., 161.

[58] Ibid., 163.

Conclusion

To survive travels at sea, to endure the grief and emotion associated with the loss of two wives, and to labor incessantly as a colonial minister, demands no other conclusion but that Gilbert Tennent was no weak man. He labored arduously for the cause of Christ. Even when he sinned, as in the case of his revivalistic and pietistic fits of enthusiasm and criticism, he sinned boldly playing a manly role in controversy. We also saw him repent boldly, playing a manly role in bringing the divided Colonial Church back into union. The latter, the repentant and conciliatory Tennent, is perhaps the most desirable and imitable portrait of the revivalist. Part of the fruit of his repentance also provides the reader with perhaps the most memorable period in Tennent's doctrinal life—when he finally saw Whitefield for the populist and ecumenist he truly was.

For the church of some three hundred years post-Tennent, many other lessons may be drawn. For one, pietism and exclusivism breed division in the church and ought to be condemned. A second lesson to be learned from Tennent's life is that order in the church is precious and while it does not thwart God's sovereign work of revival in the hearts of his people, it does stand against extra-biblical measures. A third lesson, following on the first and second, is that there is no good place for individualism in the church. Tennent's penchant for doing whatever he perceived to elicit "smiles from heaven,"[59] landed him in a self-confidence that contradicts the biblical notion of the communion and interdependence of the saints. A fourth lesson concerns the power of feelings. If Charles Hodge is correct, and we think he is, the great schism of 1741 was not caused by lack of orthodoxy or disregard for biblical church government, it was caused by the "alienation of feeling" which was largely produced by the pietistic, revivalistic New Side men.[60] A church cannot long stand once alienation of affection occurs. Another obvious lesson is that zeal without love and knowledge may bring grave harm to the church. A sixth lesson from Tennent's life is his evangelistic zeal. While his pietism may have skewed his ecclesiastical activities, his zeal for communicating the gospel to the needy is exemplary and imitable. A final lesson which all should extract from this revivalist's life is that the sovereignty of God is an absolute truth. Despite the weaknesses of this controversial Presbyterian,

[59] Gilbert Tennent, *Remarks Upon a Protestation Presented to the Synod of Philadelphia* (Philadelphia: Benjamin Franklin, 1741) 4.

[60] Hodge, *Constitutional History*, 2:207.

much good came from his life. A life summarized in a final tribute from his Arch Street congregation.

> Under this marble are buried the remains of
> Gilbert Tennent,
> first pastor of this Church; . . .
> The son of William Tennent,
> born in Armagh, Ireland
> on February 5th, 1702;[61] . . .
> He was a prudent, experienced, venerable man;
> in manners and piety eminent; as a Husband, Brother, Father and Friend,
> among the most excellent:
> a bold, learned, faithful, successful
> Defender of true religion;
> and finally,
> a Christian without guile.
> The congregation, his former hearers,
> have caused his name
> to be commemorated by this eulogy.[62]

[61] 1702 is apparently the wrong date and should read 1703.

[62] Eulogy found in Coalter, *Gilbert Tennent,* 163–64.

8

Old Side / New Side Schism and Reunion

D. G. Hart

On June 1, 1741, the Synod of Philadelphia, the highest judicatory in the infant American Presbyterian Church, received a protest signed by a large group of its members that had dire consequences for Presbyterianism in the New World. Indeed, the author of the protest, Robert Cross, believed that the American church had reached a fork in the road. He maintained that the Presbyterian Church in colonial America was "in no small danger of expiring outright, and that quickly, as to the form, order and constitution of an organized church. . . ."[1] The protest went on to say in its introductory paragraphs that its signers were convinced that their "indispensable" duty was to try as much as possible "to preserve this swooning church from a total expiration." The way to save the church from death, then, was akin to the work of a surgeon removing a malignant tumor. It involved eliminating from the Presbyterian fold those members of synod who were guilty of "unwearied, unscriptural, antipresbyterial, uncharitable, divisive practices" in the previous twelve months especially but also for "some years before."[2]

Those assembled for Synod had little trouble discerning to whom this protest, written by Cross and signed by eleven other ministers and eight elders, referred. The signers hailed mainly from the Presbytery of Donegal, an area in southeastern Pennsylvania between Philadelphia and Lancaster. Yet, figuring out the parties involved is tricky because the word

[1] "Protestation of 1741," reprinted in Richard Webster, *A History of the Presbyterian Church in America from Its Origin until the Year 1760* (Philadelphia: Joseph M. Wilson, 1857) 166.

[2] Ibid., 166–67.

"protest" was in play on both sides of the issue. For starters, the 1741 statement delivered to and ratified by Synod went into the annals of American Presbyterian history as "The Protestation of 1741," thus identifying its author and signers as "protesters." But the Protestation, in attempting to identify the Presbyterians responsible for the impasse to which the young church had come, referred to those divisive ministers as "the protesting brethren."[3] Hence the protesters were protesting against the protesters. Translated, this description meant that the ministers and elders who signed the Protestation were objecting to members of Synod who had for the better part of a year been protesting against the power of presbyteries and Synod to make and enforce rules that determined the teaching and conduct of Synod's members. Those that the Protestation had specifically in view were ministers from the recently created Presbytery of New Brunswick, led by Gilbert Tennent and Samuel Blair, and who would play a major role in founding the College of New Jersey (later Princeton University). The division clarified by the Protestation was the one later referred to as the Old Side/New Side split of colonial Presbyterianism.

This division in American Presbyterianism has been the most difficult one to explain in the history of the church thanks in large part to the way it was eventually settled. Perhaps the most significant aspect of the conundrum of the Old Side/New Side division was theological. The New Side party promoted revivals and in turn made an issue out of whether ministers supported these awakenings as evidence of God's work among the colonies. In addition, the New Side was generally Calvinistic in its understanding of the doctrines of grace, stressing that people could not be saved by any meritorious work on their part. Institutionally, the New Side established Princeton as a beach head for their labors, first with the College, which later in 1812 became a propitious cite for the establishment of Princeton Theological Seminary. All of these factors have prompted contemporary American Presbyterians to look favorably upon the New Side in the division of 1741 and to regard their opponents, the Old Side, as obstructers of the work of God and the growth of the Presbyterian Church.

Still, the picture becomes murkier when examining those figures in the shadows and others somewhat removed from the center of the frame. On closer inspection, the Old Side was the conservative party that was trying to uphold strict subscription to the Westminster Standards as well as Presbyterian polity as the divinely revealed rule for Christ's church. In fact, one of the Old Side's complaints against the revivals of the First Great

[3] Ibid., 168.

Awakening, even if generating genuine conversions, was that a true work of God could never be the source of division or acrimony in the church. Here the New Side did not distinguish itself as the party dedicated to preserving the peace and purity of the church. Its leaders regularly conducted themselves in ways that undermined the ministry of pastors in good standing. What is more, in later histories of colonial Presbyterianism not only have evangelical but also mainline church historians sided with the New Side, an alignment of interests that should strike many as curious.[4] If mainline Presbyterian historians, some of whom were outspokenly critical of conservatives in the Orthodox Presbyterian Church and of evangelicals at Fuller Seminary, saw the New Side as the "good guys" in colonial Presbyterianism, then surely more is going on in that struggle than any simple break down between evangelicals and liberals will allow.[5] The following chapter examines the controversy with an eye to the claims made in the Protestation of 1741. What this episode in colonial American Presbyterian history suggests is that the controversy among the original American Presbyterians determined to a large degree the character of Presbyterianism in the United States, even to the point of misreading the significance of the Old Side/New Side controversy.[6]

[4] Compare, for example, the positive assessments of the First Great Awakening offered by Leonard J. Trinterud, *The Forming of an American Tradition: A Re-Examination of Colonial Presbyterianism* (Philadelphia: Westminster, 1949); and Iain H. Murray, *Revival and Revivalism: The Making and Marring of American Evangelicalism, 1750–1858* (Edinburgh: Banner of Truth Trust, 1994).

[5] Trinterud wrote the report for the PCUSA which studied whether the call to teach at Fuller Seminary constituted a legitimate one according to the Presbyterian constitution. This statement also clarified the constitutional basis for the Mandate of 1934 which ruled the illegality of being a member of a parachurch organization, in this case, J. Gresham Machen's Independent Board for Presbyterian Foreign Missions. See "Los Angeles Presbytery Memorial," Presbyterian Church in the U.S.A. General Assembly, *Minutes* (1953) 110–33.

[6] The literature on colonial American Presbyterianism is by no means skimpy, but neither is it as thorough as it might be. This is partly the function of the decline of denominational history during the last thirty years. As such, Trinterud's *Forming of an American Tradition* remains the unsurpassed study of Presbyterians in the period. Other works that have informed this chapter, aside from those cited, are: Milton J. Coalter Jr., *Gilbert Tennent, Son of Thunder: A Case Study of Continental Pietism's Impact on the First Great Awakening in the Middle Colonies* (Westport, CT: Greenwood, 1986); Leigh Eric Schmidt, *Holy Fairs: Scottish Communions and American Revivals in the Early Modern Period* (Princeton: Princeton University Press, 1989); Marilyn J. Westerkamp, *Triumph of the Laity: Scots-Irish Piety and the Great Awakening, 1625–1760* (New York: Oxford University Press, 1988); and Bryan F. LeBeau, *Jonathan Dickinson and the Formative Years of American Presbyterianism* (Lexington: University of Kentucky Press, 1997); Guy Soulliard Klett, *Presbyterians in Co-*

Indecently and Without Order

One theme dominated the Protestation of 1741—namely, order. The ministers and elders who signed the protest were intent to preserve the moderation, uniformity and control within the young Presbyterian church. And they were convinced that the New Side Presbyterians, mainly operating in the Presbytery of New Brunswick, were essentially disorderly in the way they conducted themselves, related to other presbyters, and even in their patterns of pastoral ministry. The seven examples the Old Side cited as support for their motions to dismiss the New Side from Synod were all variations on the need for some authoritative norm in the church and the disorder fomented by the other party. First, specific New Side pastors had denied "that presbyteries have authority to oblige their dissenting members" and that Synod's decisions in appeals and references was merely the rendering of "their best advice." Second, the Presbytery of New Brunswick had defied Synod by ordaining men "in contempt of" guidelines set down by Synod. Third, the New Side's practice of itinerant preaching took them uninvited to towns where their preaching competed with that of the local settled clergy. These "irregular irruptions upon the congregations to which they have no immediate relation" were responsible for sowing the "seeds of division."[7] Fourth, the New Side's "rash judging and condemning all who do not fall in with their measures" was another source of division in the infant church.

If the New Side's activities upset the corporate order and authority of church authorities, according to the Protestation, the New Side's theology also indicated a chaotic scheme of grace and divine activity that was disruptive for individual Christians. Here the Old Side's fifth example of error concerned God's call to men for the ministry. The Protestation asserted that the New Side taught people the internal call from God "does not consist in their being regularly ordained and set apart to that work." Instead, it involved "invisible motions and workings of the Spirit" that were known exclusively by the man experiencing the call. Sixth, the New Side preached "the terrors of the law" in a manner that disrupted the lives of hearers and prompted them to respond in disorderly and unbecoming ways. This style of proclamation was designed to work on "the passions and affections of weak minds, as to cause them to cry out in a hideous manner, and fall

lonial Pennsylvania (Philadelphia: University of Pennsylvania Press, 1937); Ned Landsman, *Scotland and Its First American Colony* (Princeton: Princeton University Press, 1985); and Elizabeth I. Nybakken, "New Light on the Old Side: Irish Influences on Colonial Presbyterianism," *Journal of American History* 68 (1981–82) 813–32.

[7] "Protestation," 169.

down in convulsion-like fits. . . ."[8] Finally, the Protestation complained that the form of assurance promoted by the New Side made converts so certain about their own conversion and faith that they were incapable of carrying on an orderly relationship with their pastor. The faith of conversion gave believers the confidence that they "were under no sacred tie or relation to their pastors . . . but may leave them when they please, and ought to go where they think they get most good."[9]

This was a fairly long list of grievances and each point was designed to make obvious the need for Synod to defend its legitimate authority and to eject those who would not abide by its rules and procedures. In some ways, one could read the Protestation as a technical affirmation of the Presbyterian concern for decency and order. But these matters went deeper than simply whether the Form of Church Government was still in effect. It also indicated an organic connection between church order and theology, or between the form of practice and the content of faith. Here the declaration of George Whitefield in 1740 is instructive, the revivalist who turned the colonial awakenings into one singularly great and who garnered the support of most New Side Presbyterians. After over a year of itinerant preaching in the American colonies among the variety of Protestant groups represented, the evangelist concluded, "It was best to preach the new birth, and the power of godliness, and not to insist so much on the form: for people would never be brought to one mind as to that; nor did Jesus Christ ever intend it."[10] As much as Whitefield's sentiment would eventually dominate evangelical Protestantism, Old Side Presbyterians were questioning precisely this formulation. For them forms such as creeds and church polity did matter and Reformed Christianity possessed patterns of ministry and teaching that could not be dismissed in favor of the mysterious workings of the Spirit or heart-felt expressions of Christian sincerity. Forms and content were much more intimately connected than the revivalists supposed.

Even ten years before Whitefield's remark, a consensus on forms in the young American church was fragile. In 1729 Synod had embraced the Westminster Standards as the basis for holding office through the Adopting Act. Presbyterian interpreters have generally come to two different conclusions about the form of subscription implied by Synod's action.

[8] Ibid., 170.

[9] Ibid.

[10] *George Whitefield's Journals* (London: Banner of Truth, 1960) 458, quoted in Mark A. Noll, *The Rise of Evangelicalism: The Age of Edwards, Whitefield and the Wesleys* (Downers Grove, Ill.: InterVarsity, 2003) 15.

Conservatives read the Act as requiring a tight form of subscription that only allowed dissent on the Westminster Divines' teaching about the civil magistrate. More liberal renderings put great weight upon the words, "essential and necessary," and conclude that men who could affirm the basic truths of the Westminster Standards, as deciphered by their presbyteries, were eligible for licensure and ordination.[11]

Still, beyond the question of the strictness of subscription lay an equally troubling issue, namely, that of church power. Some ministers like Jonathan Dickinson, pastor in Elizabethtown, New Jersey, argued against subscription because it violated liberty of conscience. "I have no worse opinion of the Assemblies Confession," he explained, "for the second article in the twentieth chapter; 'God alone is Lord of the Conscience, &c. . . .' and I must tell you that to subscribe this article, and *impose* the rest, appears to me the most glorious contradiction."[12] Those who argued for subscription, such as John Thomson of Lewes, Delaware, believed that carefully adhered to doctrinal standards would not only fortify the witness of Presbyterians but that the church possessed the authority to require such doctrinal conformity from its officers. "As an ecclesiastical jurisdiction of Christ," Thomson wrote, "clothed with ministerial authority to act in concert in behalf of truth and in opposition to error," the church was within its rights to adopt the Standards.[13] Consequently, well before the difficulties of the 1740s over order and uniformity in the church spawned by revivalism, American Presbyterians were divided over the very form that such order could take, with some regarding even subscription as an instance of ecclesiastical tyranny and others contending that placing limits on acceptable views was part of the work Christ called his church to perform.

[11] For examples of the diversity of views on subscription among American Presbyterians, see David W. Hall, ed., *The Practice of Confessional Subscription* (Oak Ridge, TN: Covenant Foundation, 1997).

[12] Letter of Jonathan Dickinson, April 10, 1729, quoted in Charles Briggs, *American Presbyterianism: Its Origin and Early History* (Edinburgh: T. & T. Clark, 1885) 213.

[13] Thomson, as quoted in Briggs, *American Presbyterianism*, 211. Worth noting is that Thomson's understanding of church power is closer than Dickinson's to the Westminster Confession of Faith, Chap. 20 on liberty of conscience, which reads "because the powers which God hath ordained, and the liberty which Christ hath purchased, are not intended by God to destroy, but mutually to uphold and preserve one another, they who, upon pretense of Christian liberty, shall oppose any lawful power, or the lawful exercise of it, whether it be civil or ecclesiastical, resist the ordinance of God" (paragraph 4).

Into the fragile settlement to emerge from the Adopting Act of 1729 came the challenge of a new form of Protestant devotion, later known as revivalism. The Scottish clan largely responsible for introducing a new factor into colonial Presbyterianism was the Tennent family. The father, William, Sr., originally ordained an Anglican in the established church in Northern Ireland, in 1718 brought his family to the British colonies. His first stop was in Bedford, New York, where he joined forces with Presbyterians. From there in 1727 he relocated to Bucks County, Pennsylvania, just north of Philadelphia, where the elder Tennent established an academy, the Log College, an institution whose students were known for their promotion of revivalism. Although by the 1730s the Log College would become a major source of controversy within the Synod of Philadelphia, arguably the Tennents' most factious contribution was the oldest son, Gilbert Tennent. After receiving his undergraduate training at Yale College, Gilbert ministered briefly in Delaware before taking a call to the Presbyterian church in New Brunswick, New Jersey. There the introspective piety that he learned from the Puritans at Yale received additional support from the Dutch pietism of the nearby Reformed minister, Theodore Frelinghuysen, who sought greater zeal from his flock and new conversions by preaching "the terrors of the law." This was a technique designed literally to scare hearers into turning to Christ in faith and repentance.[14]

Another twist in the younger Tennent's ministry, something likely learned from Frelinghuysen, was a pattern of pastoral visitation that went beyond the accepted practices of ministers' interactions with their congregations. The New Brunswick pastor later described his method to George Whitefield in the following way:

> Since you were here, I have been among my people dealing with them plainly about their souls' state in their houses; examining them one by one as to their experiences, and telling natural people the danger of their state; and exhorting them that were totally secure, to seek convictions; and those that were convinced, to seek Jesus Christ; and reproved pious people for their faults; and blessed be God, I have seen hopeful appearances of concern amongst a pretty many in the places I belong to.[15]

The reason behind Tennent's approach was to be able to decipher the different states of the people in his congregation. He believed that his

[14] On Tennent Coalter's *Gilbert Tennent, Son of Thunder,* remains the best study.

[15] Tennent to Whitefield, in J. Gillies, *Historical Collections*, 350, quoted in Trinterud, *Forming of An American Tradition*, 59–60.

hearers could be divided into four classes: first, those converted who had a comfortable assurance; second, those seeking conversion but not satisfied with progress; third, people who needed help and were not awakened to their need; and finally, rebellious headstrong sinners. Tennent believed that older forms of ministry were insufficiently attentive to these different stages of spiritual life and his style of preaching and visitation was designed to redress the problem. Ultimately, his purpose, like some strains of Puritanism and pietism, was to eliminate nominal Christianity, that is, church goers who simply went through the motions or only had an external awareness of the gospel. By preaching intensely about the perilous state of the unconverted and by following up with pastoral counsel to foster greater awareness among the flock about their personal dedication to Christ, Tennent hoped to yield a greater sense of assurance and more strenuous forms of Christian devotion.

The initial returns on Tennent's labors were not entirely favorable. In fact, to some of the older Presbyterian ministers these revivalistic practices looked bizarre. In 1733 Synod received an overture, which was eventually passed, that called upon Presbyterian ministers "to use some proper means to revive the declining power of godliness." The remedy recommended was not the new one advocated by Tennent but the older practices outlined in the Westminster Directory. Here Synod believed that ministers should visit with families, but in doing so they should press upon them the importance of "family and secret worship," and inquire of members their "diligence" in the pursuit of such practices.[16] The message implicit here was that Tennent's methods were too personal and intimate, prompting an introspective piety that could easily subvert the regular ministry of pastors and their relationship to members of the congregation. This vote by Synod in 1733 was the first sign of the emergence of an anti-revival party and it seemed to coincide with most of those Presbyterians who advocated subscription since in 1734 Synod followed up with an overture, also ratified, that recommended to presbyteries that they be more diligent in requiring subscription from those licensed and ordained to the ministry of the word. Interestingly enough, Tennent also brought to the 1734 Synod an overture recommending that presbyteries examine candidates about their "experiential knowledge" of salvation.[17] The following year Synod tried to split the difference by passing two overtures, one urging greater scrupulousness

[16] *Records, Presbyterian Church U.S.A.*, quoted in Trinterud, *Forming of An American Tradition*, 61.

[17] Ibid., 62.

in admitting men to the ministry—a concession to the anti-subscriptionists—the other for ministers to be adequately diligent in their pastoral relations with their congregants—the concern of Tennent and other proponents of revival.

Important to notice about the issues that the Tennents introduced into colonial Presbyterianism is that revivalism gave a new twist to the older debate between subscriptionists and anti-subscriptionists. The question now was not one of liberty of conscience versus church power but of a faith enlivened by the working of the Spirit versus a faith ordered by properly ordained ministers and a disciplined body of presbyters. The revivalists' brief for the Spirit did not line up exactly with the concerns of the anti-subscriptionists. But for the defenders of order in and the rightful authority of the church, revivalism and liberty of conscience seemed to be making the same challenge, namely, whether the rules and procedures established by Synod were necessary for a faithful church. Leonard Trinterud summarized the difference between subscriptionists and anti-subscriptionists well, and what this divergence meant for the reception of revivalism:

> An unworthy minister in the eyes of the subscriptionists was one whose ideas were out of harmony with the authoritatively established creed. To Dickinson (a moderate), an unworthy minister was one who was unregenerate, unethical, and careless in his holy calling, whatever his creedal notions were. When accordingly, these two groups joined in confessing that their infant church was in danger from unworthy ministers, in danger from straying from the true Gospel, and that urgent measures were needed, it is not remarkable that their plans for reform proved well-nigh irreconcilable. As long as Dickinson and some of the moderate Scotch-Irish ministers could keep the compromise symbolized in the adopting act alive and in force, there was hope of co-operation and success.[18]

In addition to the challenge posed by Gilbert Tennent's pietistic Presbyterianism, the Tennent family's influence included more than simply the personal idiosyncracies of father and sons. Revivalism threatened the young American church at an institutional level as well through the instruction and graduates of Log College, the school located outside Philadelphia through which William, Sr. trained men preparing for the ministry. Founded in 1735, the new school became another battleground in the contest between those favoring a regulated and uniform church

[18] Ibid., 51.

and those who were more nonchalant about the Presbyterian hierarchy and stressed the importance of the local congregation. Some objected to the new school because it offered an education inferior to the one that universities in Scotland and Ireland provided. These opponents of the Log College argued that prospective Presbyterian ministers should be trained either in the Old World at Glasgow or Edinburgh, or in the New World at Harvard or Yale, institutions where the standards were high and the curriculum predictable. Defenders of Log College countered that the senior Tennent's instruction was virtually identical to his own training in Scotland, thus making the school's academic reputation as reliable as older, more established institutions. Since college instruction at the time relied more on directed readings than on lectures, Log College might well have been able to rival at least its New World competitors. A crucial factor in that calculation would be the quality of Tennent's library and whether he could match the texts assigned at the older colleges or universities.[19]

Underneath concerns about academic standards was one about the spiritual ethos of Log College. Students might have received an education the equivalent of one offered elsewhere, but were they also imbibing the devotional brew that the Tennents mixed in their ideal of introspective piety and the Presbyterian pastor's duty to nurture it? Log College, consequently, raised not only the issue of educational standards for a learned Presbyterian ministry but also that of revivalism and its promotion of heart religion. Was instruction in the liberal arts and theology what a man training for the ministry needed or should he also have a conversion experience and recognize his duty as a pastor to encourage such a personal encounter with divine mercy among his congregation?

Nevertheless, aside from the quality of education, political maneuvering in the Synod of Philadelphia was also an important factor that shaped perceptions of Log College and the sort of theological education that the Presbyterian Church expected for men to be qualified for licensure and ordination. The new school threatened to change dramatically the character of the young church because of the constant need for ministers and the lack of colleges or universities under Presbyterian control. Most of the pastors had either trained in Scotland if they had been born in Great Britain or at Harvard or Yale if born in America. Some of the tensions surrounding subscription may have stemmed from this difference. But Log College threatened to up end this minor rivalry by becoming the major

[19] For some background on New Side theological education, see Nina Reid-Maroney, "Science and the Presbyterian Academies," in *Theological Education in the Evangelical Tradition,* ed. D. G. Hart and R. Albert Mohler Jr. (Grand Rapids: Baker, 1996) 203–16.

source of Presbyterian pastors because it was conveniently located near the most populous presbyteries and it was run by members of Synod. The older party that favored subscription was particularly suspicious of the new school because subscriptionists lacked their own training ground and because the institutions with which they were most comfortable were across the Atlantic ocean. In the 1740s the Old Side would try to start their own school in Delaware, an academy from which the University of Delaware eventually emerged. But this effort failed and the Old Side resorted to relying on the University of Pennsylvania in Philadelphia, a school at which some of their ministers taught but was interdenominational at best. Meanwhile, Log College provided the resources and institutional impetus for the formation of the College of New Jersey in Princeton. Whatever the theological affiliation of the various schools, the second generation of Presbyterians knew that they could not rely on British universities to supply the ministers needed to nurture the American church.[20]

Despite the friction created by Log College, the Synod of Philadelphia continued to try to accommodate the Tennents and the men they were training. On the one hand, Synod continued to be in the hands of ministers who insisted on subscription to the Westminster Standards for ordination. In 1736, only a year after Log College's formal beginning, Synod passed a motion that interpreted the Adopting Act of 1729 in a strict or conservative manner; it placed the emphasis on subscribing the entirety of the Confession and Catechisms except for teaching on the civil magistrate instead of requiring only adherence to the "essential and necessary" articles as some presbyteries were interpreting it. On the other hand, although this ruling might have implied a measure of hostility to any minister or party that would place other qualifications for ministry higher than subscription, two years later Synod approved the creation of the Presbyterian of New Brunswick in the region of New Jersey north of Trenton. This new presbytery became in effect the pro-revival judicatory, the place where many of the graduates of Log College ministered, and accounts for the eventual relocation of Log College to Princeton in 1746, reconstituted as the College of New Jersey. Clearly, the new form of ministry and piety encouraged by the Tennents and Log College had upset the fragile balance of the young American church. Just as clear, however, were the signs that members of Synod were going to attempt to work with the new style of Presbyterianism while also trying to ease older tensions over subscrip-

[20] On Presbyterian higher education in the colonial era, see Howard Miller, *The Revolutionary College: American Presbyterian Higher Education, 1707–1837* (New York: New York University Press, 1976).

tion. In other words, American Presbyterians were still hoping to form an orderly and disciplined church no matter how disorderly some of its ministers and congregations might appear.

The crisis of revivalism among Presbyterians culminated with the advent of George Whitefield, the extraordinarily energetic Anglican itinerant evangelist who transformed the local awakenings of the 1730s into a trans-Atlantic quickening that contemporaries and historians called "Great." He had come to North America to raise money for an orphanage in Georgia and consequently traveled throughout the colonies speaking and preaching wherever he could. Whitefield was no ordinary fund-raiser, however. His power of delivery alone accounted for much of his appeal. Jonathan Edwards' wife, Sarah, remarked that Whitefield was "a born orator." "You have already heard his deep-toned, yet clear and melodious voice," she continued. "It is wonderful to see what a spell he casts over the audience by proclaiming the simplest truths of the Bible. I have seen upwards of a thousand people hang on his words with breathless silence, broken only by an occasional sob."[21] Another aspect of the sensation surrounding Whitefield was the publicity that he generated and cultivated. The large crowds and related success of his revivals attracted coverage in the press and Whitefield himself, having learned the benefits of publicity, used advertizing to set the stage for his speaking engagements in the larger towns and cities.

Another important ingredient in Whitefield's appeal was one that also proved to be the most offensive to some of the Presbyterian Church's opponents of revivalism. The evangelist's itinerancy was a cause of great concern to settled clergy. Not only did ordinary pastors suffer in comparison to the eloquence of a noted celebrity visiting their town, especially since Whitefield could deliver the same sermons over and over while ministers in local congregations needed to prepare new sermons each and every week. But in many cases Whitefield would arrive in a place without an invitation from the local clergy and preach to anyone who assembled to hear him. In the eighteenth century when state churches were the norm and religion was part of the social order, Whitefield's brand of itinerancy was a direct threat to clerical authority. Even in places like the middle colonies where a religious establishment was non-existent, Whitefield's uninvited appearance in a town often generated rivalry with the settled pastors who were naturally concerned over what their church members might be

[21] Letter of Sarah Edwards, Oct. 22, 1740, quoted in Harry S. Stout, *The Divine Dramatist: George Whitefield and the Rise of Modern Evangelicalism* (Grand Rapids: Eerdmans, 1991) 127.

exposed to from someone whose methods appeared to be questionable and whose preaching style struck some as manipulative.

Itinerancy was already an issue in the Presbyterian Church before Whitefield underscored revivalism's threat to the legitimate authority of pastors, presbyteries and Synod. The Tennents and other ministers in their circle had already begun to travel to preach in places without the permission of Synod or the local presbytery. Some of this irregularity was the understandable result of a society still in flux and people living in areas without regular pulpit supply. In fact, many of the earliest Presbyterian ministers in America engaged in itinerancy for a living because clergy were few and Presbyterians were scattered over large areas. But when itinerancy was tied to questionable and novel tactics and bred factionalism, it moved from simply a condition of ministering on the frontier to something that threatened the order and stability of the Presbyterian Church. One effort to regularize the itinerancy of the Tennents was the construction in 1738 of the Presbytery of New Brunswick, an area originally but unnaturally within the bounds of the Presbytery of Philadelphia. If revivalists were going to preach in an area without authorization, why not turn that locale into a presbytery that the revivalists themselves would oversee? This was one effort to solve the problem of itinerancy.

But the Presbyterian answer was no match for the Anglican evangelist, Whitefield. His elevation of the experiential over the formal, mentioned at the outset of this essay, led him to be indiscriminate about where he preached and with whom he associated. Indeed, Whitefield's larger than life presence, something that even endeared him to the skeptical Benjamin Franklin, further polarized the already conflicted Presbyterian Church. To say that the Great Awakening split the church into pro- and anti-revivalist factions is accurate but misses what may be a better way of describing the different groups in the church. Whitefield's conduct revealed that those Presbyterians associated with the Log College and in the vicinity of the Presbytery of New Brunswick were revivalists first and Presbyterians second. On the other side were ministers who stressed Presbyterianism as the proper context for revival, meaning that the work of the Spirit needed to be orderly and disciplined, not chaotic and enthusiastic. Whitefield's disregard for denominational forms, along with revivalistic Presbyterians' indifference to the rules and procedures of their own communion for the sake of the Awakening, greatly troubled those ministers who were already upset by the irregularities of Log College, the Tennents, and their associates.

For instance, between 1739 the time of Whitefield's arrival, and 1741, the date of the Old Side's Protestation, these two groups of Presbyterians squared off on the degree to which the revivals were of benefit to the church. Presbyterian traditionalists published a set of their concerns under the group name of "The Querists." In their reply to a letter from Whitefield in which he defended the revivals as a work of God, these critics of the revivals summarized their concerns about the order and stability of the institutional church. For them, Whitefield and the revivals of the Great Awakening were characterized by anarchy and enthusiasm. His methods and teachings were not simply objectionable to Presbyterian teaching and ecclesiology but even to the norms of the Church of England. The Querists asked Whitefield:

> How can you reconcile Gospel-Order with the vain, disorderly and illegal Practice of Men's conducing their Deportment, as Church-Members one to another, according to the blind Guesses Men form of one another's carnal or gracious State, upon the bare verbal Declaration of their Experiences? And seeing every ordinary Minister is called to the Oversight of a particular Flock; where is the Order and Decency of leaving a Man's own Flock, and industriously entering other Men's Labours? When Men strive so hard to dissolve the solemn Tye of the sacred Relation between Ministers and People, under the Notion of Liberty; why may not they plead for the same Liberty in other Relations, if it may be supposed to be for the Benefit of the *Orphan-House in Georgia*?[22]

The point of these rhetorical questions was that because God is a God of order, not chaos, his works will necessarily encourage regularity and stability in his church. As they concluded in their reply, "If therefore Mr. *Whitefield*, and others, have good Designs, it is our hearty Prayer that they may be directed to take God's Way to prosecute them, for God's Glory and Welfare of his Church." Otherwise, the revivals would end up corrupting "the true Power of Godliness and the Order of God's House, under the fair Pretence of Declaiming against the Corruption of the Times, when in Reality none more corrupt than themselves, and their corruption never broke out faster than at present."[23]

[22] The Querists, *A Short Reply to Mr. Whitefield's Letter Which he wrote in answer to the Querists. . .* (Philadelphia, 1741), reprinted in *The Great Awakening: Documents Illustrating the Crisis and Its Consequences,* ed. Alan Heimert and Perry Miller (Indianapolis, IN: Bobbs-Merrill, 1967) 141.

[23] Ibid., 145, 146.

But the proponents of revival were not convinced by the arguments for decency and order because they looked for a different sort of evidence of God's saving work. Their model was not the corporate one of a disciplined church but the personal one of an individual Christian zealously pursing a godly life. Samuel Blair, the pastor of Fagg's Manor church just outside Philadelphia, for instance, responded to the Querists by calling them formalists, "who are entirely destitute of the powerful Operations of the regenerating sanctifying Spirit of God, who can tell nothing of live Heart-Exercises in Religion, nothing of deep Heart-Distress for Sin and Guilt, of the lively Power and Consolations of Faith in the Redeemer. . . ."[24] Samuel Finley, another member of the Tennent circle who would be the fifth president of the College of New Jersey, argued in a similar fashion in a sermon during the months leading up to the Protestation. He believed that the Old Side was guilty of an inconsistency in the way they evaluated the revival. Finley caricatured them as arguing that "A dry Formalist, who shows no Relish, nor Power of Godliness, [but] seems to live chaste, honest and sober,"—such a person was deemed a genuine believer. But someone "who was drunken and unclean, becomes chaste and sober, lively and zealous withal" through the benefits of conversion, the Old Side regarded as having been influenced by "the Power of the Devil."[25] For Finley this kind of evaluation of the Great Awakening was "plainly the unpardonable Sin."[26] He added by warning his hearers not to resist "these Evidences that are as clear as you are capable of, until God give you to know the Things of his Spirit." If they did doubt, "it will be more tolerable for *Sodom* and *Gomorrah* for *Tyre* and *Sidon*, in the Day of Judgment," than for such critics of the Awakening.[27]

The problem with such accusations against critics of revival was that the Awakening's proponents failed to address the question of church authority and order. The closest they came was to try to show that if they were splitting the church, they had good precedent from church history for doing so, whether Christ and the apostles against the Jewish authorities, or the Protestant Reformers against Rome. Nevertheless, a concession of creating mistrust and antagonism in the church did not prove that the revivals' critics lacked the authority and responsibility to judge

[24] Samuel Blair, *A Particular Consideration of a Piece, Entitled, The Querists* . . . (Philadelphia, 1741), reprinted in Heimert and Miller, eds., *Great Awakening*, 131.

[25] Samuel Finley, *Christ Triumphing, and Satan Raging. A Sermon on Matt. 12:28* . . . (Philadelphia, 1741), reprinted in Heimert and Miller, eds., *Great Awakening*, 163–64.

[26] Ibid., 164.

[27] Ibid., 167.

whether the Awakening was in fact a work of God. The Old Side began with church authority as a given, thus invalidating the revivalists' charge that anyone opposed to the revivals was unregenerate or committing the unpardonable sin. This was exactly one of the points that John Thomson made in his book, *The Government of the Church of Christ* (1741). The two sides held "vastly different and opposite Judgment and Sentiments . . . of Church Government." He explained that it was plain from the revivalists' remarks that "Presbyteries and Synods, when regularly constituted, have no Authority at all, . . . either over their Members or People. . ."[28] And because of the basic disrespect that the revivalists showed for the deliberations and rulings of Synod, Thomson and other Old Side ministers questioned whether "Irregularity, Anarchy and Confusion were the Properest Means to restore the decayed Life of Religion . . ."[29]

Left with this accusation, the most compelling response was to charge the existing Presbyterian authorities of unbelief, thereby denying the legitimacy of their power. This was in fact the logic of Gilbert Tennent's most controversial contribution to the conflict, his sermon, "The Danger of An Unconverted Ministry" (1740), the proverbial straw that broke the camel's back. His initial proposition was not entirely controversial, namely, that "Natural Men have no Call of GOD to the Ministerial Work under the Gospel-Dispensation."[30] From this assertion Tennent had little trouble showing how unprofitable the ministry of such unconverted men. Nor did he back away from the implication that if church members sat under such unregenerate ministers, "Then it is both lawful and expedient to go from them to hear Godly Persons."[31] Indeed, "To bind Men to a particular Minister, against their Judgment and Inclinations, when they are more edified elsewhere, is carnal with a Witness; a cruel Oppression of tender Consciences, a compelling of Men to Sin: For he that doubts, is damn'd if he eat; and whatsoever is not of Faith, is Sin."[32] Although Tennent did not take the next step in his logic it was already evident in his actions that a similar verdict applied to members of Synod who were bound to uncon-

[28] John Thomson, *The Government of the Church of Christ, and the Authority of the Church Judicatories* . . . (Philadelphia, 1741), reprinted in Heimert and Miller, eds., *Great Awakening*, 113.

[29] Ibid., 121.

[30] Gilbert Tennent, *The Danger of an Unconverted Ministry, Considered in a Sermon on Mark 6:34* . . . (2d ed., Philadelphia, 1741), reprinted in Heimert and Miller, *Great Awakening*, 76.

[31] Ibid., 87.

[32] Ibid., 89.

verted ministers ruling over them in church courts. If church members could rightfully disregard and leave their minister in search of a regenerate man, so too Presbyterian ministers could not be bound by the determinations of godless men through the agency of Synod or presbytery.

Aside from being an obvious recipe for anarchy, as Thomson and others noted, it was also a break with Reformed teaching about the nature of pastoral office and church authority. At least one of the Reformed churches had included in its confession of faith the idea that the authority of the minister did not depend on his status as a regenerate believer. The Second Helvetic Confession, chapter nineteen, for instance, has a lengthy description of the power and authority of ministers. "The ecclesiastical power of the ministers of the Church," it declares, "is that function whereby they indeed govern the Church of God, but yet so do all things in the Church as the Lord has prescribed in his Word." This authority was an objective one that Christ delegated to his church. So strong was this authority that the efficacy of the minister did not depend on his spiritual state. The Second Helvetic Confession added that "we know that the voice of Christ is to be heard, though it be out of the mouths of evil ministers." The Confession made a very similar point in its opening chapter on the Word of God where it asserted that the preaching of ministers "lawfully called" was "the very Word of God," even "if he be evil and a sinner, nevertheless the Word of God remains still true and good." Of course, Heinrich Bullinger, the author of the Second Helvetic Confession, was not implying that the ordination of sinful, evil or unregenerate men to the ministry was desirable. He was only stating the obvious conclusions to follow from both the Donatist controversy and the Protestant doctrine of the office of the keys of the kingdom. From the former Protestants deduced that the efficacy of the ministry of word and sacrament is not dependent on the pastor but on the God who ordained and promised to bless those instruments. From the office of the keys Protestants also taught that ministers held legitimate authority to open and shut the gates of heaven through the power Christ delegated to the "stewards of the mysteries of God." New Side Presbyterians, however, seemed to be unaware of this teaching. More important, by tying the efficacy of the ministry to a pastor or evangelist's regeneration they were close to repeating the error of the Donatists, one that had been condemned throughout the history of the church by Roman Catholics and Protestants alike.

With the Great Awakening, then, the young American Presbyterian Church faced a substantial crisis of authority. Even before the revivals of Tennent and Whitefield, the debates over subscription had revealed reservations among some members of Synod, especially those from New England Puritan backgrounds, over the power of the church to set the theological boundaries for licensure and ordination. But the revivals put the question of church power in a new light, taking the liberty of conscience advocated by anti-subscriptionists and adding to it the free operation of the Spirit. From this angle, concerns about church power and ordered relations among ministers, presbyteries and Synod looked to the proponents of revivals like barriers or impediments to an amazing work of God. But in so construing the revival, the advocates of the Awakening separated the work of the Spirit from the ministry of the church. This was a distinction that most of the Old Side ministers were unprepared to make. This is why the Protestation presented to the Synod of 1741 that initiated the breach between the Old and New Side Presbyterians summarized its signers' grievances by asserting that the pro-revival party's "principles and practices are so diametrically opposite to our doctrine, and principles of government and order, which the great King of the Church hath laid down in his word."[33]

From Protestation to Reunion

The Synod of 1741 was not actually the time of the final break between the Old and New Side Presbyterians. But the issues that prompted the Old Siders to issue the Protestation of 1741 were substantially the same for the next four years before the formal divide between Old and New Sides with each group having its own Synod. Moderates on both sides of the Synod of Philadelphia, such as Jonathan Dickinson, a supporter of the revivals, and George Gillespie, a defender of church authority, tried to work out a compromise that would keep the New Brunswick men within the church. In 1742 Synod addressed the matter and the signers of the Protestation were adamant that Tennent and other revivalists remain excluded from Synod until they repented for their conduct and manner. The next year Synod received two sets of proposals, one from the Old Side again insisting on the terms of the original Protestation, the other from the Presbytery of New York, led by Dickinson, which urged that the Protestation be withdrawn and that laid out procedures for dealing with grievances among members of Synod. Synod rejected this compromise, a decision that prompted the New Yorkers after another year of negotiations to found their own ecclesiastical body. On September 19, 1745 the Presbytery of New York joined with the Presbyteries of Londonderry and New Brunswick to found the

[33] "Protestation," 170.

Synod of New York. It was in effect, the New Side Synod with Philadelphia remaining Old Side. But unlike the frustration reflected in the Protestation of 1741, the Synod of Philadelphia's determination to allow New York to withdraw implied resignation and good will. "Though we judge they have no just ground to withdraw from us," the Old Side Synod declared, "yet . . . we shall endeavour to maintain charitable and christian affections toward them, and show the same upon all occasions by such correspondence as we shall think duty, and consistent with a good conscience."[34]

The good will explicit in the Synod of Philadelphia's decision carried over even to the staunchest revivalists who had accused their opponents of being unregenerate or sinning against the Holy Spirit. In 1749, for instance, Gilbert Tennent more or less recanted from the vituperation of his earlier, "Danger of an Unconverted Ministry." By then he had moved to Philadelphia to pastor a New Side congregation in the heart of Old Side Philadelphia, a transfer that may have enabled Tennent to see another side of his antagonists. He also had witnessed the excesses of the revival that forced him and other revivalists to try to distinguish themselves from the enthusiasm that gave the Awakening a bad name. His 1749 sermon, "*Irenicum Ecclesiasticum,*" was based on 1 Cor. 1 and the problems of factionalism in the church. Tennent conceded that the revival party had been guilty of this by "cruel and censorious Judging" of those whose states "we know not."[35] Tennent also cautioned his hearers against pride and implied that he and his co-revivalists may have been guilty of it. "Pride inclines us to obtrude with Violence our Opinion even in lesser Things upon others, and unjustly deny them the Liberty we desire for ourselves. . ."[36] Even so, Tennent was not willing to say that the Awakening's understanding of religious experience and conversion was in error, only that its proponents may have gone overboard. Tennent was still convinced that the Awakening's insistence upon the need for conversion was correct and that it was clearly taught both by Scripture and the Westminster Standards.[37] He also attempted to smooth off the edges of his earlier sermon by explaining that the unconverted he had in mind were "principally and directly *erroneous* and *heretical Teachers.*" But "to *separate* from such as are sound in essen-

[34] *Records, Presbyterian Church, U.S.A.*, 163, quoted in Briggs, *American Presbyterianism*, 269.

[35] Gilbert Tennent, *Irenicum Ecclesiasticum, or a Humble Impartial Essay upon the Peace of Jerusalem* . . . (Philadelphia, 1749), reprinted in Heimert and Miller, eds., *Great Awakening*, 371.

[36] Ibid., 374.

[37] Ibid., 370.

tial and necessary Articles, of Faith, regular in Life, and edifying in their Ministry, merely or only because they differ from us in some circumstantial Points . . . is uncharitable, unscriptural, and of dangerous Tendency!"[38] In fact, a "misguided and ill-tempered *Zeal*, and severe narrowness of Soul, is directly contrary to right Reason and to the Christian Revelation."[39]

Tennent's irenic expression was a harbinger of the reunion to come almost a decade later. In between the division of 1745 and the reunion of 1758, the New Side grew more than its Old Side counterpart thanks partly to the more aggressive style of revivalism and to having a school to train ministers. During the period of separation the attempt to start an Old Side academy failed and the Synod of Philadelphia had to rely upon the training supplied through the University of Pennsylvania. Meanwhile, the difficulty of obtaining Old Side ministers made it more likely for the new Scottish and Scotch-Irish immigrants settling in Virginia and North Carolina to call pastors trained at the College of New Jersey and licensed and ordained by the Presbytery of New Brunswick. Despite the New Side's growth, compared to the Old Side's stasis, good reasons existed for reunion, most of them having to do with the political situation. In Pennsylvania politics, for Presbyterians to challenge the Quakers in the colony a divided church was not ideal. In addition, the Seven Years War (1756–1763) had direct consequences for Presbyterians on the frontier, another reason for political if not religious unity. The obstacles to reunion were still formidable. But with Tennent indicating a willingness to be less demanding on the question of conversion, the list of problems began to look less insurmountable. The sticking points were the power of Synod (whether Synod could overrule presbyteries or dictate the terms of ordination), and the doctrinal norms for ordination. Once both sides began to discuss the possibility of reunion as early as 1754, another issue emerged, namely, whether Old Side and New Side presbyteries in the same region should be merged as part of the proposed reunion. During that same year, both groups agreed in principle to reunion. It still took four years to make it official, which they did on May 15, 1758, when the Synod of New York held its annual meeting in Philadelphia while the Synod of Philadelphia was already in session.

The key provisions in the eight points affirmed in the *Plan of Union of 1758* could be read to indicate a genuine compromise even if the Old Side had less leverage given its size. The first affirmed the Adopting Act of 1729

38 Ibid., 372.

39 Ibid., 373.

and the church's standard for subscription. Paragraphs two, three, five and six all affirmed Old Side convictions about the importance of order in the church and the legitimate authority of church judicatories. Five was arguably the greatest concession for the New Side, though Tennent had already proposed it in his 1749 sermon, which read "That it shall be esteemed and treated as a censurable evil, to accuse any member of heterodoxy, insufficiency, or immorality, in a calumniating manner, or otherwise than by private brotherly admonition, or by a regular process according to our known rules of judicial trial in cases of scandal."[40] Where the Old Side appeared to have given ground was in paragraph four, which followed a statement affirming the rights of members to protest the acts of Synod. Although ministers had such a right, the *Plan of Union* ruled that the Protestation of 1741 was "never judicially adopted," could not be counted as a "Synodical act," but should be considered "the act of those only who subscribed it." As such it could not become the basis for opposing the reunion of the Old and New Sides.[41]

As much as the *Plan of Union of 1758* forced both sides to make concessions, in terms of sheer word count the statement was a decisive victory for the New Side and revivalism more generally. The eighth plank in the Plan was no mere paragraph but contained four that in their entirety took up as much space as the preceding seven points plus the preamble. This concluding provision concerned the revival and the nature of religious experience. On the one hand, Synod declared that the recent awakening was "a blessed work of God's Spirit in the conversion of numbers. . . ." From there the Plan elaborated what a true form of conversion is and walked through an order of salvation that began with human sinfulness, the need for the work of the Spirit, a conviction of sin, turning to Christ in faith, and endeavoring to live in a manner pleasing to God. Why members of Synod felt a need to discuss the order of salvation in terms different from the Westminster Standards which already gave one of the more precise accounts in all the Reformed creeds of the sixteenth and seventeenth centuries is something of a mystery. They could have simply reaffirmed the nature of true conversion along the lines established by the Westminster Divines. But clearly the revivals of the Great Awakening raised questions about the Westminster consensus and forced another statement on the matter. The context of the awakening became explicit when after describing a true conversion point eight declared, "this is to be acknowledged as

40 "The Union of 1758," reprinted in Briggs, *American Presbyterianism*, cix.

41 Ibid.

a gracious work of God, even though it should be attended with unusual bodily commotions or some more exceptionable circumstances, . . . and wherever religious appearances are attended with the good effect above mentioned, we desire to rejoice in and thank God for them."[42] The *Plan of Union* thus clearly refuted Old Side's reservations about conversions that displayed enthusiasm.

On the other hand, Synod did draw the line about some forms of enthusiasm. "When persons seeming to be under a religious concern, imagine that they have visions of the human nature of Jesus Christ, or hear voices, or see external lights, or have fainting and convulsion-like fits, and on the account of these judge themselves to be truly converted, . . . we believe such persons are under a dangerous delusion, wherever it attends any religious appearances in any church or time." Synod went on to concede that a certain amount of disagreement might still exist in the church about conversion "respecting particular matters of fact."[43] But the goal of reunion was to "take heed to ourselves that our hearts be upright, our discourse edifying and our lives exemplary for purity and godliness. . . ."[44] With this acknowledgment of differences coupled with an assertion of unity and good will, Synod in effect tabled all further discussion of revivalism and conversion among American Presbyterians. From 1758 on American Presbyterians, whether Old School or New School, conservative or liberal, would reserve a special place for religious experience, perhaps not insisting on conversion for membership or ordination, but clearly affirming its importance to true godliness and conceiving the church's purpose as principally to cultivate such experience.

In his still unchallenged and deftly executed history of colonial Presbyterianism, Leonard J. Trinterud characterized the dynamics of the young church in a way that underscores the significance of the *Plan of Union of 1758* and the way it resolved the disputes from the Old-Side-New-Side Controversy. He wrote:

> The driving force that shaped American Presbyterianism in its formative years, and thereby determined also its later course, was the reinterpretation of the Christian life which inspired the Great Awakening. This conception of the Christian life was introduced by the Log College men, who in turn had heard it preached and taught by William Tennent. Against it one group in the Church

42 Ibid., cl–cxi.

43 Ibid.

44 Ibid.

> had united in what came to be known as the Old Side. . . . After 1745, when the Synod of New York was founded, this conception of the Christian life became normative for most of American Presbyterianism.[45]

The "reinterpretation of the Christian life" that Trinterud identified was one that stressed the individual's experience above the corporate life of the church, whether through the ordained ministry or church judicatories. It was a form of Christian devotion that favored the free movement and sovereignty of the Holy Spirit over a view that regarded the work of the Spirit as ordinarily applied through the work and ministry of the institutional church, both in the local congregation and in the wider assemblies. This New Side form of devotion did strive to work within the constraints of Presbyterian theology and church government, as the *Plan of Union of 1758* indicates. But because it exalted experience and the spirit over forms and the church, as Whitefield himself had done, it was an unstable compound that left American Presbyterianism with a precarious foundation on which to construct a church that would develop the true genius of the Reformed faith as a churchly form of Christianity.

45 Trinterud, *Forming of an American Tradition*, 169.

9

Samuel Davies—Preacher, Teacher, and Pastor

James H. Smylie

We begin this story when an Ulster-Scots immigrant Francis Makemie (c. 1658–1708) landed on the Eastern Shore of Virginia in colonial America and wrote a pamphlet, *A Plain and Friendly Persuasive to the Inhabitants of Virginia and Maryland* (1705). In it he urged readers to build communities, schools and churches and establish businesses for the public good. He urged tradesmen to compete domestically with foreigners, and even control "sots" as he called them—drunkers who might need to be constrained by a "pair of stocks" in towns. Makemie traveled north to New York where he was able to organize, after reassuring legal authorities that Presbyterians made good citizens, the first church and then Presbytery which embraced New York and Philadelphia as well as points north, south and west. He reassured readers that Presbyterians held allegiance to the Mother country, and actually provided a balance of power to European nations. This would add to Britain's "Advancement," "Greatness" and "Glory."

People flowed south into Virginia, out toward the Valley and began to organize religious communities. A John Thomason from the University of Glasgow, for example, began to preach in Prince Edward County; as a good Presbyterian, he went to Williamsburg and was granted a permission to do so. Baptists and Methodists felt they did not have to get such permission to do the Lord's work. Meanwhile, some settlers were meeting in the home of a Samuel Morris, and "other gentlemen of respectability" to read and study together. They, among other things, read Martin Luther's Commentary of Galations, and John Knox's Confession of Faith of the Church of Scotland. They decided, under the preaching of a

William Robinson of New Brunswick, to organize and identify themselves as Presbyterians.

Samuel Davies (1723–1761) stepped into this picture. Davies was born in New Castle, Delaware to David and Martha Davies who were farmers of Welch ancestry. Martha developed a dislike for her Baptist pastor and took her family into a Presbyterian Church. The Davies sent the bright young Samuel to the Reverend Samuel Blair's Log College at Fagg's Manor, Pennsylvania where he received his Classical Greek and Latin ministerial education in which he excelled as a student. He was licensed to preach by the New Side Presbytery of New Castle in 1747 at the age of twenty and his Presbytery sent him into Virginia as an evangelist. The New Side was more evangelical than the Old Side. Although others had preached there, Davies was the first Presbyterian to settle in the area, in a very large parish for one pastor extending from the Atlantic Ocean to the East, Pennsylvania to the North, and the Appalachian Mountains to the West. Decently and in good order, as a Presbyterian, unlike other clergy, e.g., Methodist and Baptist—he traveled to Williamsburg, to obtain a license to preach from the General Court. He confessed his faith to the authorities not only in the *Westminster Confession and Catechisms*, but also the *Thirty-Nine Articles* of the Church of England, with a few qualifications which were accepted. While some of the political leaders were wary of the young man, the Court granted him licenses in five western counties, to which two more were eventually added as preaching stations not churches, since "church" was claimed by the Anglicans. Personally, he did not like to be dubbed an "itinerant," since he knew that Anglican clergy of the Establishment also traveled to two or three places of worship known as "chapels of ease," to serve their members. Davies provided a place of worship for those who had none and who had been forced to attend the Anglican churches on the frontier. Many found their way over several miles to hear Davies' preaching. He published two defenses of his role entitled the *Impartial Trial, Impartially tried and Convicted of Partially* (1748) and an *Appendix Proving the Right of the Synod of New York to the Religious Liberties and Immunities Allowed to Protestant Dissenters* (1748). In the meantime, because of the fact that some authorities believed Davies an asset to Virginia's faith as well as life, they welcomed him and his ministry. He even stimulated Anglicans to more responsible faith and lives. Meanwhile, Davies nurtured his own congregations along the way covering a multitude of concerns, only a few of which can be mentioned here. It should be noted that the French held the territory to the west of the areas where Davies' congregations were located.

Preacher of the Gospel

Samuel Davies was primarily a preacher, teacher and pastor to a growing number of Virginians of all denomination in the Southwest who flocked to hear him on Sundays and other days of the week. As already indicated, he started out with five meeting places and added two more as his congregations spread and grew. Many congregants had little or no formal education. Davies' sermons were lectures as well as sermons that often lasted more than an hour. His sermons touched upon the educational, pastoral and emotional needs of his people who flowed to hear him when he visited their houses of worship, often only once a month and during the week as well as on the Sabbath. His sermons were often published and many of them appeared in a three volume set in 1760 when he finished his ministry in the colony. Davies was an ecumenist, in part because of his own spirit, but also because of the diversity of his hearers who came from no church or other denominations. He was suspicious of Roman Catholics as were other Protestants during his ministry. With his knowledge of Greek, Latin and Hebrew, he introduced his hearers to Adam and Eve, Moses, the Prophets, the Psalmist, and Ecclesiastes. He introduced them to Matthew, Mark, John, Peter, Paul, and Timothy—all the books of the Scripture. He drew as well from Classic figures and Christian theologians, such as Cicero, Demosthenes, Augustine, and Tacitus. He also spoke of Reformation leaders—Martin Luther, John Knox, John Calvin, Thomas Cranmer, and later contemporaries, such as John and Charles Wesley, Joseph Addison, Alexander Pope, Isaac Watts, and George Whitefield, who along with John Wesley visited the colonies and preached to Virginians a number of times. And as already noted, he employed the *Westminster Confession and Catechisms* along with the *Thirty-Nine Articles* of the Church of England in his teaching.

Unfortunately, some Virginian Anglican officials and clergy thought he was out to "presbyterianize" the colony. He tried to reassure them in his sermons. He stressed the commonality of Virginia's religious communities as an ecumenist. He preached about "The Sacred Importance of the Christian Name" and "Is Christ Divided." Of course, he recognized, as a student of Christian history that there had been "Paulists, Peterites, Johnites, Barnabites, and later Jesuits, Jansenites, Dominicans, and Franciscans." No, he proclaimed from the pulpit! We are not baptized in our own names. We are baptized in Christ's name, as born again, born anew again as Christians. We were baptized in Christ's name! We should all know Christ's teaching, depart from iniquity, and practice Christ's precepts.

To do this, he noted, pastors must be able to read "Men as well as books," as, indeed, did Davies. With regard to Presbyterian worship, he called upon his hearers to keep the Sabbath Day holy. They should remind themselves that God is sovereign Lord over all, a God to be "feared, loved, praised," and "called upon, trusted in, and served with all the heart and with all the soul, and with all the might." Worship, he taught, should be given in the name of "God the Father, Son and Holy Ghost," not to any angel, saint, or other creature—since the fall, through the "mediation" of Christ alone. Worship should involve thanksgiving to God, prayer for all things lawful, and for all sorts and conditions of living persons. It should take place on the first day of every week which should be kept holy to the Lord, "kept for rest from, works, words, and thoughts" about worldly employments and recreations. The day was for "duties of necessity and mercy," as he put it.

Davies was an impressive figure in the pulpit, driving his message to the heart without gesture, but with "modulation" of voice and motion of his body. He was concerned about the spiritual condition of his people which he addressed in numerous sermons. Davies administered the sacrament of baptism, of infants and adults. Baptism he held was a "badge" of our Christian profession, and a memorial of Christ's suffering for all his people through the ages and in the present. God was a "great God of Wonder," as he put it in another sermon. He expressed this in one of his poems, which he often used in his services:

> Ah! what are Worlds compar'd to Thee,
> Great everlasting *All!*
> But Atoms hovering in the Air
> Bubbles and Vanity
> That at thy great Command appear,
> And at thy Word to nothing fail,
> Whose pleasure gives them Leave to be.
> Thou viewest, independent, from on high
> A sparrow or a Hero die,
> Atoms or Systems moulder into Dust,
> And now a World, and now a bubble Burst.

But God was a "Great God of Wonders," as he put it in another poem. God was also a pardoner of "grace as rich and free."

Davies expressed God's watchful care over and challenges to his people. His eloquence may be measured in a sermon on "God is Love" in which he included another passage based on 1 John 4:8. According to Davies, God showed his love to the world, to him and his parishioners through the work of Christ's death on the cross as he maintains in another moving sermon on the "Preaching of Christ Crucified, The Means of Salvation." Such preaching,

> gives such a presentation of the evil of sin, and the dreadful punishment due to it, as naturally tends to turn sinners from it, and bring them to repentance. In the Cross of Christ the sinner may see how God hates it, when he punished it so severely in his beloved Son. If the almighty Redeemer sunk under the load, how shall the feeble sinner bear up under it? If God spared not his own Son, who was but a surety, how can the sinner escape, who was the original debtor! Oh sinners! Never call it cruel that God should punish you for your sins; so he dealt with Jesus, his favourite; and can you hope for more favour? Hear the nature of sin, as written in characters of blood on the cross of Christ, and surely you can make light of it no more. You must tremble at the very thought of it: and immediately reform and repent of it.

In his worship services, while a low churchman, Davies invited the worshipers on occasions—not too often, however—to the Lord's Supper. This is indicated in his sermons concerning the importance of Christians coming to the Table to receive God's forgiveness. In a sermon entitled "The Christian Feast" based on 1 Corinthians 5:8, the Virginian called his parishioners to take the Last Supper seriously, to prepare for it diligently, to remember the Savior's death for all people, to repent the neglect of the Table as a renewal of God's covenant, and to avail themselves of it. He considered the neglect of the ordinance by Christians the "national sin in our country" since it was appointed by God to acknowledge Jesus Christ, the "Founder" of Christian faith and life. In "The Gospel Invitation, A Sacramental Discourse," Davies preached on Luke 14: 21–24, opening with these words:

> So vast and various are the blessings proposed to our acceptance in the gospel, that they can never be fully represented, though the utmost force of language be exhausted for that purpose in the sacred writings. Among other lively images, this one is my context, whether the gospel is compared to a feast, a marriage-feast of royal magnificence. The propriety and significance of this representation

> are obvious at first sight; for what is more rich and elegant, and what more agreeable to mankind, that such an entertainment!

It was for Davies a sadly, neglected joy.

The Virginia native, among other things, reminded his congregations of "The Sacred Import of the Christian Name" based on Acts 9:26: "The disciples were called Christians first in Antioch." He thought they should be called Christians in Virginia because of their faith and lives. He reminded his hearers that early disciples were not known at first by this name. Christian enemies in the first century called them Galileans, Nazarenes, and other names of contempt. Among themselves they are called saints, from their holiness; disciples, from learning their religion from Christ as their teacher; believers, from their believing in him as the Messiah; and brethren, from their mutual love and their relation to God and each other. He reminded his listeners that Christians first received their name in Antioch, a "heathen" city, infamous for all manner of vice and evil. He called on his parishioners to be worthy of their Christian name in America.

A be a Christian, he preached, was not an "hereditary" gift through a natural birth. He reminded his congregations that a Christian must be "born anew" of the Spirit to be entitled to the new name. Then he proceeded to inform Christians of what is expected of them.

> The Christian has exalted sentiments of the Supreme Being, just notions of duty, and a proper temper and conduct towards God and man. A Christian is a devout worshipper of the God of heaven, a cheerful observer of his whole law, and a broken-hearted penitent for his imperfections. A Christian is a complaisant of all amiable and useful graces and virtues; temperate and sober, just, liberal, compassionate, and benevolent, humble, meek, gentle, peaceable, and in all things conscientious. A Christian is a good parent, a good child, a good master, a good servant, a good husband, a good wife, a faithful friend, an obliging neighbour, a dutiful subject, a good ruler, a zealous patriot, and an honest statesman; and as far as he is such, so far, no father, he is a Christian. And can there be a more amiable and excellent character exhibited to your view? It is angelic, a divine character. Let it be your glory and your ambition to wear it with a good grace, to wear it so as to adorn it.

To be a Christian was, according to Davies, every bit as important as having the title of kings and lords, as heroes, even scholars and philosophers. Davies wondered how much better off the whole world would be with more people who were such Christian professors.

In order to make such Christians, Davies did not believe that he or any other clergyman could produce them in church by sermons without home help. He preached another sermon on "The Necessity and Excellence of Family Devotion" based on 1 Timothy 5:8. This should be provided by leaders of households, as indicated in the Scriptures. He ran through a list of excuses his parishioners made to excuse themselves from a household of faithful living. Objection 1. "I have no time, and my secular business would suffer by family religion." Objection 2. "I have no ability to pray; I am too ignorant." 3. "I am ashamed." 4. "But alas! I know not how to begin it." 5. "But, I shall be ridiculed and laughed at." Davies warned such a protester: Are you then more afraid of a laugh or a jeer than the displeasure of God? Would you rather please men then God? Davies then invited his hearers: "Therefore, wherever you have your habitation, there let Jehovah, may I so speak, have an altar, and there let morning and evening prayers and praises be presented, til you are called to worship him in his temple above, where your prayers should be swallowed up in everlasting praise. Amen." In this way, Davies helped his frontier Virginian congregations to trust in, as he put it in another sermon title based on Luke 16:27-31, "The Divine Authority and Sufficiency of the Christian Religion." Through sermons such as these he addressed the hearts, minds and lives of his parishioners, and he inspired many to devote themselves to the Christian faith and life.

Trip to the British Isles

Not long after Davies' own ordination to the ministry and the beginning of his work of founding churches in Virginia, he began to participate in the New Light Synod of New York. In 1753 he was asked to leave his congregations—and family—in the South, and joined northerner Gilbert Tennent, thirty years older than the Virginian, and sail to the British Isles to raise money for a new college in Princeton, NJ, to train laity and also clergy for the ministry. Tennent was still known for his preaching, notably "The Dangers of an Unconverted Ministry" (1747), so important for the Awakening. Davies agreed to go, leaving his family on a mission which lasted almost two years. Perhaps Davies was asked because of his own eloquence. But he believed in the purpose of the trip, and also because he thought he could raise funds for Native and African Americans in the South. In the North he lodged with David Brainerd, the noted Missionary to Native Americans. Before he and Tennent sailed he preached and was honored with a degree of Master of Arts in Newark where the college was located at this time. The embassaries sailed on their four week trip across the Atlantic Ocean on a ship which was tossed to and fro like a cork. He was often sick and low-spirited on the long voyage. But he and Tennent were greeted enthusiastically upon their arrival by friends who wanted to help the cause in the New World.

Davies and Tennent were troubled by what they saw in the Old World—the impiety, corruption, crime which led to countless hangings. In the young clergy whom he met, he found little "serious faith," in some believers a "dry and rigid" Calvinist orthodoxy. Perhaps restless with his young companion, Tennent took off to Scotland and Ireland to raise funds and also search for ancestors and relatives, and to avoid some Englishmen. They had copies of his infamous sermon which they did not appreciate. Davies met with George Whitefield, the noted preacher who counseled him in what to expect from the British as he traveled, preached, and solicited funds. He did preach in numerous churches in London, Scotland, and elsewhere. He preached with eloquence mixed with diffidence as he sought support. He "waited on" John and Charles Wesley with all their "wild Notions," as he put it, but who gave birth to Methodism now so strong in the New World. He was sympathetic to their desires and labors, as he put it, to "awaken the secure World to a sense of Religion." But he was also concerned that they were encouraging so many "illiterate Men to preach the Gospel," the result of which might have "bad consequences." While in Britain he remembered help from friend Philip Doddridge, who died before Davies could meet with him on his journey.

In order to reassure his own audiences, Davies made sure that they understood the faith and life of Virginian Presbyterians whose cause he represented—as well as that of Princeton. Unlike Methodists and Baptists, he registered his "preaching stations," and reassured his hearers of Presbyterian loyalty to the Williamsburg government. He apparently made an impression, since people in places like London, Edinburgh, and Glasgow where he preached where anxious to have copies of his sermons. Davies sought advice as to how he could reassure officials in Virginia about Presbyterian loyalty. While on his tour Davies was reminded of his own British roots. He preached, for example, to a grandson of Oliver Cromwell. His discourse caused tears, he reports, to swell up in the descendant's eyes. He also visited the tomb of John Locke whose political ideas were so very important to American political development in the eighteenth century. Moreover, Davies took notice of a young clergyman, John Witherspoon of Scotland, who wrote *Ecclesiastical Characteristics* (1753)—a humorous burlesque on the high flying, so-called "moderate men" who were undercutting, according to the Scot, the Gospel. It was humor, Davies thought, worthy of Jonathan Swift.

Because of his busy schedule among "strangers in a strangeland," as he put it, Davies, never robust, fell sick during his trip and almost died. While Davies was raising funds in the Isles, Tennent did the same in Ireland. Tennent was now known also for his *Irenicum Ecclesiasticum* (1745), which he had published in America to help mend fences broken during the Awakening in which he and Davies had played such an important roles. He also made an impression and he and Davies were able to raise considerable sums before returning to America—on separate ships. Davies had a long three-month voyage before he returned to the homeland and his Virginia family. He remembered his Atlantic voyage in verse:

> Sure 'tis the War of Elements; the shock
> of Nature in Convulsions: 'tis the Wreck
> of Worlds! What horrid Images can shew
> The dreadful Scene! What loud tremendous Sounds,
> What wild, tumultuous Verse can represent
> The blended Roar of Thunder, Winds and Waves
> In Tumult—Now how naturally Distress
> Casts up to Heaven the wild imploring Eye
> And eager cries for Help—Now, now we sink!
> —O thou Ruler of the Seas,
> Send forth thy mighty Mandate, "Peace, be still,"
> And calm their Rage—But can even Mercy hear
> Such daring Rebels, who in one vile Breath
> Blend Prayers and Curses? But alas! My Heart
> Look home; thou art not innocent; my Guilt
> My hurl these curious Hurricanes in Air
> And arm each Billow of the Sea against me.

Davies and Tennent arrived on American soil safely!

Hanover Presbytery

When Davies returned from the British Isles he was immediately drawn into the organization of Hanover Presbytery in 1755 at Pole Green Church in Hanover. Davies was elected its first moderator. In doing this the body extended organized Presbyterian influences westward in Virginia and Southward into North Carolina, thus further taming America's frontier. In the process he inspired, instructed, and installed those young men who helped organize the presbytery. He left a legacy of some brilliant and inspiring ordination and installation sermons. He preached and installed John Todd, an early student and colleague with "The Duties, Difficulties and Rewards of the Faithful Minister" (1752), dedicated respectfully, and wisely by the way, to the "Revd Clergy of the Established Church in Virginia," "The Office of a Bishop, a Good Work" (1757) at the ordination of John Martin, "The Love of Souls, A Necessary Qualification for the Ministerial Office" (1758) at the ordination of Henry Patillo, "The Success of the Ministry of the Gospel, Owing to a Divine Influence" (1757), and "The Tender Anxieties of Ministers for Their People" (1758), as well as several others in which he showed his skill in the pulpit and his vision of ministry.

It must be remembered that Davies himself had received an excellent classical education himself and was able to draw upon not only the Bible, but classical authors in his sermons. He taught, as he himself had learned, that a minister had to "read Men as well as the Book," beginning with self-examinations. A minister, he preached, had to look in his own heart, for, as he wrote, as in "water face answereth to Face, so doth the heart of Man to Man." Davies was concerned not only about himself but clergy in general—even Virginia's Anglican clergy. In his ordination sermon for John Martin, a protégé, he observed that some might think of ministry as another task, e.g., like that of lawyers, physicians, or merchants, and enter the church simply for a living. To be sure, he observed ministers deserved "competent maintenance," but they should not be greedy for "superfluous" luxuries. He maintained that was a "sordid" motive to seek Christ's "ministry of souls." Moreover, he condemned those who preached,

> a little *smattering* of human literature, a *superficial* acquaintance with Divinity and experimental religion, a stock of useless *Pedantries*, a volubility of Tongue, a Dexterity to amuse the Populace with empty Harangues; these are not sufficient: and much less, a capacity to play the *Plagiary* in reading the Sermons of others as their own; which is but stealing the Word of the Lord from our Neighbor and strutting Majesty in borrowed Feathers.

Of course, some Anglican clergy may not have appreciated such purple passages from the dissenter's own oratory. Davies was preaching to himself as well as to others. Davies did, however, dedicate the sermon "To the rev. Clergy of the Established Church of Virginia."

Davies did consider that the preaching of the "good news of God's grace" (Acts 20:24), the text of Todd's sermon, was serious business. It had to do with human sinfulness documented in the Bible, human history, reflected in the "mirror" of current history. God's grace had been demonstrated in Jesus Christ—his witness to love, his redemptive suffering, and his resurrection, giving humans hope for this life in the next. Because of his Christ centeredness Davies condemned in no uncertain terms the rationalistic, optimistic Deism growing so fashionable during these years. In his ordination of Todd he assured the Virginian Anglicans that he preached "Catholic Christianity" laid down not only in his *Westminster Confession of Faith* but also in the *Thirty-Nine Articles* of the Church of England, established in Virginia. So he addressed and instructed those whom he welcomed into the ministry to preach repentance unto life. The "Great God" cries to you all, he once preached, "Repent, Repent young and old, rich and poor, white and black, free and bond." But he also urged ordinands to preach to faith, hope and love as did Christ. Davies preached with tears in his eyes. In preaching this Christ, Davies held, properly trained ministers are co-workers together with God and the Holy Spirit, and in concert with "angels in heaven." Thus they would be, as Augustine held, true "bishops of souls."

In addition, Davies preached that clergy not only should be educated and educate their congregations, but also preach Christ in such a way as to move the heart, not simply the head. Christ, he held must be planted in the heart, there to grow and mature, as Paul wrote in Galatians (Gal 4:19-20). This was the text for Davies' sermon in 1758 on "The Tender Anxieties of Ministers for Their People." As he informed Williamsburg Anglicans about his own preaching so he urged his own preaching colleagues to make "Catholic Christians." Also, he maintained that Presbyterians and other ministers were not simply called to sow Presbyterianism, or Anglicanism, or Roman Catholicism, or Methodism, or Baptist seed, but true Catholic Christian faith and life. With regard to his own Presbyterian family, divided as it was, he urged students and colleagues not to "choke" on small points of doctrine and become "firebrands of contention," but to convert and care for the souls of people. He used metaphors of farmers in his preaching. He urged them to plant the "embryo of Christ" in the hearts of believers and nurture Christ's growth in their lives. Moreover, in this matter the minister must not "lord" it over parishioners, but join them in their pilgrimages, showing tender anxiety for them as well as for himself.

To minister affectively and effectively, the pastor must consider members of his congregations as a "circle of friends" and must remember his own humanity as well as their need of salvation. Thus the minister must not "lord" it over his people. Davies may have used this word "lord" to send a message to Anglicans too. He must rather in that "circle of friendship," aim his arrows, not as a "scold," but with "tears in his eyes," as did Christ, as one in need himself. Thus the arrows will make their proper "medicinal wound." Thus he and others would deal with the anxieties of the people. Davies had a realistic approach to preaching.

The effectiveness of preaching depended on God's work and the receptiveness of parishioners at any particular time in their lives. So Davies read and interpreted 1 Corinthians 3:7 while he preached in 1752 and 1757 in Hanover. He was realistic. Sometimes a good sermon will have no impact whatever, while a poor one will reach the heart. Sometimes reading a sermon will be helpful whereas those delivered without manuscript, even with zeal, will not move any one at all. Sometimes a sermon will touch one person, while it may leave another unresponsive. Sometimes an old truth preached many times by a clergyman, may leave a flash upon a congregation as a new discovery in an entirely different situation. Every one responds to a sermon not according to the discourse, but according to his or her "sensations" at the time, an insight Davies may have had as a good eighteenth-century psychologist. For him it is God who always "gives the increase." He also applied this to the preacher. They had to aim their sermons at themselves as well as their parishioners. Of course, as Davies reminded preachers and church goers, God, in the end, had to bring the preached texts from Corinth, Galatia, Ephesus, and Rome, to Virginia, and bring forth the fruits of the Spirit. Davies did complain that some of his own parishioners had "uncircumcised ears," even with regard to his own eloquence.

In addition, Davies suggested that ministers themselves should not be "sour" ascetics, "Morose, mophish, melancholy." But he also noted that they were not likely to "dance and frolic" themselves into heaven. It should be noticed, however, that he did not pass the same judgment on music, dancing, and feasting, that he did on careless sinners, the drunkards, swearers, thieves, and the infidels and the scoffers. He also highly recommended that preachers preach as one human being to other human beings "out of the pulpit" by example. He was to visit families in their homes, to learn about their lives and share with parishioners experiences, in other words, to show a "love of Souls" so that the "embryo of Christ" within the heart might be nurtured and mature.

And this suggests another aspect of Davies preaching. He did urge upon his hearers responsible living, to be, in a word, "co-workers with

Christ" through the power of the Holy Spirit. As he supported a learned ministry, he also championed an educated laity. He often sent away for books which he distributed among his members. He urged them to read them and share them with one another. And he urged Bible reading and study when no other books were available. Thus while he did not establish a school himself, he turned his church into a schoolroom, and trained other clergy to do the same—to spread education throughout the Old Dominion.

Ministry to Slaves

In 1700 Samuel Sewall, a Congregationalist published *The Selling of Joseph* which supplied evidence for rejecting the institution. Despite Joseph's experience and deliverance from slavery, Davies accepted slavery as an institution he found in the Bible and which was supported by American Presbyterians and other Christians. The Virginian probably owned one or more slaves. It was a custom in the South to present a slave to a pastor. Davies noted the growth of the institution in the region and gave his attention to the matter especially to the slaves and their families. He was deeply concerned about slaves as individuals, God's children, their need of salvation, therefore their need to know about Christian faith and life, and to be able to read and understand the Scripture, and to deepen their devotion and quest for holiness. He believed that slaves were being neglected and he was concerned for them. Even many of his parishioners were concerned. He reported to the Society for Promoting Religious Knowledge among the poor how slaves took to reading:

> Every new benefaction of Books sets hundreds upon attempting to read with fresh eagerness. Such of them as had already learned, I furnish with *Bibles, Testaments, Psalm Books, Catechisms*, &c. immediately upon their application to me. Many come to me, who have not yet learned, but tell me, they are eager to make trail, and want books for that purpose: Among these I have divided the Spelling Books, which were sent to me from private hands, and I bid them come to me when them have learned them, and let me see they can read, and then I shall furnish them with other books.

The slaves were especially influenced by Isaac Watts' hymnal, and took "ecstatic delight" in the Psalmody. In fact, Davies remarked that some slaves had lodged "all night in my kitchen: and sometimes, when I have awaked about two or three o'clock in the morning, a torrent of sacred harmony poured into my chamber, and carried my mind away to heaven. In this seraphic exercise, some of them spend almost the whole night."

Davies, by 1755, was able to say that almost three hundred slaves attended his worship services regularly and that he was able to educate and baptize about a hundred of them. Much of his time was spent in teaching them to read. He also was concerned about training some African Americans to enter the College of New Jersey and prepare for mission work in Africa, an idea which never actually materialized. The Presbyterian pastor continued his concerns for those whom he called "African Savages" at one point whom he wished to civilize:

> I am told, that in almost every house in my congregation, and in sundry other places, they spend every leisure hour in trying to learn, since they expect Books as soon as they are capable of using them. Some of them, I doubt not, are excited to it by a sincere desire to know the Will of God, and what they shall do to be saved. Others, I am afraid, are actuated by the mean principles of curiosity, ambition, and vanity. However, be that principle what it will, I cannot but rejoice in the effect, as it renders them more capable of Instruction, in the great concerns of Religion.

Davies took this concern to the British Isles when he visited the place.

Davies took his view of Christian faith and life seriously with regard to this institution, and identified Christ and himself as identified with them. Christ was considered a malefactor and a slave and was treated as such. But he maintained the dignity of the most powerful kings. "All his subjects are kings." The Lord has peopled heaven with "redeemed slaves, and advanced them to royal dignity." People in this life find themselves in different stations and consequently have different responsibilities and obligations toward one another. These relationships must be regulated by the principle of equity not by "self love." Humans should treat one another as they would be treated if in the same position. A prince must govern subjects as he would like to be governed if a subject. So this precept is "universal and extends to all mankind, in all circumstances; to superiors, inferiors, and equals." And a true follower of Christ should be able to transcend his own special interest and empathize with those under authority: "If you were a servant, how would you have your master to behave towards you? Consider and determine the matter: and you will know how you should behave towards your servants. The same thing may be applied to rulers and subjects in general, to parents and children, husbands and wives, neighbour and neighbour." We can see how Davies attempted to treat the few slaves he may have owned. Davies' sermon, "The Duty of Christians to

Propagate Religion among Heathen," earnestly recommended to the masters of Negro Slaves in Virginia was published in London in 1757, based on "I am a debtor both to the Greeks, and to the Barbarians; both to the wise, and the unwise" (Rom 1:14), a sermon which helped him raise funds for fulfilling his goals of educating American slaves.

War and Call to Princeton

Colonial Presbyterians, as were other colonists were drawn into what is known as the French and Indian War. They had been concerned under the leadership and sacrifices of several missionaries. As was for example, David Brainerd who was dedicated to the cause. Brainerd had a vision of a large "nation" of Christian Indians on the Virginia and Carolina frontier. He thought that seven or eight hundred Christian "Cherokees and Creeks" would provide protection against other frontier "Savages." Davies promoted such work when he went to the British Isles. Of course, his concerns for such evangelism was stymied by what became known as the French and Indian War, dangerously close to where Davies served his ministry in Western Virginia. He became a modern Demosthenes in his discourses when he warned against cowards in the battle. General Edward Braddock was defeated in 1755 by an enemy force. This caused Davies to preach about that event as well as sermons about "God the Sovereign of all Kingdoms," "Religion and Patriotism," and "The Curse of Cowardice." The latter he preached to the Hanover Militia. In this sermon he made a reference to an "heroic youth, Col. Washington" about whom he hoped "Providence has hitherto preserved in so signal a manner, for some important service to his country." How prophetic he was!

Meanwhile, Davies had to face another challenge. At Princeton, New Jersey, two presidents, Aaron Burr and Jonathan Edwards, whom Davies had tried to persuade to join him in Virginia, died shortly after assuming their official duties. At first Davies resisted the call to the office. But the Princeton board persisted. Davies finally consented. "Service to God and Mankind," he was taught as a youngster at Fagg's Manor, was not a "local" matter. He left in the summer of 1759 after preaching on an "Apostolic Valediction" based on II Cor. 8:11. He concluded with these words:

> I preach to you as a dying man to dying men, and—now the time of my departure is at hand—I must take my farewell of you. Receive, all of you, my brethren, the word of exhortation, from the lips of him, whose voice has so often sounded alarm in your ears; though I fear, as to many of you, with out the desired effect.

> My voice, it is probable, will never or more be heard by you. . . . O recollect the many invitations I have given you on the one hand, and threatenings on the other. Heaven forbid that any of them should arise in judgment against you another day! Behold, now is the accepted time: behold, now is the day of salvation. . . . Flee, flee, all of you, from the wrath to come—lay hold on the hope that is set before you.—O forget it not. Lay it seriously to hear. . . . Farewell—'finally brethren; be perfect, be of good comfort, be of one mind, live in peace, and the God of love and peace shall be with you, - which may God grant for Christ's sake. *Amen.*'

Conclusion

When Davies arrived in Princeton, he found an institution of the church with 150 male students. Nassau Hall had been completed in the center of the community by 1756, and held not only classrooms but a library with approximately 1,500 books. Davies dedicated himself to raising the standards of the institution as well as its endowment. He was also a regular pastor of the Princeton congregation. One of his most important sermons he preached shortly after his arrival was "On the death of His Late Majesty, King George II" (January, 1761). It was an exposition of II Sam. 1:19: "How are the Mighty Fallen!"

> George is no more! George, the Mighty, the just, the gentle, and the wise; George, the father of Britain and her colonies, the guardian of laws and liberty, the protector of the oppressed, the arbiter of Europe, the terror of tyrants and France; George, the friend of man, the benefactor of millions, is no more! Millions tremble at the alarm. Britain expresses her sorrow in national groans. Europe re-echoes to the melancholy sound. The melancholy sound circulates far and wide. This remote American continent shares in the loyal sympathy. The wide intermediate Atlantic rolls the tide of grief to these distant shores; and even the recluse sons of Nassau Hall feel the immense bereavement, with all the sensibility of a filial heart; and must mourn with their country, with Britain, with Europe, with the world—George was our Father too.

He concluded his tribute to the King with a call to loyalty, not only to the royal family but to God: "Let every soul be subject to the higher powers." "This is," he held, "my dear youth, this is the great precept of Christianity which this day demands your attention."

> Therefore, it becomes you to know your own importance to your king and country, that you may exert your influences in your re-

> spective spheres, to execute all his patriot designs. . . .Your education, both at home and in Nassau-Hall, has invincibly pre-engaged your incluation, your reason, and your conscience in favor of our incomparable constitution, and the succession in the Hanover family of liberty, the protestant religion, and George the Third, which are inseparably united. Therefore act up to your principles, practice according to your political creed, and then my most benevolent wishes, nay the highest wishes of your kind and fellow-subject, will be amply accomplished in you. Then you will give the world an honorable and just specimen of the morals and politics inculcated in the College of New Jersey; and convince them that it is a seminary of loyalty, as well as learning and piety; a nursery for the state, as well as the church. Such may it always continue, You all concur in your cordial Amen.

Little did he know what would happen in 1776 when an American revolution broke out against another George, and that a Scottish immigrant who admired Davies, John Witherspoon, would succeed him as President of Princeton. He would be the only clergy to sign the Declaration of Independence, and educate James Madison, a key author of the United States Constitution. Madison's parents who admired Davies had sent their son to Princeton rather than to William and Mary.

Davies was honored by being elected moderator of the Synod of Philadelphia and New York where he sought help for the New Jersey Indians, recalling his earlier concerns for Virginia's natives. Davies died "unto the Lord" in 1761 and was mourned and celebrated in Virginia where he had such an influential ministry, as well as in New York and Philadelphia and London. We still remember him through his inspiring sermons printed often during his lifetime, in sets of two, three and five volumes in New York, Philadelphia, Baltimore and Boston. This essay is based in part on a three-volume set published as late as 1993.[1] Davies is certainly worthy of study in our own times.

[1] Samuel Davies, *Sermons of the Rev. Samuel Davies,* 3 vols. (reprinted, Pittsburgh: Soli Deo Gloria, 1993); see also, Samuel Davies, *Sermons on Important Subjects.* 3 Vols (New York: Robert Carter & Brothers, 1867). Other sources used in this essay include: William Henry Foote, *Sketches of Virginia*, First Series (1850; reprinted, Richmond: John Knox Press, 1966); Wesley M. Gewehr, *The Great Awakening in Virginia, 1740–1790* (Durham, NC: Duke University Press, 1930); Alan Heimert and Perry Miller, *Religion and the American Mind: From the Great Awakening to the Revolution* (Cambridge: Harvard University Press, 1966); George William Pilcher, *Samuel Davies: Apostle of Dissent in Colonial Virginia* (Knoxville: University of Tennessee Press, 1971); and Leonard J. Trinterud, *The Forming of an American Tradition: A Re-Examination of Colonial Presbyterianism* (Philadelphia: Westminster, 1949).

10

John Witherspoon's Prescription for a Nation Strong, Free, and Virtuous

L. Gordon Tait

"He who makes a people virtuous, makes them invincible."[1]

IT may seem strange to say that John Witherspoon's prescription for a strong, free and virtuous nation begins and ends with piety, not political theory, not constitutions, not ethics, but piety. He sometimes substituted for the word piety the phrase "holiness of life" or "true religion," but whatever he called it, he knew it was based on a person's love of God ("Thou shalt love the Lord thy God with all thy heart, and with all thy soul, and with all thy mind." Matthew 22:37). In his many sermons he showed how that love of God leads to a few select beliefs and those beliefs to concrete practical application. Thus, without any hesitation he always insisted that his piety was very practical.

What he meant, of course, was that Christians ought always to be looking outward to the larger world even as they nurtured and deepened their spirituality. While in Scotland, later in America, he recognized and proclaimed a piety that constituted the life of the Christian in society.

The construct of that piety was simple and clear. Also, it was Biblical, Protestant and practical, he declared. There were four core beliefs, four "truths of the everlasting gospel," as he called them, which constituted the Christian faith. They were, in his words, "the lost state of man by nature [human sinfulness]; salvation by the free grace of God; justification by the imputed righteousness of Christ; and sanctification by the effectual opera-

[1] John Witherspoon, "The Druid," in *The Works of the Rev. John Witherspoon,* ed. Ashbel Green, 4 vols. (Philadelphia, 1802: reprinted, with an Introduction by L. Gordon Tait, Bristol, UK: Thoemmes, 2003) 4:430; [hereafter *Works*].

tion of the Holy Spirit."[2] This was the kind of religion that would be the salvation of persons and the very foundation of a nation. What he has to say about the practicality of the four eternal truths is significant:

> These doctrines I am persuaded are not only true in themselves, but the great foundation of all practical religion. Wherever they are maintained and inculcated, strictness and purity of life and manners will be their natural effect. On the contrary, where they are neglected and a pretended theory of moral virtue substituted in their room [place], it will immediately and certainly introduce a deluge of profanity and immorality in practice.[3]

Indeed, Witherspoon thought that they were so important that everywhere they ought to be "clearly explained, strongly inculcated, and frequently repeated."

The story of Witherspoon's piety begins in Scotland. Born near Edinburgh in 1723, he was reared in a Presbyterian manse and attended a local grammar school. Later he enrolled in and graduated from the University of Edinburgh, completing his studies in the arts in 1739 and divinity in 1743. Ordained in the Church of Scotland in 1745, he was the minister for twelve years in the parish of Beith and eleven years in the Laigh (Low) Kirk in Paisley.[4] In both churches he preached expository sermons based more directly on the Bible than the historic Westminster Confession of Faith (1646).[5] Even in the sermons of the young Witherspoon it is possible to discern a concern for the well-being of the nation as well as the church. Always in the background, however, were the central convictions of the Confession. It is not too difficult to find in the sermons he preached in his two parishes his critique of certain aspects of national and church life. His assumption, of course, a common one at the time, was that a faithful church made up of pious members would be the basis of a strong, healthy society. He made this argument, for example, in the

[2] These four "truths" are to be found scattered throughout his sermons. See especially, *Works* 2:404, 443. The "truths" are developed at some length in L. Gordon Tait, *The Piety of John Witherspoon: Pew, Pulpit and Public Forum* (Louisville: Geneva, 2001) 41–71.

[3] *Works* 3:294, 2:515.

[4] For a full account of Witherspoon's life see Varnum L. Collins, *President Witherspoon: A Biography*, 2 vols. (Princeton: Princeton University Press, 1925: reprint, New York: Arno Press, 1969).

[5] Forty-seven of his sermons have been preserved in the *Works*, vols. 1–3. For The Westminster Confession of Faith, see John H. Leith, ed., *Creeds of the Churches* (Chicago: Aldine, 1963) 192–230 [hereafter *The Confession*].

sermon "The Absolute Necessity of Salvation Through Christ"[6] that he preached on January 2, 1758, in St. Giles' Cathedral, "The High Church of Edinburgh" as it was called. He surveyed the Scottish citizenry and noticed that there were not only non-Christians who needed to hear the gospel, but more importantly, there were those nominal Christians who interpreted the gospel in such a way as to "render it palatable to a corrupt and worldly mind." This would have dire consequences. Later in the sermon he softened his message somewhat by admonishing his hearers to care for the body, as well as for the souls of those who know not the gospel. He concluded with a memorable phrase: "True religion always enlarges the heart, and strengthens the social tie."[7]

This 1758 Edinburgh sermon is notable for another reason: the emphasis on salvation. A close reading of all his sermons reveals his urgency to preach salvation through Christ to all who would listen. Witherspoon did lip service to the Westminster Shorter Catechism's definition of God, "a Spirit, infinite, eternal, and unchangeable, in his being, wisdom, power, holiness, justice, goodness and truth," but he consciously went beyond this formal definition by stating that the very best one could say about God was "the boundless mercy of the Father, and the infinite condescension of the Son, when we reflect on his incarnation, and on the Astonishing end of his appearance in our nature, that 'he might bear our sins in his own body on the tree.'" For Witherspoon, God is a God who saves sinners.[8]

Witherspoon adhered to the Confession's declarations on predestination, election, and a limited design of the atonement, but frequently he quietly set aside these beliefs to stress that it was up to each sinner to decide for or against the redemption made effective by Christ. To give equal emphasis to the divine initiative and human responsibility in the plan of redemption, he resorted to Paul's letter to the Philippians that joins both actions: "Work out your own salvation with fear and trembling, for it is God that worketh in you to will and to do his good pleasure" (Philippians 2:12, 13).[9]

In a second sermon also preached in 1758, on a Public Fast day, Witherspoon's outlook moves from the individual to the whole of society. The title indicates clearly what the preacher intends: "Prayer for National

6 *Works*, 2:339–67.

7 Ibid., 2:362.

8 "A Practical Treatise on Regeneration," *Works* 1:246. In both this treatise, published in 1764, and an earlier one in 1756, "An Essay on Justification," the theme of salvation looms large. See *Works* 1:43–265 for both treatises.

9 "Treatise on Regeneration," *Works*, 1:102. See also Tait, *Piety*, 56–58.

Prosperity, and for the Revival of Religion Inseparably Connected."[10] He is convinced that Britain is in trouble. He asks, "Is not our state [condition] both as a nation, and as a church, exceedingly fallen and low?" He answers his own question by declaring that "we are at present in a distressed, and in a contemptible state." He even proposes that Britain's fallen state has brought on the Seven Years War with France (1755–1763)[11] as God's punishment. His recommendation to rescue Britain is a "remarkable revival of religion among all ranks." In other words, we must pray that the work and power of the Holy Spirit:

> May appear in all his gracious influences, convincing and converting sinners, sanctifying, quickening and comforting believers. That this may be a common blessing on all corners of the land, on persons of every class and denomination, of every rank and degree, . . . of every station and office, civil and sacred."[12]

We now see how in Witherspoon's mind piety was so essential to the welfare of the nation.

It is important to note that John Witherspoon occupied a prominent position in eighteenth-century Scottish church life. While still in Beith, he became one of the leaders of the Popular party, a conservative faction in the national church. This meant that he viewed the nation and the church through the prism of the beliefs and standards of that party. A dominant principle of this faction was the right of each congregation to choose its own pastor and manage its own affairs. Also, Popular party ministers preached sermons on sin and salvation based on the Confession. They stressed personal piety. Witherspoon and his compatriots opposed the Moderate party, which held that wealthy landowners should appoint ministers to parishes (thus upholding the parliamentary law of lay patronage). The Moderates also took a relaxed approach to the Confession, emphasizing instead moral teaching and preaching. They strove to make their sermons fine literary exercises. Moderate leaders were known to endorse more liberal patterns of thought on many subjects, to socialize with the nobility and mix with the patrons of the arts. Witherspoon's reputation as a vigorous critic of Moderate views increased after he wrote a biting satire in 1753 on Moderate beliefs and lifestyle called "Ecclesiastical Characteristics." At one point in this essay, he lists four basic rules that a

[10] Ibid., 2:453–77.

[11] What is called in Britain the Seven Years War is known in American history as the French and Indian War.

[12] *Works*, 2:474.

Moderate preacher must exemplify. Witherspoon's exaggerations are obvious:

> 1. His subjects must be confined to social duties.
>
> 2. He must recommend them only from rational consideration, viz. the beauty and comely proportions of virtue . . . .
>
> 3. His authorities must be drawn from heathen writers, *none* [Witherspoon's italics], or as few as possible, from Scripture.
>
> 4. He must be very unacceptable to the common people [respected only by the upper classes].[13]

In sum, if Scotland was to be a strong, virtuous nation, Moderate views would have to be repressed and the Popular party would have to become dominant: Strong vital religion would make a strong vital nation.

Witherspoon also saw a danger to the nation in the emerging public theater. In 1756, a play, *The Tragedy of Douglas*, had opened in Edinburgh, prompting members of the Popular party, especially Witherspoon, to speak and write in opposition to the corrupting influences of the theater. His essay, "A Serious Inquiry into the Nature and Effects of the Stage" appeared in 1757 and was widely circulated. A long treatise, its message was chiefly "that contributing to the support of a public theatre, is inconsistent with the character of a Christian."[14] Christians do not need this kind of amusement, he went on to say. Going to plays also "agitates the passions too violently;" the subjects of love, pride and ambition are distorted in order to entertain; attending the theater supports actors in an unchristian vocation—these were some of the reasons why a Christian should shun the theater. He repeated his opposition in the last sermon he preached in Paisley before emigrating to America, noting that "the best and wisest men in all ages have borne witness against [the pernicious entertainments of the stage], as the great means of corrupting the morals of a people . . . ."[15]

By 1768, Witherspoon's reputation had stretched beyond Scotland, and in that year he accepted an invitation to come to America and become the sixth president of the small Presbyterian College of New Jersey (now Princeton University). After nearly three months at sea, he, his wife and their five children landed at Philadelphia and went on to Princeton where they received an enthusiastic welcome by the staff and the entire student

[13] "Ecclesiastical Characteristics," *Works*, 3:219.

[14] Works, 3:121–90. See also Tait, *Piety*, 11–12, 47–48.

[15] *Works*, 2:550.

body. Providence, Witherspoon said, had guided him to new opportunities and new duties in America, and he quickly and energetically entered into his teaching and preaching in the new colonial environment.

Before long, he began to notice the rising opposition to Britain on the part of many in America. Students at the College also helped him eventually to transfer his loyalty from the British government to the American patriots. He allowed the students, without censoring them, to compose orations and conduct demonstrations expressing their anti-British views. At one commencement, the seniors chose to wear only clothes made in America. In 1774, after news of the Boston Tea Party had reached Princeton, the students gleefully burned the winter's supply of tea in a huge bonfire, along with an effigy of the colonial governor of Massachusetts, who had "a Tea canister tyed about his neck."[16] Many of Witherspoon's students took to heart their professor's instruction on sound government and the right of resistance, and served in the Continental army. Because there were no class rolls prior to 1787, an exact count of the students fighting in the army is impossible. Varnum Collins, Witherspoon's biographer, has written that "it is startling to note that, even if commissions were cheap, among these young graduates of his were eleven captains, six majors, four colonels, and ten lieutenant-colonels. Four of these officers died in service. Of the eleven army chaplains found among his students of theology seven gave up their lives on the same altar."[17] That same year Witherspoon cast his lot with the Americans, expressing support for the Continental Congress and publishing an essay, "Thoughts on American Liberty." Small wonder that John Adams called him "as high a Son of Liberty, as any man in America."[18]

It is important to observe here that Witherspoon's theology took on a new emphasis in the new world. I have explained elsewhere how he, while still retaining his focus on God as Redeemer, added a new dimension to his understanding of how God acts, namely, God as Providence.[19] No doubt his new situation and the unfolding events leading to war with

[16] Collins, *President Witherspoon*, 1:157–58.

[17] Ibid., 2:229.

[18] Tait, *Piety*, 152–54. Witherspoon preached regularly to the Princeton Presbyterian congregation and elsewhere in the colonies in his travels. At the College he taught Moral Philosophy, Eloquence or Belles Lettres, Chronology and History, Divinity (to pre-ministerial students), and on demand, Hebrew and French! His administrative duties included such responsibilities as staffing, oversight of finances, admissions, student life and discipline, development, and alumni relations. The Adams quote can be found in Lyman H. Butterfield et al., eds. *The Diary and Autobiography of John Adams* (Cambridge: Harvard University Press, 1961) 2:112.

[19] See my chapter, "Providence" in *Piety*, 143–77.

Britain prompted this addition to his thought. And whereas in Scotland when he preached on Providence, referring more to God's care of persons, in America he thought and spoke about Providence in a larger more expanded way: God rules over nations and peoples as well as individuals. Before, during and after the Revolutionary War, Witherspoon related, sometimes at length, how God seemed to direct political and military affairs. Nowhere is this better illustrated than in the laudatory speech that he delivered when George Washington visited Princeton in 1783:

> We contemplate and adore the wisdom and goodness of divine Providence, as displayed in favour of the United States, in many instances during the course of the war; but in none more than in the unanimous appointment of your Excellency to the command of the army. When we consider the continuance of your life and health—the discernment, prudence, fortitude and patience of your conduct, by which you have not only sacrificed . . . personal ease and property . . . in the public cause, chusing rather to risque your own name than expose the nakedness of your country—when we consider the great and glowing attachment of the army, and the cordial esteem of all ranks of men, and of every state in the Union, which you have so long enjoyed–we cannot help being of [the] opinion, that God himself has raised you up as a fit and proper instrument for establishing and securing the liberty and happiness of these States.[20]

Providence guided Witherspoon to the new world in 1768, and he brought with him the same impulse for a virtuous society that he had nurtured in Scotland. Specifically, he was transporting to America a conviction long sustained and deeply embedded in the culture of British and European society: The social and political health of a nation depended entirely upon the religion of both the ruler and the ruled. In practice, this meant that the well-being of a nation rested upon a vital national church. Historian Edwin Gaustad makes the point emphatically: "No Holy Roman Empire without a Holy Roman Church, no English king without an English bishop, no German prince without a uniformity of religion in his region, no Mother Russia without a structured Orthodoxy. . . ."[21] Later, we will see how Witherspoon and the other founders of the American republic were forced to adapt this ancient principle for the new nation.

[20] *Works*, 4:363, 364.

[21] Edwin S. Gaustad, *Faith of the Founders: Religion and the New Republic, 1776–1826* (Waco, TX: Baylor University Press, 2004) 4.

Of the several courses Professor Witherspoon taught, none was more important than Moral Philosophy. The lectures that were the content of this course reveal much of his thinking with regard to the formation and well-being of society. They bear closer examination.

Required for seniors, this course was a mixture of philosophy, sociology, political science, psychology and jurisprudence. More of a compend or a syllabus, the "Lectures on Moral Philosophy" as we have them are incomplete. No doubt aware of their imperfections, Witherspoon refused to publish them in his lifetime. Ashbel Green (1762–1848), Witherspoon's former student, who edited his professor's collected *Works* in 1800, included the "Lectures," explaining that though they were not a finished product, they deserved to be printed lest "a very valuable work should be consigned to oblivion."[22]

Jack Scott, who edited the "Lectures," has noted that "the one characteristic that stands above all else in this work is eclecticism."[23] This feature is both a weakness and a strength. The professor did not hesitate to borrow from several philosophical traditions and numerous thinkers, both ancient and contemporary, but he did not always integrate successfully the views of those he discussed. Also, if he had presented fewer thinkers, he might have developed their ideas at greater length. However, it must be acknowledged that he did introduce his students to a wide range of thought.

The "Lectures" are divided into two main parts: ethics, in which he treated epistemology, human nature, the moral sense, virtue, rights and duties; and politics, which encompassed such topics as political theory, domestic and civil society, law of nature and nations, war and just war theory, and the right of resistance. An important feature of Witherspoon's ethical thought is his insistence that humans possess a moral sense. He proclaimed in Lecture III "that a sense of moral good and evil, is as really a principle of our nature, as either the gross external or reflex senses . . . ."[24] This assertion enabled him on this occasion to reconcile his philosophical ideas with his religious beliefs. He explained that the "moral sense is precisely the same thing with what, in scripture and common language, we call conscience. It is the law which our Maker has written upon our

[22] The "Lectures on Moral Philosophy" can be found in the *Works*, 3:367–472. The Green quotation is included in the one-page introduction to the "Lectures" on page 366.

[23] Jack Scott, ed. *An Annotated Edition of Lectures on Moral Philosophy by John Witherspoon* (Newark: University of Delaware Press, 1982) 27. Green admitted that Witherspoon "took freely and without acknowledgment from writers of character such ideas . . . as he found suited to his purpose"; *Works*, 3:366.

[24] *Works*, 3:379.

hearts, and both intimates and enforces duty, previous to all reasoning."[25] Witherspoon never relinquished his belief in "the lost state of man by nature," but his teaching on the moral sense permitted human beings to live a virtuous life, an important condition for a virtuous society.[26]

Another feature of the section on ethics is the professor's desire to link virtue and duty. As I have recounted elsewhere,[27] he believed "whatever God commands is virtue and duty, and true virtue promotes the general good." True virtue relies on our sense of duty. Then in four lectures (Lectures VI–IX) and in some detail he described our duties to God, to our neighbor and to ourselves.[28] Our obligation to our neighbor, stated simply, is: "Love to others, sincere and active, is the sum of our duty." He continues with a discussion of benevolence since it is "the principle of that branch of duty which regards others." Love to others must be expressed with a due regard to rights, which are to be classified as natural and acquired, perfect and imperfect, alienable and inalienable. In this whole presentation there is no question that John Witherspoon regarded the individual as a member of society whose personal good must always be balanced with the good of society.

In the second part of the "Lectures" called politics, the professor took up several topics which constituted the framework of a free moral society. He began with a discussion of the state of nature, followed by a discussion of the social state created by common consent. Here three major agreements must prevail:

> (1.) The consent of every individual to live in, and be a member of that society. (2.) A consent to some particular plan of government. (3.) A mutual agreement between the subjects and rulers; of subjection on the one hand, of protection on the other—These are all implied in the union of every society, and they compleat the whole.[29]

[25] Ibid.

[26] Roger J. Fechner, "The Godly and Virtuous Republic of John Witherspoon," in *Ideas in America's Cultures*, Hamilton Cravens, ed. (Ames: Iowa State University Press, 1982) 7–25. In this essay, Fechner overlooks Witherspoon's piety and his critique of church and nation, relying solely on Witherspoon's ideas of a virtuous republic that he developed in his "Lectures on Moral Philosophy."

[27] L. Gordon Tait, "Lectures on Moral Philosophy by John Witherspoon," *American Presbyterians* 66 (1988) 225.

[28] *Works*, 3:393–416.

[29] Ibid., 3:430.

Witherspoon took the concept of the social contract so seriously that he could think of only one circumstance when the citizens would be justified in breaking it: When their government had become so corrupt and tyrannical that it could no longer be reformed. Only then could the citizens "resist and overthrow it" and a new government be created that would restore the civil contract, guaranteeing the citizens their natural rights. "But," he warned, "this is only when it becomes manifestly more advantageous to unsettle the government altogether, than to submit to tyranny."[30] With this explanation Witherspoon proved himself to be no hot-headed radical, no violent revolutionary. Resistance to established authority could be undertaken only when there was no other option.

His understanding of society assumed the traditional divisions of rulers and subjects, masters and servants, rich and poor.[31] Such an ordering of society, providentially decreed he thought, was not original with him. One can find the idea present in John Calvin (1509–1564) who claimed that God had ordered a "varying mixture of rich and poor."[32] It is interesting to observe that Witherspoon could preach that there were indeed rich folk who misused their wealth and thought only of feeding their appetites. At the same time he tried to placate the poor by telling them that God knows what is best for them: "The Lord knoweth . . . what state of life will be upon the whole most convenient for us."[33] The poor should not "secretly murmur" at their present state, he advised. It certainly sounds like social control, assigning and keeping everyone in some predetermined place in society, but Witherspoon would say he was merely recognizing the divisions that do exist in society while prescribing the necessity of piety for everyone. He concluded, "God is certainly the best judge of what is good for us, so resignation to him is a most acceptable expression both of our worship and obedience."[34]

One must be careful in calling Witherspoon a Calvinist. He was indebted to Calvin on several counts, but he saw fit to modify certain Calvinistic beliefs: God is an omnipotent being, yes, but no arbitrary deity; reason is not depraved and it can validate revelation; humans are

[30] Ibid., 3:436. Fechner, "The Godly and Virtuous Republic," 21.

[31] Ibid., 3:424–39.

[32] William J. Bouwsma, *John Calvin: A Sixteenth Century Portrait* (New York: Oxford University Press, 1988) 196.

[33] *Works*, 2:225.

[34] Ibid., 2:226.

self-centered sinners so there must be checks and balances in any government.[35]

As the author of the "Lectures on Moral Philosophy" probes deeper into his analysis of civil society, he considers governmental organization and function. For instance, he argued that a just society needs a government that successfully performs four functions: Legislation, taxation, jurisdiction (the administration of justice), and representation. When he considered the actual form of government, he predictably rejected monarchy and aristocracy, but to the surprise of most modern readers, he also rejected democracy. "Aristocracy always makes vassals of the inferior ranks," he observes, but democracy is undesirable because "it is very subject to caprice and the madness of popular rage." There is also the danger of citizens in a democracy choosing "a favorite, and [vesting] him with such power as overthrows their own liberty . . . ."[36]

What he does propose is a government of checks and balances "so that one principle may check the other." This would be a balanced political structure, a "complex" or mixed form of government, so that when there is misuse of power or self interest pervades the whole, a correction can be undertaken. What he was advancing, of course, was a republican form of government, balanced and representative.[37]

He concluded the notable Lecture XIII, Of Civil Society, by posing and answering a timely question: "What then is the advantage of civil liberty? I suppose it chiefly consists in its tendency to put in motion all the human powers. Therefore it promotes industry, and in this respect happiness,—produces every latent quality, and improves the human mind.—Liberty is the nurse of riches, literature [learning] and heroism."[38] Liberty, certainly, but as he stated so many times, a free people must be a pious people. True religion or piety and civil liberty are "inseparable." To summarize: Witherspoon was able to hold together two central convictions which made a moral republican government possible, namely, a realistic belief in a certain degree of human depravity along with a measure of optimism that humans could live and govern themselves responsibly. This was made possible by their moral sense, as well as their experience and reason.

[35] Scott, *Annotated Edition* 69, 144.

[36] *Works*, 3:432–35.

[37] Ibid. Later, when discussing the responsibilities of magistrates, he specifies the three branches of government—legislative, executive and judicial. Ibid., 3:83.

[38] Ibid., 3:439.

Another course that Witherspoon taught which was important for educating leaders in a new America was called simply Eloquence. The aim of this course was to train young men to be persuasive and, yes, eloquent expert writers and speakers in the public sphere. In his published "Lectures on Eloquence,"[39] one can readily observe and appreciate his commitment "to form the scholars to taste, propriety and accuracy, in that language which they must speak and write all their life . . . ."[40]

Early in these "Lectures" he offered two pieces of good advice to his students—first, study and imitate the great writers and speakers, classical and contemporary, and second, put into practice useful rules, which he supplied, on how to speak and write well. These rules include sensible advice, such as organizing carefully one's thoughts in speeches and compositions, and practical tips on speaking, such as avoiding "unnatural rants or ridiculous gestures."[41] This general instruction applies to all those who would hold positions of leadership in society, but the Eloquence professor singled out three professions for special attention: the pulpit, the bar, and what he called "deliberative assemblies."[42] In his judgment these are the professions which have the most influence in society, which insure the strength and virtue of a nation. His requirements for each are at once substantial and practical.

The Pulpit. During the time Witherspoon was at Princeton and there were no theological seminaries, he supervised the training of many young men for the ministry. He insisted that it was not sufficient for them to have a vital religious experience, believe the "truths of the everlasting gospel," and know their Bible from cover to cover. They must be acquainted with secular disciplines as well. He wrapped his specific recommendations in six qualities of an ideal minister: Piety ("a lively sense of religion upon his own heart"), simplicity, accuracy, force and vehemence, tempered by judgment and propriety, and extensive knowledge. To modern ears some of his advice seems quaint yet pointed: "Simplicity is beautiful everywhere," or a minister's personal "example is more intelligible than precept," or ministers "ought to avoid all turgid declamation, to keep to experience, and take things as they really are."

The Bar. Under this heading, Witherspoon places five qualities that should be found in the ideal lawyer. "Probity or real untainted integrity"

[39] Ibid., 3:475–592.

[40] "The Druid" Number 5, ibid., 4:458–63.

[41] "Lecture XII," ibid., 3:550–5.

[42] "Lectures XIV and XV," ibid., 3:561–81.

heads the list. Then comes "assiduity [diligence] and method in business." He strongly approves what some in derision might call "dull plodding fellows" because they manifest "form and good order." Never doubt, Witherspoon admonished, that "the greatest men have been and are remarkable for order and method in every thing they do." A third quality in a model lawyer is "address and delicacy." This is just another way of saying a lawyer must always consider the propriety of time and place in his public addresses. The fourth quality is "extensive knowledge in the arts and sciences," necessary because a lawyer never knows what kinds of opponents he may have to deal with, and "the causes he may have occasion to treat, are exceedingly various." Finally, the lawyer must demonstrate "quickness and vivacity," that is, he must be able to think on his feet and speak quickly. These, then, are the qualities of the kind of lawyer a strong virtuous nation requires.

Deliberative Assemblies. Here Witherspoon describes what is required of those who might serve as legislators, senators, or members of any political body. Witherspoon knows politics; he knows the nature and behavior of deliberative bodies; he knows that when lawmakers gather there is often more fervor and passion than calm and reason. In this regard, it is a surprise to find him citing David Hume (1711–1776), whom elsewhere he calls an infidel (atheist), with approval because Hume once announced that "the eloquence which kindles and governs the passions, will always have great influence in large assemblies."[43] Witherspoon thought that was a timely observation. Again, he has his list of qualities for this kind of speaking: (1) Dignity of character and disinterestedness, (2) Knowledge of men and manners, of history, and of human nature, (3) Power over the passions.

John Witherspoon, ever practical, ever the professor, and ever the statesman, wanted very much for the new nation to be led by outstanding individuals in the church, in law, and in political bodies. Thus, he selected these three professions for special attention. And his instruction, particularly in the courses on Moral Philosophy and Eloquence, bore fruit. Significant numbers of his students became ministers, lawyers, and entered government service. By one count, twelve were members of the Continental Congress, five were delegates to the Constitutional Convention, forty-nine became U.S. representatives, twenty-eight were elected U.S. senators,

[43] Ibid., 3:574.

three were appointed as Supreme Court justices and three as attorneys general, and one, James Madison, became a U.S. president.[44]

Not only in the classroom but also in the pulpit he set forth his views on the war and on the new nation about to be formed. On May 17, 1776, a day of public prayer in the colonies, the Rev. John Witherspoon preached a long sermon with the title "The Dominion of Providence over the Passions of Men" (text: Psalm 76:10).[45] He admitted that it was "the first time of my introducing any political subject into the pulpit." It actually is a sermon on providence as the title makes clear, but buried in the discourse is an analysis of the current political situation and a prescription for a positive outcome to the war, which had begun a year earlier.

In the first part of the sermon the preacher discusses three ways in which human wrath actually praises God. First, such wrath "clearly points out the corruption of our nature;" second, human wrath serves to bring sinners to repentance; and third, God in his power sometimes turns tragedy into blessings, as seen in the sufferings and death of Jesus, the persecution of the Protestant reformers, and the attacks on the English Puritans.

In the second part of the discourse there is another threefold declaration, this time explaining how human wrath praises God–in the present situation. First, each person must attend to the salvation of his or her soul; second, notice carefully, he declares, "the singular interposition of providence hitherto, in behalf of the American colonies;" and third, he proceeds to list and explain three ways which if realized will insure an American victory in the struggle: "If your cause is just,—if your principles are pure,—and if your conduct is prudent, you need not fear the multitude of opposing hosts." Further on, he delivers what he calls three "exhortations" to proper and prudent conduct. The first amounts to a plan for everyone to manifest "zeal for the glory of God and the good of others." The second is to be industrious ("Industry is a moral duty of the greatest moment"). And the third is simply frugality in every part of one's life—meals, dress, and "furniture and equipage," all very good advice for a people entering a war. Witherspoon's concern for the nation, that it be virtuous and victorious is effectively summarized in the last sentence of the sermon: "God grant that in America true religion and civil liberty may be inseparable, and that the

[44] See Jeffry H. Morrison, *John Witherspoon and the Founding of the American Republic* (Notre Dame, IN: University of Notre Dame Press, 2005) 4.

[45] Ibid., 3:17–46. See my longer analysis of the sermon in *Piety*, 155–60.

unjust attempts to destroy the one, may in the issue tend to the support and establishment of both."[46]

It is proper to ask how Presbyterian minister John Witherspoon could support and participate in a war even if it were absolutely necessary to preserve religious and civil liberty. It is clear by now in our discussion that Witherspoon was no pacifist. What we must recognize, however, is that he had given a fair amount of thought to how a war should be fought.[47] In his estimation there were just ways to conduct a war and unjust ones. In his "Druid Essay Number II" and in "The Lectures on Moral Philosophy," he lays out the requirements for a just war.[48]

Based on the "law of nature and nations," not on any Biblical authority, he first dealt with the causes of war: the violation of any perfect right, such as "taking away the property of the other state, or the lives of its subjects, or restraining them in their industry. . . ." An act of "notorious inhumanity" will also qualify as a legitimate cause. A war should last no longer than needed, only "till the injury be completely redressed," and there is reasonable assurance that there will be no future attacks. "Reasonable security" must be based on "solemn treaties."

When he discusses the legitimate means of conducting the war, his advice at first might surprise us: Military action can be directed to rulers and those on the battlefield—as well as civilians ("Every member of the hostile state")! He admits it is cruel that innocent subjects of the state should suffer, but practically speaking, "it would be impossible for an enemy to distinguish the guilty from the innocent." All the citizens make up the state, and if they enjoy the benefits of society, they must also be ready to suffer the blows of an enemy, he reasons.

Still, there are restrictions to total warfare. All acts of cruelty and inhumanity are forbidden as a violation of the "law of nations." Thus, an opposing army must not treat prisoners with oppression or insult nor kill them; an army must not kill, "distress or torture the weaker sex, or the helpless infant."

The following are also outlawed: burning and destroying of goods and property indiscriminately, using poisoned weapons, inventing methods of torture, and poisoning springs and provisions. Referring to the Revolutionary War itself, Witherspoon became quite exercised by the attempt on the part of the British to enlist Native American tribes to fight

[46] Ibid., 3:46.

[47] Tait, *Piety* 72–73.

[48] *Works*, 3:440–45; 4:431–38.

the patriots. They are cruel and barbaric, he charged, sometimes "putting to death women and children." Likewise, he is angry that the British have freed slaves and stirred them up to rebel against their masters. As a summation to his discussion of a just war, he wrote "That all acts of cruelty which have no tendency to weaken the resisting force, are contrary to reason and religion, and therefore to the law of nature and nations."[49]

To ascertain Witherspoon's program of what was required for a new strong prosperous America, the sermon he preached at the end of the war is just as important as the 1776 "Dominion" sermon. Based on Psalm 3:8, the untitled sermon is a lively thanksgiving for the numerous ways providence had blessed America during the conflict.[50] At the same time it was an opportunity for Witherspoon to explain what was required if the new nation were to prosper. My analysis of this sermon elsewhere[51] will bear repeating, at least in part, since it demonstrates how Witherspoon used the occasion to address the needs of the emerging republic.

In this sermon he explained at length ways in which God had directly helped America win the war, from the victories at sea to the fortunate choice of George Washington as general of the army to the ways the "councils of our enemies were confounded." "Nothing appears to me more manifest than that the separation of this country from Britain, has been of God," he announced.[52] The sermon was not lacking in such sentiment, but the preacher shifted his emphasis when he warned that enjoying the fruits of victory must never lead to boasting. The only proper post-war behavior, he said, was one of humility and thanksgiving. While he looked back with satisfaction and gratitude, he also peered into the future to the time when America would stand alone as a new nation. He urged a renewal of piety, which he said had suffered during the war. With the end of the war it was the duty of all Americans to show gratitude by "a concern for the glory of God, the public interest of religion, and the good of others." While these obligations fall on all of us, he explained, two kinds of public persons have special responsibilities if the republic is to be strong and virtuous: ministers and magistrates.[53]

[49] *Works*, 4:436.

[50] Ibid., 3:61–85. Here the sermon is simply headed "Sermon 45 Delivered at Public Thanksgiving After Peace." It has been customary to date this sermon, April 19, 1783. Morrison, *John Witherspoon and the Founding* (see 133–35), argues for an earlier date, November 28, 1782.

[51] Tait, *Piety*, 161–68.

[52] *Works*, 3:79.

[53] Ibid., 3:80–84.

Ministers are under the strongest obligation to holiness and usefulness in their own lives, and diligence in doing good to others, he insisted. A special obligation of theirs is "the inspection of the morals of their several societies," which will, in turn, make the members of those religious groups "more regular citizens, and the more useful members of society." Though not quite advocating a clergy police force, he expected ministers to take a measure of responsibility for the behavior of their members. It did not occur to him to employ ministers in this way in order to purify the church or enhance the standing of the clergy. Witherspoon wants to improve society and this is one way to do it. The behavior of church members is "of the utmost moment [importance] to the stability of any civil society."

Magistrates, or those who serve in any part of government, have even a greater responsibility for the health of society than ministers. We have to remember that Witherspoon must have been greatly influenced by the section "Of the Civil Magistrate" in the seventeenth-century Confession. It was only natural for him to place upon all those "vested with civil authority" a heavy responsibility for the civic health of society, a responsibility that surely exceeds what would be expected or tolerated today.

Specifically, voters must elect candidates for public office who are examples of "inward principle . . . personal integrity and private virtue."[54] Civil liberty, he believed, could not last very long unless it was based on public and private virtue. Office holders, then, must be the kind of individuals who are upright and moral. "The people in general," he advised, "ought to have regard to the moral character of those whom they invest with authority, either in the legislative, executive or judicial branches. . . ."[55] So, once in office, what exactly are the magistrates to do? The godly magistrates must maintain and advance a virtuous society. As persons they must be outstanding examples of piety. Then, as they carry out their duties, they are "under the strongest obligation to do their utmost to promote religion, sobriety, industry, and every social virtue, among those who are committed to their care." Witherspoon would take the matter even further. Magistrates have the strongest obligation to prevent impiety, since impiety promotes disorder. The health of society is a heavy burden on the rulers as they deal with wrongdoing: They are, he counseled, to be "a terror to evildoers"![56]

[54] Ibid., 3:82.

[55] Ibid., 3:83.

[56] Ibid.

He had even more to say about the duties of magistrates in Lecture XIV, Jurisprudence, in his Lectures on Moral Philosophy. There he explains, "If . . . virtue and piety are inseparably connected, then to promote true religion is the best and most effectual way of making a virtuous and regular people. Love to God, and love to man, is the substance of religion; when these prevail, civil laws will have little to do."[57] Recognizing that such a statement leads to the question of "how far the magistrate ought to interfere in matters of religion," he emphasized that there were three "particulars which must be considered:" "(1.) The magistrate (or ruling part of any society) ought to encourage piety by his own example, and by endeavoring to make it an object of public esteem." "2.) The magistrate ought to defend the rights of conscience, and tolerate all in their religious sentiments that are not injurious to their neighbors." On this point we see Witherspoon stoutly defending the freedom of one's conscience, adding "that everyone should judge for himself in matters of religion." On the other hand, such freedom does have certain limits." "(3.) The magistrate may enact laws for the punishment of acts of profanity and impiety."[58] Witherspoon could well have added a fourth "particular" for he immediately defines a major duty of the magistrate:

> Many are of opinion that besides all this, the magistrate ought to make public provision for the worship of God, in such manner as is agreeable to the great body of the society; though at the same time all who dissent from it, are fully tolerated. And indeed there seems to be a good deal of reason for it, that so instruction may be provided for the bulk of common people, who would, many of them, neither support nor employ teachers, unless they were obliged. The magistrate's right in this case, seems to be something like that of the parent, they have a right to instruct, but not to constrain.[59]

One is forced to conclude that in this discussion of the duties of the magistrate Witherspoon was undertaking a balancing act with the recognition of religion as a necessity for public order on the one hand, countered by an equal weight given to freedom of conscience on the other.

In this regard, his attitude toward the Catholic Church is of interest. When Witherspoon employed the term "Christian religion" it is almost certain that he intended Protestant Christianity. He observed, however,

[57] *Works*, 3:447–48.

[58] Ibid., 3:448, 449.

[59] Ibid., 3:449.

that in Great Britain "Popery is not tolerated," but in Holland "Papists are tolerated without danger to liberty." Revealing a spirit of openness, he concluded that in America toleration should prevail. His advice was that "we ought in general to guard against persecution on a religious account as much as possible, because such as hold absurd tenets are seldom dangerous."[60]

What, then, was Witherspoon's position on religious liberty, given the extent of the several duties he assigned to the rulers? He was not able to prescribe full religious liberty as we would understand it today. He and his contemporaries did come to realize that there could be no national church in America.[61] Nevertheless, they could not rid themselves of the notion that religion must undergird society if it were to be moral, free and strong. Thus, when Witherspoon described the character and duties of the magistrate, he was assuming that the state would give recognition but not concrete support to the Christian religion, though not to any particular denomination.[62] The government must not merely maintain neutrality when the issue is religious belief. Government would recognize and approve Christianity, undoubtedly in its Protestant form, since in the late eighteenth century the Christian religion was the dominant religion in America, at the same time providing liberty to those who did not accept Christianity.

Witherspoon was not alone by any means in contending that religion was the bedrock of a strong, virtuous nation. He belongs in the mainstream of early American political thought. Two examples will suffice: John Adams declared that "Statesmen . . . may plan and speculate for liberty, but it is religion and morality alone which can establish the principle upon which freedom can surely stand." Likewise, George Washington in his Farewell Address asserted that a strong free government required religion as a foundation. "Of all the dispositions and habits which lead to political prosperity, Religion and morality are essential supports. . . . And let us with caution indulge the supposition, that morality can be maintained without religion."[63]

60 Ibid.

61 However, the idea of an ecclesiastical establishment did not quickly disappear. In New England, for example, Congregational Churches were supported by taxation well into the nineteenth century (until 1833 in Massachusetts).

62 By using the word "denomination" Witherspoon already appears to recognize the plurality of religion, which came to characterize the state of religion in America.

63 Adams and Washington are quoted in Morrison, *John Witherspoon and the Founding*, 30. It is only fair to point out that when Witherspoon, Washington, Adams and others drew up

Neither Adams nor Washington was that explicit when providing the details of the kind of religion that the republic should have in place.[64] Witherspoon was. We have learned that in his ministry he had defined the kind of piety that would make and keep a nation's political arm strong and moral. His piety was embedded in the eternal truths of the gospel, a piety that became practical and dynamic when it was lifted from the Bible and transferred to the life of a nation. Politics always rested on the bedrock of virtue, and civic virtue itself was the outgrowth of Christian piety. John Witherspoon knew for a fact that authentic piety would make a people strong and free, which is why he concluded his "Dominion of Providence" sermon with the prescription for the new America that has a timeless ring to it: "It is in the [person] of piety and inward principle," he said, "that we may expect to find the uncorrupted patriot, the useful citizen and the invincible soldier."[65]

plans for the new nation, they could hardly imagine the size and diversity—racial, social, religious—of the United States today. It was easy enough in the late eighteenth century when America consisted of thirteen colonies on the east coast, and religion was centered in a few Christian denominations, to postulate a kind of general Protestant Christianity as the moral support of the nation. Today, one must be very cautious in transferring early American views to the present and in recommending any kind of religious uniformity.

64 David Holmes has explained that John Adams, though technically a church-going Congregationalist, evolved into a "Unitarian Christian or Christian Deist." He rejected the Trinity and the divinity of Christ, but retained belief in a personal God ("a benevolent all-powerful and all-merciful Creator"), Jesus as the Redeemer of humanity, and the Biblical miracles. George Washington, on the other hand, a lifelong Episcopalian, also attended church but not always weekly. He seemed to have little interest in theology. In his official documents, "Providence" is the most commonly used name for the deity. Washington rarely referred to Jesus. After he died there was an Episcopalian funeral service, but on his deathbed, while attended by physicians and servants, he never asked for an Episcopal priest and none was present when he died. Holmes explains that after his death there were serious attempts to portray Washington as a devout Christian, even though the evidence points to him being "a Deistic Episcopalian." See David L. Holmes, *The Faiths of the Founding Fathers* (New York: Oxford University Press, 2006) 59–78.

65 *Works*, 3:46.

Appendix A

The Saybrook Platform

This text of the Saybrook Platform is taken from Williston Walker, *The Creeds and Platforms of Congregationalism* (New York: Pilgrim, 1991) 503–6. The spelling and punctuation have been modernized.

In compliance with an order of the General Assembly, May 13, 1708.

After humble addresses to the throne of grace for the Divine presence, assistance, and blessing upon us, having our eyes upon the Word of God and the constitution of our churches for the advancement of God's glory and the further order and edification of our churches,

We agree that the Confession of Faith owned and consented unto by the elders and messengers of the churches assembled at Boston in New England May 12, 1680, being the second session of that Synod, be recommended to the honorable General Assembly of this colony at the next session for their public testimony thereto as the faith of the churches of this colony.

We also agree that the Heads of Agreement assented to by the united ministers formerly called Presbyterian and Congregational be observed by the churches throughout this colony.

And for the better regulation of the administration of church discipline in relation to all cases ecclesiastical both in particular churches and in Councils to the full determining and executing of the rules in all such cases.

It is agreed

1. That the elder or elders of a particular church, with the consent of the brethren of the same, have power and ought to exercise church discipline according to the rule of God's Word in relation to all scandals that fall out within the same. And it may be meet in all cases of difficulty for the respective pastors of particular churches to take advice of the elders of the churches in the neighborhood before they proceed to censure in such cases.
2. That the churches which are neighboring each to other shall consociate for the mutual affording to each other such assistance as may be requisite upon all

occasions ecclesiastical. And that the particular pastors and churches within the respective counties in this government shall be one Consociation (or more if they judge meet) for the end aforesaid.

3. That all cases of scandal that fall out within the circuit of any of the aforesaid Consociations shall be brought to a Council of the elders and also messengers of the churches within the said circuit; i.e., the churches of one Consociation if they see cause to send messengers when there shall be need of a Council for the determination of them.
4. That according to the common practice of our churches, nothing shall be deemed an act of judgment of any Council which has not the major part of elders present concurring and such a number of the messengers present as make the majority of the Council, provided that if any church shall not see cause to send any messengers to the Council or the persons chosen by them shall not attend, neither of these shall be any obstruction to the proceedings of the Council or invalidate any of their acts.
5. That when any case is orderly brought before any Council of the churches, it shall there be heard and determined which (unless utterly removed from thence) shall be a final issue, and all parties therein concerned shall sit down and be determined thereby. And the Council so hearing and giving the result or final issue in the said case as aforesaid shall see their determinations or judgment duly executed and attended in such way or manner as shall in their judgment be most suitable and agreeable to the Word of God.
6. That if any pastor and church doth obstinately refuse a due attendance and conformity to the determinations of the Council that has cognizance of the case and determines it as above, after due patience used, they shall be reputed guilty of scandalous contempt and dealt with as the rule of God's word in such case doth provide, and the sentence of non-communion shall be declared against such pastor and church, and the churches are to approve of the said sentence by withdrawing from the communion of the pastor and church which so refuses to be healed.
7. That in case any difficulties shall arise in any of the churches in this colony which cannot be issued without considerable disquiet, that church in which they arise or that minister or member aggrieved with them shall apply themselves to the Council of the consociated churches of the circuit to which the said church belongs, who, if they see cause, shall thereon convene, hear, and determine such cases of difficulty unless the matter brought before them shall be judged so great in the nature of it, or so doubtful in the issue, or of such general concern that the said Council shall judge best that it be referred to a fuller Council consisting of the churches of the other Consociation within the same county (or of the next adjoining Consociation of another county if there be not two Consociations in the county where the difficult arises) who

together with themselves shall hear, judge, determine, and finally issue such case according to the Word of God.

8. That a particular church in which any difficult doth arise may, if they see cause, call a Council of the consociated churches of the circuit to which the said church belongs before they proceed to sentence therein, but there is not the same liberty to an offending brother to call the said Council before the church to which he belongs proceed to excommunication in the said case unless with the consent of the said church.

9. That all the churches of the respective Consociations shall choose if they see cause one or two members of each church to represent them in the Councils of the said churches as occasion may call for them, who shall stand in that capacity till new be chosen for the same service unless any church shall incline to choose their messengers anew upon the convening of such Councils.

10. That the minister or ministers of the county towns, and where there are no ministers in such towns, the two next ministers shall, as soon as conveniently may be, appoint a time and place for the meeting of the elders and messengers of the churches in the said county in order to the forming themselves into one or more Consociations and notify the said time and place to the elders and churches of that county, who shall attend at the same, the elders in their own persons, and the churches by their messengers if they see cause to send them, which elders and messengers so assembled in Councils as also any other Council hereby allowed of shall have power to adjourn themselves as need shall be for the space of one year after the beginning or first session of the said Council and no longer, and that minister who was chosen at the last session of any Council to be Moderator shall with the advice and consent of two more elders (or, in case of the Moderator's death, any two elders of the same Consociation) call another Council within the same circuit when they shall judge there is need thereof, and all Councils may prescribe rules as occasion may require and whatsoever they shall judge needful within their circuit for the well performing and orderly managing the several acts to be attended by them, or matters that shall come under their cognizance.

11. That if any person or persons orderly complained of to a Council or that are witnesses to such complaints, having regular notification to appear, shall refuse or neglect so to do in the place and time specified in the warning given, except they or he give some satisfying reason thereof to the said Council, they shall be judged guilty of scandalous contempt.

12. That the teaching elders of each county shall be one Association (or more if they see cause) which Association or Associations shall assemble twice a year at least, at such time and place as they shall appoint, to consult the duties of their office and the common interest of the churches, who shall consider and resolve questions and cases of importance which shall be offered by any among

themselves or others, who shall have power of examining and recommending the candidates of the ministry to the work thereof.

13. That the said associated elders shall take notice of any among themselves that may be accused of scandal or heresy unto or cognizable by them, examine the matters, and, if they find just occasion, shall direct to the calling of the Council where such offenders shall be duly proceeded against.

14. That the associated pastors shall also be consulted by bereaved churches belonging to their Association and recommend to such churches such persons as may be fit to be called and settled in the work of the Gospel ministry among them, and, if such bereaved churches shall not seasonable call and settle a minister among them, the said associated pastors shall lay the state of such bereaved churches before the General Assembly of this colony that they may take such order concerning them as shall be found necessary for their peace and edification.

15. That it be recommended as expedient that all the Association of this colony do meet in the General Association by their respective delegates, one or more out of each Association, once a year, the first meeting to be at Hartford at the time of the General Election next ensuing the date hereof and so annually in all the counties successively at such time and place as the said delegates shall in their annual meetings appoint.

Appendix B

The Adopting Act (1729)

THIS text is taken from the *Minutes of the Synod*, September 19, 1729, as found in Guy S. Klett, *Minutes of the Presbyterian Church in America*, 1706–1788 (Philadelphia: Presbyterian Historical Society, 1976) 103, 104. The original spelling and punctuation are preserved.

❧

MORNING MINUTE

Altho' the Synod do not claim or pretend to any Authority of imposing our faith upon other men's Consciences, but do profess our just Dissatisfaction with and Abhorrence of such Impositions, and do utterly disclaim all Legislative Power and Authority in the Church, being willing to receive one another, as Christ has received us to the Glory of God, and admit to fellowship in sacred ordinances all such as we have Grounds to believe Christ will at last admit to the Kingdom of Heaven; yet we are undoubtedly obliged to take Care that the faith once delivered to the Saints be kept pure and uncorrupt among Us, and so handed down to our Posterity. And do therefore agree, yt all the Ministers of this Synod, or that shall hereafter be admitted into this Synod, shall declare their agreement in and approbation of the Confession of Faith with the larger and shorter Catechisms of the assembly of Divines at Westminster, as being in all the essential and necessary Articles, good Forms of sound words and systems of Christian Doctrine; and do also adopt the said Confession and Catechisms as the Confession of our Faith. And we do also agree, yt all the Presbyteries within our Bounds shall always take Care not to admit any Candidate of the Ministry into the Exercise of the sacred Function, but what declares his Agreement in opinion with all the Essential and Necessary Articles of said Confession, either by subscribing the said Confession of Faith and Catechisms, or by a verbal Declaration of their assent thereto, as such Minister or Candidate shall think best.

And in Case any Minister of this Synod or any Candidate for the Ministry shall have any Scruple with respect to any Article or Articles of sd. Confession or Catechisms, he shall at the Time of his making sd. Declaration declare his Sentiments to the Presbytery or Synod, who shall notwithstanding admit him to ye Exercise of the Ministry within our Bounds and to Ministerial Communion if the Synod or Presbytery shall judge his scruple or mistake to be only about articles not Essential and necessary in Doctrine, Worship or Government. But if the Synod or Presbytery shall judge such Ministers or Candidates erronious in Essential and necessary Articles of Faith, the Synod or Presbytery shall declare them uncapable of Communion with them. And the Synod do solemnly agree, that none of us will traduce or use any opprobrious Terms of those yt differ from us in these extra-essential and not-necessary points of doctrine, but treat them with the same friendship, kindness and brotherly Love, as if they had not differed from us in such Sentiments.

AFTERNOON MINUTE

All the Ministers of this Synod now present except one yt declared himself not prepared vizt. Mastrs. Jedidiah Andrews, Thomas Creaghead, John Thompson, Ja. Anderson, Jno. Pierson, Saml. Gleston, Joseph Houston, Gelbert Tenant, Adam Boyd, Jonathan Dickinson, Jno. Bradner, Alexder Hutcheson, Thomas Evans, Hugh Stevenson, Willm. Tenant, Hugh Conn, George Gillespy, and John Willson, after proposing all the Scruples yt any of them had to make against any Articles and Expressions in the Confession of Faith and larger and shorter Catechisms of the Assembly of divines at Westminster, have unanimously agreed in the solution of those Scruples, and in declaring the sd. Confession and Catechisms to be the Confession of their faith excepting only some Clauses in ye 20. and 23. Chapters, concerning which Clauses, the Synod do unanimously declare, yt they do not receive those Articles in any such sense as to suppose the civil Magistrate hath a controlling Power over Synods with Respect to the Exercise of the ministerial Authority; or Power to persecute any for their Religion, or in any sense contrary to the Protestant succession to the Throne of Great-Britain.

The Synod observing that Unanimity, Peace and Unity which appeared in all their Consultations and Determinations relating to the Affair of the Confession did unanimously agree in giving Thanks to God in solemn Prayer and Praises.

Appendix C

Colonial Presbyterian Chronology

❧

1667 Presbyterian congregation is established in Newark, New Jersey

1682 Francis Makemie becomes a Presbyterian missionary to America

1706 First Presbytery in America meets in Philadelphia

1707 Makemie's Arrest and Trial for preaching in New York

1708 Congregationalist *Saybrook Platform* adopts a Presbyterian-like form of order

1717 Synod of Philadelphia is established with three presbyteries

1722 Jonathan Edwards serves as supply pastor of a Presbyterian Church in New York

1727 Log College in Pennsylvania provides education for young revivalist ministers

1729 American Presbyterians adopt the Westminster Confession and Catechisms

1735 Heresy Trial of Samuel Hemphill tests the meaning of confessional subscription

1740 Gilbert Tennent preaches the sermon, "Dangers of an Unconverted Ministry"

1741 Old Side/New Side Schism over the Great Awakening and other issues

1745 Revivalists and Presbytery of New York unite to form Synod of New York

1747 Jonathan Dickinson serves as first President of College of New Jersey

1755 Samuel Davies organizes the Presbytery of Hanover in Virginia

1758 Reunion of Synods of Philadelphia and New York

1768 John Witherspoon comes to America to serve as President of College of New Jersey

1776 Witherspoon is only active clergyman to sign *Declaration of Independence*

1788 Presbyterians ratify a Constitution including a *Plan of Government*

1789 First General Assembly convenes which encompasses four Synods

Bibliography

Ahlstrom, Sydney E. *A Religious History of the American People*. New Haven: Yale University Press, 1972.

Aldridge, Alfred Owen. *Benjamin Franklin and Nature's God*. Durham, NC: Duke University Press, 1967.

Alexander, Archibald. *Biographical Sketches of the Founder and Principal Alumni of the Log College. Together with an Account of the Revivals of Religion under Their Ministry.* Philadelphia: Presbyterian Board of Publication, 1851.

[Alexander, Archibald]. *Sermons and Essays by the Tennents and Their Contemporaries.* Philadelphia: Presbyterian Board of Publication, 1855.

Andrews, Jedidiah. To "Reverend and Dear Sir." June 14, 1735. Photocopy in the Presbyterian Historical Society, Philadelphia.

Armstrong, Maurice, Charles Anderson, and Lefferts Loetscher, eds. *The Presbyterian Enterprise: Sources of American Presbyterian History.* Philadelphia: Westminster, 1956.

Bainton, Roland H. *Yale and the Ministry: A History of Education for the Christian Ministry at Yale from the Founding in 1701.* New York: Harper, 1957.

Bailyn, Bernard. *The Ideological Origins of the American Revolution.* Cambridge: Belknap, 1967.

Baldwin, Ebenezer. *Annals of Yale College.* New Haven: Hezekiah Howe, 1831.

Barker, William S. "The Hemphill Case, Benjamin Franklin, and Subscription to the Westminster Confession." *American Presbyterians* 69 (winter 1991) 243–56.

———. "Subscription to the Westminster Confession and Catechisms." *Presbuterion: The Covenant Seminary Review* 10 (1984) 11–14.

Brands, H. W. *The First American: The Life and Times of Benjamin Franklin.* New York: Doubleday, 2000.

Briggs, Charles. *American Presbyterianism: Its Origin and Early History.* Edinburgh: T. & T. Clark, 1885.

Bumsted, J. M., and John E. Van de Wetering. *What Must I Do to be Saved? The Great Awakening in Colonial America.* Hinsdale, IL: Dryden, 1976.

Butterfield, Lyman H., ed. *John Witherspoon Comes to America: A Documentary Account Based Largely on New Materials.* Princeton: Princeton University Press, 1953.

Buxbaum, Melvin H. *Benjamin Franklin and the Zealous Presbyterians.* University Park: Pennsylvania State University Press, 1975.

Cameron, Henry Clay. *Jonathan Dickinson and the College of New Jersey.* Princeton: C. S. Robinson, 1880.

Christensen, Merton A., "Franklin on the Hemphill Trial: Deism Versus Presbyterian Orthodoxy." *William and Mary Quarterly*, 3d series, 10 (July 1953) 422–40.

Coalter, Milton J., Jr. *Gilbert Tennent, Son of Thunder: A Case Study of Continental Pietism's Impact on the First Great Awakening in the Middle Colonies.* Westport, CT: Greenwood, 1986.

Collins, Varnum Lansing. *President Witherspoon: A Biography*. 2 vols. Princeton: Princeton University Press, 1925; reprinted, New York: Arno, 1969.

The Constitution of the Presbyterian Church in the United States of America. Philadelphia: Thomas Bradford, 1792.

Cross, Robert. *The Danger of Perverting the Gospel of Christ, Represented in a Sermon Preach'd before the Commission of Synod at Philadelphia. April 20th, 1735*. New York: John Peter Zenger, 1735.

Demos, John Putnam. *Entertaining Satan: Witchcraft and the Culture of Early New England*. New York: Oxford University Press, 1986.

DeWitt, John. "Historical Sketch of Princeton University." In *Memorial Book of the Sesquicentennial Celebration of the Founding Fathers of the College of New Jersey and of the Ceremonies Inaugurating Princeton University*. New York: Scribner, 1898.

Davies, Samuel. *Sermons on Important Subjects*. 3 vols. New York: Robert Carter & Brothers, 1867.

———. *Sermons of the Rev. Samuel Davies*. 3 vols. Reprint. Pittsburgh: Soli Deo Gloria, 1993.

Dickinson, Jonathan. *Familiar Letters to a Gentleman, upon a Variety of Seasonable and Important Subjects in Religion*. Boston: Rogers and Fowle, 1745.

———. *The Reasonableness of Christianity, in Four Sermons, Wherein the Being and Attributes of God, the Apostasy of Man, and the Credibility of the Christian Religion Are Demonstrated by Rational Considerations. And the Divine Mission of Our Blessed Savior Proved by Scripture Arguments, Both from the Old Testament and the New; and Vindicated Against the Most Important Objections, Whether of Ancient or Modern Infidels*. Boston: S. Kneeland and T. Green, 1732.

———. *Remarks upon a Discourse Entitled An Overture Presented to the Reverend Synod of Dissenting Ministers Sitting in Philadelphia, in the Month of September, 1728*. New York: J. Peter Zenger, 1729.

[Dickinson, Jonathan?] *Remarks upon a Pamphlet, Entitled, A Letter to a Friend in the Country, containing the Substance of a Sermon preached at Philadelphia, in the Congregation of the Rev. Mr. Hemphill*. Philadelphia: Andrew Bradford, 1735.

Duncan, J. Ligon. "Owning the Confession: Subscription in the Scottish Presbyterian Tradition." In *The Practice of Confessional Subscription*, ed. David W. Hall, 77–92. Lanham, MD: University Press of America, 1995.

Dunn, Elizabeth E. "From a Bold Youth to a Reflective Sage: A Revelation of Benjamin Franklin's Religion." *Pennsylvania Magazine of History and Biography* 111 (1987) 501–24.

Edwards, Jonathan. "Memoirs of Jonathan Edwards" in *The Works of Jonathan Edwards. Volume I*. Edinburgh: Banner of Truth Trust, 1974.

An Extract of the Minutes of the Commission of the Synod, Relating to the Affair of the Reverend Mr. Hemphil. Philadelphia: Andrew Bradford, 1735.

Fechner, Roger J. "The Godly and Virtuous Commonwealth of John Witherspoon." In *Ideas in America's Cultures from Republic to Mass Society*, edited by Hamilton Cravens, 7–25. Ames: Iowa State University Press, 1982.

Fiering, Norman S. "Will and Intellect in the New England Mind." *William and Mary Quarterly*, 3d series, 29 (October 1972).

Foote, William Henry. *Sketches of Virginia*, First Series, 1850. reprinted, Richmond: John Knox, 1966.

Franklin, Benjamin. *The Autobiography of Benjamin Franklin: A Genetic Text*. Edited by J. A. Leo Lemay and P. M. Zall. Knoxville: University of Tennessee Press, 1981.

[Franklin, Benjamin]. *A Defence Of the Rev. Mr. Hemphill's Observations: or, An Answer to the Vindication of the Reverend Commission.* Philadelphia: B. Franklin, 1735.

[Franklin, Benjamin]. *A letter to a Friend in the Country, Containing the Substance of a Sermon Preach'd at Philadelphia, in the Congregation of the Rev. Mr. Hemphill, Concerning the Terms of Christian and Ministerial Communion.* Philadelphia: B. Franklin, 1735.

———. *The Papers of Benjamin Franklin.* ed. Leonard W. Labaree *et al.* 24 vols. New Haven: Yale University Press, 1959–.

———. "Dialogue between Two of the Presbyterians Meeting in This City." In *The Papers of Benjamin Franklin.* Vol. 2. Edited by Leonard W. Labaree. New Haven: Yale University Press, 1960.

[Franklin, Benjamin]. *Some Observations on the Proceedings Against the Rev. Mr. Hemphill; With a Vindication of His Sermons.* 2d ed. Philadelphia: B. Franklin, 1735.

———. *Some Observations on the Proceedings against the Reverend Mr. Hemphill; with a Vindication of His Sermons.* In *The Papers of Benjamin Franklin.* Vol. 2. Edited by Leonard W. Labaree. New Haven: Yale University Press, 1960.

Fraser, James W. "The Great Awakening and New Patterns of Presbyterian Theological Education." *Journal of Presbyterian History* 60 (Fall 1982) 189–208.

Gaustad, Edwin H. *Faith of the Founders: Religion and the New Republic, 1776–1826.* Waco, TX: Baylor University Press, 2004.

Gewehr, Wesley M. *The Great Awakening in Virginia, 1740-1790.* Durham, NC: Duke University Press, 1930.

Gillespie, George. *A Letter to the Reverend Brethren of the Presbytery of New York, or of Elizabeth Town. In Which Is Shown the Unjustness of the Synod's Protest, Entered Last May at Philadelphia, Against Some of the Reverend Brethren.* Philadelphia: Benjamin Franklin, 1742.

———. *A Treatise against the Deists or Free-Thinkers, proving the Necessity of Revealed Religion.* Philadelphia: A. Bradford, 1735.

Gillett, E. H. *History of the Presbyterian Church in the United States of America.* 2 vols. Philadelphia: Presbyterian Publication Committee, 1864.

———. "The Men and the Times of the Reunion of 1758." *American Presbyterian and Theological Review* 6 (July 1868) 414–43.

———. "The True Character of the Adopting Act." *American Presbyterian and Theological Review* 7 (Jan 1869) 29–58.

Green, Ashbel. *Life of the Revd. John Witherspoon, D.D., LL.D.* Edited by Henry Lyttleton Savage. Princeton: Princeton University Press, 1973.

———. Review of *Letters to Presbyterians on the Present Crisis in the Presbyterian Church in the United States,* by Samuel Miller. *Christian Advocate* (July 1833) 318–25; (Aug. 1833) 358–66; (Sept. 1833) 411–22; (Oct. 1833) 458–65; (Nov. 1833) 495–507; (Dec. 1833) 547–53; (Jan. 1834) 27–35; (Feb. 1834) 78–86; (Mar. 1834) 128–33; (Apr. 1834) 181–82.

———. editor. *The Works of the Rev. John Witherspoon.* 4 vols. Philadelphia, 1802. Reprint, with an Introduction by L. Gordon Tait. Bristol, UK: Thoemmes, 2003.

Gura, Philip. A *Glimpse* of *Sion's Glory: Puritan Radicalism in New England, 1620–1660.* Middletown, CT: Wesleyan University Press, 1984.

Hall, David W., editor. *The Practice of Confessional Subscription.* Oak Ridge, TN: Covenant Foundation, 1997.

Haller, William. *The Rise of Puritanism.* New York: Harper & Row, 1957.

Hanzsche, William T. "New Jersey Molders of the American Presbyterian Church." *Journal of the Presbyterian Historical Society* 24 (June 1946).

Hardman, Keith J. *Jonathan Dickinson and the Course of American Presbyterianism.* Ph.D. diss., Univ. of Pennsylvania, 1971.

Harlan, David C. "The Travail of Religious Moderation: Jonathan Dickinson and the Great Awakening." *Journal of Presbyterian History* 61 (Winter 1983).

Hart, D. G. and Mark A. Noll, ed. *Dictionary of the Presbyterian and Reformed Tradition in America.* Downers Grove, IL: InterVarsity, 1999.

Heimert, Alan, and Perry Miller, editors. *The Great Awakening: Documents Illustrating the Crisis and Its Consequences.* Indianapolis: Bobbs-Merrill, 1967.

———. *Religion and the American Mind: From the Great Awakening to the Revolution.* Cambridge: Harvard University Press, 1966.

Hodge, Charles. *The Constitutional History of the Presbyterian Church in the United States of America,* Part I, 1705–1741. Philadelphia: Presbyterian Board of Publication, 1851.

Holmes, David L. *The Faiths of the Founding Fathers.* New York: Oxford University Press, 2006.

Humphrey, David C. "The Struggle for Sectarian Control of Princeton, 1745–1760." *New Jersey History* 91 (summer 1973) 71–90.

Isaacson, Walter. *Benjamin Franklin: An American Life.* New York: Simon and Schuster, 2003.

Jacobsen, Douglas. *An Unprov'd Experiment: Religious Pluralism in Colonial New Jersey.* Brooklyn: Carlson, 1991.

Jenkins, Obadiah. *Remarks upon the Defence of the Reverend Mr. Hemphill's Observations: In a Letter to a Friend.* Philadelphia: Andrew Bradford, 1735.

Kempshall, Everard. *The Centennial of the Anniversary of the Burning of the Church Edifice of the First Church of Elizabeth, New Jersey.* Elizabeth, NJ: Elizabeth Daily Journal, 1881.

Klett, Guy S., editor. *Minutes of the Presbyterian Church in America 1706–1788.* Philadelphia: Presbyterian Historical Society, 1976.

———. *Presbyterians in Colonial Pennsylvania.* Philadelphia: University of Pennsylvania Press, 1937.

Knight, George W. III. "A Response to Dr. William Barker's Article 'Subscription to the Westminster Confession of Faith and Catechisms.'" *Presbuterion: The Covenant Seminary Review* 10 (1984) 56–63.

———. "Subscription to the Westminster Confession of Faith and Catechisms." *Presbuterion: The Covenant Seminary Review* 10 (1984) 20–55.

Landsman, Ned. *Scotland and Its First American Colony.* Princeton: Princeton University Press, 1985.

Le Beau, Bryan F. "The Subscription Controversy and Jonathan Dickinson." *Journal of Presbyterian History* 54 (1976) 317–35.

———. *Jonathan Dickinson and the Formative Years of American Presbyterianism.* Lexington: University of Kentucky Press, 1997.

Lodge, Martin E. "The Great Awakening in the Middle Colonies." Ph.D. diss., University of California at Berkeley, 1964.

Loetscher, Frederick W. "The Adopting Act." *Journal of the Presbyterian Historical Society* 13 (December 1929) 337–55.

Loetscher, Lefferts. *A Brief History of the Presbyterians.* Philadelphia: Westminster, 1978.

MacLean, John. *History of the College of New Jersey, 1746–1854.* Philadelphia: Lippincott, 1887.

Marsden, George M. *Jonathan Edwards: A Life.* New Haven: Yale University Press, 2003.

Mather, Cotton. *Magnalia Christi Americana.* Vol. 1. Edinburgh: Banner of Truth, 1979.

Maxson, Charles Hartshorn. *The Great Awakening in the Middle Colonies.* Gloucester, MA: Peter Smith, 1958

Miller, Howard. *The Revolutionary College: American Presbyterian Higher Education, 1707–1837.* New York: New York University Press, 1976.

Miller, Perry. The *New England Mind: From Colony to Province.* Boston: Beacon, 1981.

———. *Orthodoxy in Massachusetts, 1630–1650.* Gloucester, MA: Peter Smith, 1965.

———. and Thomas H. Johnson, editors. *The Puritans: A Sourcebook of Their Writings.* New York: Harper & Row, 1963.

Morgan, S. Edmond. *American Slavery, American Freedom: The Ordeal of Colonial Virginia.* New York: Norton, 1975.

———. *Benjamin Franklin.* New Haven: Yale University Press, 2002.

———. *The Puritan Dilemma: The Story of John Winthrop.* Boston: Little, Brown, and Co., 1958.

———. *Visible Saints: The History of a Puritan Idea.* Ithaca: Cornell University Press, 1963.

Morrison, Jeffry H. *John Witherspoon and the Founding of the American Republic.* Notre Dame, IN: University of Notre Dame Press, 2005.

Murphy, Thomas. *The Presbytery of the Log College; or, The Cradle of the Presbyterian Church in America.* Philadelphia: Presbyterian Board of Publication, 1889.

Murray, Iain H. *Revival and Revivalism : The Making and Marring of American Evangelicalism, 1750–1858.* Edinburgh: Banner of Truth Trust, 1994.

Murray, Nicholas. *Notes, Historical and Biographical, Concerning Elizabeth Town, Its Eminent Men, Churches, and Ministers.* Elizabeth Town, NJ: E. Sanderson, 1844.

Nevin, Alfred. ed. "Adopting Act" in *Encyclopedia of the Presbyterian Church in the United States of America: Including the Northern and Southern Assemblies.* Philadelphia: Presbyterian Encyclopedia Publishing Co., 1884.

Nichols, James Hastings. "Colonial Presbyterianism Adopts Its Standards." *Journal of the Presbyterian Historical Society* 34 (March 1956) 53–66.

———. "John Witherspoon on Church and State." In *Calvinism and the Political Order,* edited by George L. Hunt and John T. McNeill, 130–39. Philadelphia: Westminster, 1965.

Noll, Mark A. *Princeton and the Republic: 1768–1822.* Princeton: Princeton University Press, 1989.

———. *The Rise of Evangelicalism: The Age of Edwards, Whitefield and the Wesleys.* Downers Grove, Ill.: InterVarsity, 2003.

Nybakken, Elizabeth I. "New Light on the Old Side: Irish Influences on Colonial Presbyterianism." *Journal of American History* 68 (1981–82) 813–32.

Olin, John C., ed. *A Reformation Debate.* New York: Harper & Row, 1966.

Pahl, Jon. *Paradox Lost: Free Will and Political Liberty in American Culture, 1630–1760.* Baltimore: Johns Hopkins University Press, 1992.

Payton, James R., Jr. "Background and Significance of the Adopting Act of 1729." In *Pressing Toward the Mark: Essays Commemorating Fifty Years of the Orthodox Presbyterian Church.* Edited by Charles G. Dennison and Richard C. Gamble. Philadelphia: Committee for the Historian of the Orthodox Presbyterian Church, 1986.

Pears, Jr., Thomas Clinton. "Colonial Education among Presbyterians," *Journal of the Presbyterian Historical Society* (June 1952) and (Sept. 1952).

Pemberton, Ebenezer. *Sermon Preach'd before the Commission of the Synod, at Philadelphia. April 20th, 1735.* New York: John Peter Zenger, 1735.

Pilcher, George William, editor. *The Reverend Samuel Davies Abroad.* Urbana: University of Illinois Press, 1967.

———. *Samuel Davies: Apostle of Dissent in Colonial Virginia.* Knoxville: University of Tennessee Press, 1971.

Prince, Thomas. ed., *The Christian History Containing Accounts of the Revival and Propagation of Religion in Great Britain and America for the Year 1744.* Boston: S. Kneeland and T. Green, 1745.

Records of the General Synod of Ulster, From 1691 to 1820. 3 vols. Belfast, 1890–98.

Records of the Presbyterian Church in the United States of America. Edited by William H. Roberts. Philadelphia: Presbyterian Board of Publication and Sabbath School Work, 1904.

"Records of the Presbytery of New Castle upon Delaware." *Journal of the Presbyterian Historical Society* 15 (December 1932).

Reed, Charles Robert. "Image Alteration in a Mass Movement: A Rhetorical Analysis of the Role of the Log College in the Great Awakening." Ph.D. diss., Ohio State University, 1972.

Reid-Maroney, Nina. "Science and the Presbyterian Academies." In *Theological Education in the Evangelical Tradition,* edited by D. G. Hart and R. Albert Mohler, Jr., 203–16. Grand Rapids: Baker, 1996.

Samworth, Herbert L. "Those Astonishing Wonders of His Grace: Jonathan Dickinson and the Great Awakening." Ph.D. diss., Westminster Theological Seminary, 1988.

Schafer, Thomas A. "The Beginnings of Confessional Subscription in the Presbyterian Church." *McCormick Quarterly* 19 (1966) 102–19.

Schmidt, Leigh Eric. "Jonathan Dickinson and the Making of the Moderate Awakening." *American Presbyterians* 63 (winter 1985) 341–53.

———. *Holy Fairs: Scottish Communions and American Revivals in the Early Modern Period.* Princeton: Princeton University Press, 1989.

Schnittjer, Gary E. "The Ingredients of Effective Mentoring: The Log College as a Model for Mentorship." *Christian Education Journal* 15 (Fall 1994) 86–100.

Scott, Jack, editor. *An Annotated Edition of Lectures on Moral Philosophy by John Witherspoon.* Newark: University of Delaware Press, 1982.

Sewall, Richard B. *The Life of Emily Dickinson.* New York: Farrar, Straus and Giroux, 1987.

Shriver, George H., editor. *Dictionary of Heresy Trials in American Christianity.* Westport, CT: Greenwood, 1997.

Sloan, Douglas. *The Scottish Enlightenment and the American College Ideal.* New York: Teachers College Press, 1971.

Smith, Morton H. *How the Gold Is Become Dim: The Decline of the Presbyterian Church U.S., as Reflected in Its Assembly Actions.* 2d ed. Jackson, Miss.: Steering Committee for a Continuing Presbyterian Church, 1973.

Smylie, James H. *A Brief History of the Presbyterians.* Louisville: Geneva, 1996.

———. editor. "Presbyterians and the American Revolution: An Interpretive Account." *Journal of Presbyterian History* (Spring 1976).

Stout, Harry S. *The Divine Dramatist: George Whitefield and the Rise of Modern Evangelicalism.* Grand Rapids: Eerdmans, 1991.

———. *The New England Soul.* Oxford: Oxford University Press, 1986.

Tabb, Wilfred Earnest III. "The Presbyterian Clergy of the Great Awakening." Ph.D. diss., Washington University, 1992.

Tait, L. Gordon. "Lectures on Moral Philosophy by Dr. John Witherspoon, President of the College of New Jersey." *American Presbyterians* 66 (1988) 223–28.

———. *The Piety of John Witherspoon: Pew, Pulpit, and Public Forum*. Louisville: Geneva, 2001.

Tennent, Gilbert. *Remarks Upon a Protestation Presented to the Synod of Philadelphia.* Philadelphia: Benjamin Franklin, 1741.

Thayer, Theodore. *As We Were: The Story of Old Elizabethtown*. Elizabeth, NJ: Grassmann, 1964.

Thornwell, James Henley. *Collected Writings*. Edinburgh: Banner of Truth, 1974.

Trinterud, Leonard J. *The Forming of an American Tradition: A Re-Examination of Colonial Presbyterianism*. Philadelphia: Westminster, 1949.

A Vindication of the Reverend Commission of the Synod In Answer to Some Observations on Their Proceedings against the Reverend Mr. Hemphill. Philadelphia: Andrew Bradford, 1735.

Virginia. *Session Laws 1758 Sept.* Williamsburg: William Hunter, 1758. Retrieved from Readex database Early American Imprints, Series I: Evans, Record No. 0F2F81FDD080BB40.

Walker, Williston. *The Creeds and Platforms of Congregationalism*. New York: Scribner, 1893.

Warch, Richard. *School of the Prophets: Yale College, 1701–1740.* New Haven: Yale University Press, 1973.

Webster, Richard. *A History of the Presbyterian Church in America from Its Origin until the Year 1760*. Philadelphia: Joseph M. Wilson, 1857.

Wertenbaker, Thomas J. "The College of New Jersey and the Presbyterians." *Journal of the Presbyterian Historical Society* 36 (Dec 1958).

Westerkamp, Marilyn J. *Triumph of the Laity: Scots-Irish Piety and the Great Awakening, 1625–1760*. New York: Oxford University Press, 1988.

Whitlock, Jr., Luder G. "The Context for the Adopting Act." In *The Practice of Confessional Subscription*, edited by David W. Hall, 93–104. Lanham, MD: University Press of America, 1995.

Woolley, Bruce Chapman. "Reverend Thomas Shepard and Cambridge Church Members 1636–1649: A Socio-Economic Analysis." Ph.D. diss., University of Rochester, 1973.

Woolverton, John Frederick. *Colonial Anglicanism in North America.* Detroit: Wayne State University Press, 1984.

Contributors

William S. Barker (Ph.D., Vanderbilt University) is Professor of Church History Emeritus at Westminster Theological Seminary in Philadelphia. He is the author of *Puritan Profiles: 54 Contemporaries of the Westminster Assembly* and a history of Covenant College.

David B. Calhoun (Ph.D., Princeton Theological Seminary) is Professor of Church History at Covenant Theological Seminary. He is the author of the two-volume *Princeton Seminary* and a history of First Presbyterian Church in Columbia, SC.

D. Clair Davis (Dr. Theol., Georg-August Universität, Göttingen) is Professor of Church History Emeritus at Westminster Theological Seminary in Philadelphia. He is the author of numerous articles on American Presbyterianism.

S. Donald Fortson III (Ph.D., Westminster Theological Seminary) is Associate Professor of Church History and Practical Theology at Reformed Seminary–Charlotte. He is author of several articles on American Presbyterianism and the forthcoming book, *The Presbyterian Creed.*

D. G. Hart (Ph.D., Johns Hopkins University) is Director for the Honors Program and Faculty Development at the Intercollegiate Studies Institute. He is general editor of *Dictionary of the Presbyterian and Reformed Tradition in America* and the author of numerous books and articles on American Christianity.

Bryan F. LeBeau (Ph.D., New York University) is Dean of Institutional Services at Kansas City Kansas Community College. He is the author of *Jonathan Dickinson and the Formative Years of American Presbyterianism* and numerous other books and essays on religion in America.

Samuel T. Logan Jr. (Ph.D., Emory University) is Chancellor and Professor of Church History at Westminster Theological Seminary in Philadelphia. He is co-editor with William S. Barker of *Sermons that Shaped America: Reformed Preaching from 1630 to 2001* as well as other published essays and several articles on Jonathan Edwards.

James H. Smylie (Th.D., Princeton Theological Seminary) is Professor of Church History Emeritus at Union Theological Seminary in Virginia. He is the author of *A Brief History of the Presbyterians* and a number of other publications on American Presbyterianism.

L. Gordon Tait (Ph.D., University of Edinburgh) is Mercer Professor of Religious Studies Emeritus at The College of Wooster. He is the author of *The Piety of John Witherspoon: Pew, Pulpit, and Public Forum* and has written the introduction to a recent edition of Witherspoon's works.

C. N. Wilborn (Ph.D., Westminster Theological Seminary) is Associate Professor of Church History and Biblical Theology at Greenville Presbyterian Theological Seminary. He is author of several introductions to classic reprints and a forthcoming biography of John L. Girardeau.

Made in the USA
Las Vegas, NV
25 August 2021

28866210R00138